MORE PRAISE FOR DARKNESS FOLLOWS LIGHT

Darkness Follows Light is a courageous and moving work. The clarity of writing brought back such strong memories of my knowing Pattie and Earle in the golden days of their life together. In this memoir, all aspects of their relationship have been shared, the great joys of love found and the deep sorrow of love tragically lost. Their meeting, courtship, and marriage overflows with joy and passion. Their descent into illness and death conveys unflinching revelations of grief and loss. I was struck by the great beauty in finding love, despite its painful cost. Pattie and Earle's story reminds us all that one of the greatest measures of a life well lived is how deeply we have loved. — Matt Daly, poet and recipient of 2015 Neltje Blanchan writer's award. Jackson, Wyoming.

Employed as an editor for Powder Mountain Press, I rented the apartment above Earle and Pattie's garage. I soon realized that their pleasure in each other was cherished and intentional in everything they did. Pairs of skis, hiking boots, daypacks, canoeing and other outdoor gear were neatly stowed everywhere, evidence of their active lifestyle. Their oversize bathtub had back cushions permanently mounted on both ends. Even today, it's impossible to think of one without memories entwined around the other. Written from the depths of excruciating grief, this memoir is a portrait of two people possessed with rare awareness of their good fortune and of the impermanence of all things. — Kristine Jepsen, freelance writer and editor. Dorchester, Iowa.

Passion for wild nature and each other bonded Earle and Pattie Layser. It led them on exotic adventures around the world, fueled their resolve as conservationists, and served as a balm through tragedy and loss. Their story shows how the spirit and memory of loved ones can live on in the landscapes we treasure. This is a remarkable memoir and survivor's story. — Todd Wilkinson, award winning journalist and author of *Grizzlies of Pilgrim Creek* and *Last Stand: Ted Turner's Quest to Save a Troubled Planet*. Bozeman, Montana.

DARKNESS *follows* LIGHT

A MEMOIR OF LOVE, PLACE, AND BEREAVEMENT

A Love Story

Earle F. Layser

Darkness Follows Light

Copyright © 2016 by Earle F. Layser

ISBN-13-9781519723543

ISBN-10-1519723547

For permission to duplicate any portion of this book, please contact the author

Earle F. Layser, Alta, Wyoming 83414

Cover and Graphic Design by Rossetti Designs, Wilson, Wyoming

Printed by Create Space in the United States of America

Published by Dancing Pine Publishing, Alta, Wyoming

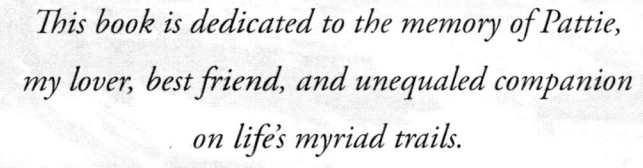

This book is dedicated to the memory of Pattie,
my lover, best friend, and unequaled companion
on life's myriad trails.
We shared an exceptionally deep love and grand passion
for life and each other.
My enduring gratitude to Pattie for all her love,
bright smiles, laughter, and joyful being.

Darkness may hide the trees and the flowers from the eyes but it cannot hide love from the soul.

— Rumi, 13th-century Persian Poet

DARKNESS FOLLOWS LIGHT

CONTENTS

PREFACE

A deep and loving relationship between two people is one of life's most meaningful experiences. This is a tale about such bonding, two people who became one—the true story of Pattie and Earle. It is an account of enduring love and tragic loss.

Earle and Pattie's romance flourished amid the glory of the Yellowstone-Teton region's spectacular natural beauty, among adrenaline-charged mountain town lifestyles, and in exotic travel to foreign places. Characterized by a singularly beautiful courtship, extraordinary joy and affection, and fairy-tale richness, their story will enrich the reader and encourage an appreciation for the preciousness of life and the miracle of love.

Their humanity is laid heartbreakingly bare when passion and love collide with sickness, death, and mourning. The tragic lessons learned shine a light onto the devastating emotional turmoil and loss of life's vision one experiences from terminal illness, loss of a beloved spouse, and complicated bereavement.

Pattie and Earle's story mirrors the human experience in that others may also find true love and a lasting relationship filled with romance and passion; multitudes are drawn to the Tetons, some of those also discover a spiritual connection to the mountains; many today engage in outdoor adventure and activities at highly skilled and athletic levels; and countless people are stricken with terminal illnesses and heartrending grief, as they were. At first glance, it may appear Pattie and Earle were not exceptional or unique. But when we examine their story from all those perspectives combined, this memoir transforms into an extraordinary tale that is uniquely *their* story.

Pattie and Earle were ordinary people, but what they enjoyed as a couple was remarkable and uncommon. The springtime of their intimacy burned bright with health and vigor, passion, joy and love. An unfathomable darkness followed bringing illness, death, incredible grief, and mourning. Grief, we learn, materializes proportionate to love; without love, commitment, or passionate involvement, there is little or no grief. The story melds memoir, obituary, eulogy, and a farewell; it is testimony that true love trumps all. It does not die when the other person is gone. Death cannot kill that which never dies.

INTRODUCTION

This ring in which you are but a grain will glitter afresh forever.
— Friedrich Nietzsche

Pattie died tragically and heartbreakingly before her time. With her death, a large part of me died, too. Thus began the winter of my life.

For a cosmic instant her mortal light had glowed warm and bright—a beacon of white light radiating infinitely exquisite colors and beauty. When it winked out, cold and darkness followed. Gone was my best friend, life companion, and lover.

As Earth hurtles through endless space and time, I can feel the distance between Pattie and me growing. How will I ever find her again? I pray the stars and heavens will realign over time so we will meet again as old souls in an everlasting love that never dies.

Over time events and circumstances can assume a chronology of their own making. Time begins to play with one's mind. Has it really been more than twenty-three years since Pattie and I met, or was it only yesterday? Do I accurately remember events and details? Has my recall been selective or shaped by an accretion of biases?

Fortunately, this narrative does not rely on the veracity of my mind alone. Much of our story took place in an earlier time, before the impersonal ephemerality of electronic mail and social media, and the potentially dystopian spin-offs of digital technology. Our history and words have been preserved because both Pattie and I possessed an old-fashioned propensity to write letters, keep journals, save photographs, correspondence and cards, and write and publish stories about our lives and adventures together.

I remember once asking Pattie, "Why are you saving all that stuff?" Grinning, she prophetically replied, "Someone may want to write about me someday."

It did not occur to me at the time that someone might be me. Now, Pattie speaks to me again, not only through my memory, but also through our preserved cards, letters, and recorded stories. Randomly selected excerpts from those precious materials are incorporated throughout this book. Those words, phrases, and passages corroborate this narrative. They exist as recorded sentiments of the heart.

Reading the words Pattie and I penned many years ago in our journals, articles, and letters transports me back to joyous times filled with love and the springtime of life's promises. Paradoxically, there is also bottomless sadness and gavel-rap finality to knowing all we will ever share in this lifetime is preserved in those writings.

Set within the spectacular natural beauty of the Yellowstone-Teton region, this is a true story—a love story and romance that begins in Bozeman, Montana. No reasonable explanation exists for Pattie and me meeting on a blustery snowy April day in 1991. Some might be inclined to attribute our meeting to chance. However, the probability of our coming together by chance alone—finding and recognizing each other over time and space—was infinitesimally small. Winning the lottery posed far better odds. More than luck, our searching for and finding each other appears to be testament for the workings of providence. Our meeting seems somehow to have been predestined.

At the ages Pattie and I were when we met, some people are already languishing in middle-aged doldrums and consider their lives to be largely over. But for us, our life together had only just begun, surpassing anything we had known before. It is not that our former lives were impoverished—far from it. Rather, it was that our new-found love and life together, combined with our maturity and experience produced such richness.

Like many who fall deeply in love, we believed our love to be special. However, I recognize we were not unique. Many others experience the good fortune to forge a durable loving relationship; and sadly, some too suffer the tragic misfortune of unfathomable personal loss and profound grief.

In sharing this tale of love and loss, I am not motivated by conceit or ego, or a need to idealize Pattie or our relationship. It is in part a labor of mourning, memorializing, and honoring her. It is also an affirmation of all we enjoyed together and recognition of our authenticity as a couple. It serves as part of our legacy. Writing this memoir was not easy; it required overcoming my discomfort with making our private lives public. It also necessitated extreme immersion into the emotional nadir and wellspring of my sorrow. I am compelled to tell this story as a tribute to her.

Pattie was an uncommonly beautiful person, both inside and out. She combined intelligence and wisdom with touching kindness and innocence. She lived graciously, loved unselfishly, and gave freely of her laughter and smiles. I will forever feel gratitude for all we shared and for our incomparable time together.

Unabashedly sentimental and romantic, Pattie was fond of characterizing deserving relationships by saying, "It's a love story." By her measures, ours was truly worthy of being labeled "a love story." We enjoyed a remarkably intimate bonding: one that imparted delight into every day and all aspects of our lives. Our story is not just about falling in love. Significantly, it is also about being and staying deeply and passionately in love.

Adventuring, globe-trotting, and road-tripping to exotic places, our lives together possessed an exceptional and enviable richness. As Bozeman mountaineer Conrad Anker identifies in the forward to *Higher Love: Skiing the Seven Summits*, our travel and adventures consisted of more than just discovering blank places on a map. It involved "discovering previously unknown places within ourselves."

For years we exalted in living a healthy, athletic, and outdoor lifestyle. Readers may glean inspiration and enjoyment from the fairy-tale richness of our courtship, relationship, love, and life together. But our experience also reflects a Buddhist principle: the impermanence of all earthly things.

Our fate calls attention to the dire unpredictability of life. We were dealt an unanticipated hand: death's specter came randomly into our happy lives. When cancer afflicted us both, our lives sadly degenerated into medical procedures, terminal sickness, despair, death and darkness. Writer Alexandria Fuller observes that "luck is capricious and life fleeting, [and] no one is too special to avoid suffering." Bad things can happen to good people. Through it all, though, one constant burned bright—our abiding love for each other.

Colliding with the insidious cruelty of cancer and barbarous medical procedures, our happy and healthy lives and lifestyles were destroyed. Pattie, much loved by all, died unjustly before her time—before the Tasha Tudor gardening she had always imagined as part of her old age. As she was younger, her untimely death before me defied logic and natural order. Our life together was left uncompleted, like final pages missing from a promising novel. To borrow author Ellen Meloy's phrase, it left our "someday country" forever unexplored—all our plans, trips, intentions and future lives with each other came to a shortened end.

I have learned firsthand that the death of a beloved spouse can be extremely deleterious for the survivor and his or her continued existence; it can top the stress and grief charts. This agonizingly painful heartache and inconsolable sorrow is difficult to comprehend, unless a person has experienced it. Processed in the same part of the brain, physical pain and emotional pain are not differentiated by our neurological circuitry.

While our society widely celebrates the beauty of courtship, enduring love, and marriage, it is comparatively silent about the inevitable outcome. Eventually, a mortal pair will be ripped apart and one left to go on alone. In *A Grief Observed*, C. S. Lewis described his struggle with despair and concluded that bereavement should not be regarded as the end of married love, but as "one of its phases, no less than the honeymoon."

I am now everywhere haunted by memories. The pleasant and familiar experiences and places Pattie and I once shared, and the photographs, keepsakes, possessions, mementoes, embodying our love, are now pervasively enshrouded in a heavy cloak of pain-filled sadness, mirroring not joy, but rather sorrow, death, and darkness.

Alone on high mountain vistas we once frequented, I mournfully cry out her name, but only echoes of my wailing return. Even the wildflowers, once seen as happily gracing mountain meadows, now impart a feeling of mourning. Visiting places that we once rejoiced in together, I am apprehensive and filled with dread because of the impossible heartache it can engender.

I am advised that passage of time will ameliorate those feelings and am reminded of the old adage, "time heals all wounds." As Latin poet Virgil wrote over two thousand years ago, "Time bears away all things, even the heart." Short of developing much-feared memory loss, I remain skeptical of that ever happening. Time may change the way mourning manifests, but it never truly ends. Great loss, like great love, remains a part of us forever.

Like an aged wine, memories are best shared. "Remember when...?" recalls and creates a close bond of shared experiences. If a tree falls in the forest and no one hears it, does it make a sound? Similarly, if one recalls a cherished memory, but no longer has someone close to share it with, did it ever even occur?

When well-intentioned friends smile and say to me, "How wonderful your memories must be," I struggle not to choke up at the invoking of memories. In the rawness of my bereavement, I find "wonderful memories" are frequently too hauntingly painful to recall. My memories must eventually lose their edge, dulling with time, but the images buried deep in my soul will remain forever.

Others, uncomfortable in the face of my anguish, advise: "be strong . . . keep busy . . . get out among people." Some suggest I seek professional help, sedatives and anti-depression drugs—pop a pill for palliative relief from the suffering, block or enhance the brain's neurotransmitters and reduce the intensity of painful emotions. Conversely, another source counsels: "There is a natural winter of the heart, naturally healing and renewing, a season we must let run its course."

This winter of my heart engulfs my very soul. If grief is as straightforward and manageable as some suggest, would it stricken me, and others who suffer from its neurological stranglehold, in such emotionally supercharged and lasting ways?

I have learned an inverse correlation exists between the joy of love and the dark despair of deep grief: the more love and joy one felt, the closer one's attachment, the greater the misery and heartache from the loss. It is Pattie's deep love that torments me through this duality of joy and sorrow. As C. S. Lewis observed, the counterpoint for great love is great loss.

Is healing and acceptance of loss really simply a matter of time and letting a natural process run its course? And can the confession of feelings to a psychologist, along with modern pharmacology, really alleviate one's grief? Perhaps it works for some. I do believe that skirting or avoiding the dark center delays reconciling the loss and the potential for any true healing. We must honor and respect the pain that results from the loss of a loved one, perhaps try to transform it into something meaningful. The enslaved must row the galley boat.

Love, death, grief, and mourning are mysteries of the human condition and psyche that have been studied by philosophers and physicians since ancient time. Remedies and timetables to heal a broken heart do not exist. The emotions of both love and grief similarly arise and reside in the neurons of the brain—our "heart." The feelings from deep grief continue to challenge mankind's means for coping despite an exuberance of pharmacology and modern psychotherapy. As Nobel Prize-winning novelist and playwright Samuel Beckett noted, "The tears of the world are a constant quantity."

My chronicling, musings, and vignettes may provide awareness, but not the means for dealing with personal loss and complicated bereavement. There is, in fact, a cottage industry designed to assist the grief-stricken, but there are no ready cures. Those tormented by grief and in mourning may find some solace, however, by the simple realization that they are not alone on those dark paths.

Since recorded time, grieving has been a part of our humanity, as demonstrated by the ancient Greeks' tragic tale of Orpheus, who searches into the very depths of hell for his lost wife, Eurydice. Paved with indescribable sorrow, the pathways of bereavement can lead into Orpheus's darkest abysses. Alone, I find myself wandering those opaque reaches. The despair comes not only from my own loss, but also from knowing the heartrending emotional and physical pain, and shattered dreams, Pattie personally suffered, too.

I believe within the over twenty-two years span of my relationship with Pattie, there is more substance than just reading entertainment. While it is not a road map, our story is meaningfully embedded with timeless and worthy issues and values that invariably touch on eternal mysteries and truths, matters of the heart: fate, destiny and free will, courtship, love, relationships, healing the past, terminal illness, death, grief, mourning, spirituality, and the importance of nature in our lives. Those are matters that resist empirical observation and literal description or definition and are commonly only describable through metaphor.

I am neither a professional psychologist nor a practicing clinician, nor are my observations and this story methodically derived. Rather, these are firsthand personal and emotional accounts, which are not static and continue to evolve. I am not recommending you follow my and Pattie's ways or approaches. I am but a solitary, grief-stricken widower—a simple, ordinary person—chronicling the path that my journey, our journey, has taken. There are multiple paths in life, and in the end, each of us is left to find, unfurl, and experience our own unique journeys, however enriching or despairing.

LEGACY

No one is as capable of gratitude as one who has emerged from the torments of darkness.
— E. Wisel, 1986 Nobel Prize Acceptance Speech

Flash forward. Missoula had been buried under a record snowstorm a day earlier. Unplowed streets were clogged with the heavy late-season snow. I was driving our Toyota 4-Runner. It had been "Pattie's car." The high clearance, four-by-four vehicle readily crawled over the piles of snow blocking side streets. Without four-wheel drive it would have been impossible.

With me in the SUV were Pattie's sister, Donna, and Gaia, my niece. Donna had flown in ahead of the storm from Austin, Texas, and Gaia, from Ashland, Oregon, to attend the dedication celebration for the *Earle and Pattie Layser Distinguished Professorship in Conservation Biology and Policy* at the University of Montana's College of Forestry and Conservation. Also joining us was Gaia's son Gavan, a freshman Presidential Scholar at the College of Forestry in wildlife biology.

People asked, "Where was Brett?" My older son who is very important to me had without reason chosen not to attend. His absence was a source of family tension. Someone inferred from his enigmatic behavior that for whatever reason he appeared determined to avoid participating in recognition for Pattie and myself. Legacy is what we leave behind for others. I suppose, as far as legacy goes, all of us have a choice about what we consciously elect to honor.

It was March 4, 2014, and Pattie had been gone for seven months already. I was in deep mourning—a deep wraithlike grief, choking up at the mere mention of her name and immobilized by intense memories of her.

On campus, we had been provided a special university parking pass. After circling a few times, we managed to locate a plowed out vacant spot conveniently located in front of Forestry School building with Mount Sentinel looming before us.

We were unsure what to expect. I had been asked to make a speech. The President of the University and Dean of the Forestry School would also be making dedication speeches. We filed into a large seating room with a stage and podium. The event was being televised for the local news. Already seated in the filled-up auditorium were friends, old classmates, and a host of university people I didn't know, as well as Montana's Commissioner for Higher Education, the Provost for Academic Affairs, CEO of the UM Foundation, and other importantly titled personages. I was surprised to see there were a hundred or more attendees. I had not expected so many. A large brass plaque that was to be installed outside of the School of Forestry honoring Pattie and me was on display up front.

We had never anticipated this kind of attention. Pattie and I had led unassuming lives. Now here I was preparing to speak before a large audience about our lives and purposes, all while I still found it difficult to even utter Pattie's name aloud without emotionally choking up.

The president and the dean both spoke giving a long list of generous introductions. Then it was my turn. I lugged my heavy feelings of grief for Pattie's absence along to the podium with me. The emotional burden I felt in my bereavement trumped any anxiety which I may have had about speaking. With frequent pauses to gather my composure, I delivered our speech, Pattie's and my speech.

Thank you, President Engstrom and Dean Burchfield . . . family, friends and guests . . . and good morning.

Pattie and I led mostly private lives. After those generous introductory words, people in the audience must be looking around wondering . . . who is it they are talking about . . . really?

This morning, I have been given the unenviable task of making a speech about what is always an audience's least favorite topic—the speaker. I didn't ask to do this, the University Foundation insisted. Little did they know. So I ask, please have patience and bear with me. It took me weeks to prepare for this impromptu speech.

First, let me say, our gift is intended as an investment in education and research on the natural world's importance and value to society and toward the continuing existence and maintenance of wildland environments—particularly in the Northern Rockies, but also worldwide—as contrasted to the virtual, digital, urban, and manufacturing and economic development of the modern human environment.

I am here representing both Pattie and myself. I'm sure you would have enjoyed hearing Pattie speak more than me— she was more personable and much better looking, too.

Pattie died tragically before her time this past year. She had felt strongly about the Northern Rockies wildlands, particularly the Greater Yellowstone, calling it her "life's landscape." One of the last things she was physically capable of signing was this Gift Agreement.

Some background narrative for us both: Growing up in Pennsylvania's forested rural backwaters, I attended a one-room school house, first through eighth grades. The region was labeled "Appalachia." There were no jobs. I enlisted in the military. There, on late night watches, a friend told me tales about smoke jumping in Missoula; another friend, about his summer on a blister-rust crew in north Idaho.

Except possibly for my beer drinking ability back then, you might rightly judge I was poorly prepared for college.

But after my military tour, I drove my '57 Chevy from Pennsylvania to Missoula and matriculated in forestry. In retrospect, it was Robert Frost's "road less traveled," and graduation from the University of Montana that "made all the difference" in my life.

Conversely, Pattie grew up in a big city—Memphis, Tennessee. Excelling academically, she was first in her class, was voted most likely to succeed, and was crowned in pageants. She graduated from Rhodes College in Memphis with distinction. She was "smart with good looks and personality too," as a classmate put it.

In her former marriage, she had attended Washington White House functions. She laughingly claimed that Alabama's infamous Governor George Wallace had an eye for her. Years later she wrote: "We celebrated the Great Indoors at highly polished places boasting four-star cuisine and garden tours for the wives . . . I was a hothouse flower of the Deep South—sheltered and protected."

In 1974, at age twenty-five, Pattie was struck down with a ruptured cerebral aneurism, which was generally fatal in those days. She was flight lifted to Birmingham, Alabama, where a skilled surgeon saved her life.

As part of a difficult convalescence, her family arranged for her to spend time at the Triangle X Guest Ranch in Jackson Hole. She fell in love with the Tetons. It changed her life forever. Embarking on a "road less traveled" odyssey also, she moved west, eventually settling in Bozeman and independently opening Quest Gallery on Main Street.

I retired from the Forest Service in 1990, intent on moving back to the Greater Yellowstone. In 1991 while temporarily living in Bozeman, providence directed me to Pattie's gallery. Pattie later wrote, "I took Earle's hand, and we stepped into the outside . . . I will always be thankful that, over time and space, a Southern girl's backyard morphed into Yellowstone Park and other Western wildlands." The Northern Rockies became our home, our life's landscape, source of our avocation and our playgrounds.

When we weren't skiing, canoeing, fly fishing, cycling or backcountry trekking, I did photography, writing, and environmental consulting work. Pattie sold her art gallery and began writing. We published a lot of stories (between us perhaps a couple hundred) on conservation, natural history, history and heritage, outdoor recreation, and travel. We were a team, able to accomplish a lot. International travels transported us to far flung places. Bear with me on some examples, the relevance of which, I trust, should become apparent.

Pattie entitled herself a "conservation journalist" and was invited to write about black rhino conservation in the Selous Game Reserve at Sand River, Tanzania, where poaching had all but eliminated the rhino.

On another trip, our travels took us to the Serengeti wilderness, where we marveled at the wildebeest migration with no other people around us except our local guide—a place where today a major road is being proposed.

We journeyed to Uganda to write about mountain gorillas in Bwindi's Impenetrable Forest and observed roadside bush meat marketing at an entrance to Queen Elizabeth National Park.

Unguided and mud-covered, we searched a snake-infested marshy jungle habitat fragment for rare red collobus monkeys on Zanzibar Island and located the island's last old-growth red mahogany tree, fondly dubbed Mama Mtondoo, "big mama."

In Madagascar, where 40 percent of the population is under fourteen years of age, we witnessed "slash and burn" agriculture to feed the expanding population destroying primary forest and rare lemur habitat (80 percent of the island's primary forest is gone). While picking leaches off each other's faces, we found and photographed the rare indri, a large, panda-like primate with green glow eyes that has become a symbol for the protection of remaining rainforest habitat.

In the Galapagos Islands, appalled by the number of visitors, but impressed with the stringent protection practices for the rare endemic plants and animals, we admired the blue-footed boobies' singular courtship dance performances within only a few feet from us.

Along the Tiputini River deep in Ecuador's Amazonian jungle—Earth's richest biological habitat—we were confronted with road and oil development activity encroaching on the 2.5-million-acre Yasuni National Park. Yet the Waroni tribe still carries on its traditional way of life here.

We were lucky enough to journey into the midst of the Porcupine Caribou herd's migration in the Arctic National Wildlife Refuge, meanwhile the Refuge's so-called '1002 lands' were being proposed for oil and gas development.

On another trek, we photographed and observed Alaskan brown bears at a hair-raising distance of less than thirty feet, and learned on the ground how storied and habituated Alaskan brown bears of Katmai and McNeil Rivers were subject to hunting when they crossed the area between the two preserves. Pattie also later participated as a journalist with a BBC film crew doing a documentary on Alaska brown bears within the Hallo Bay wilderness.

In short, what all this means is we were fortunate to observe and write about some of Earth's beautiful, wild, and biologically unique places. But in the process, we also witnessed firsthand humankind's sobering worldwide assault on natural places and wildlife.

Are the parks, wildlands, and wildlife here in the Northern Rockies—what I call the Nation's "biological heartland"—more secure than those above? We continue to see park visitations escalate yearly, overwhelming agency budgets and facilities, and hear the continual call for commoditization of wildlife and other natural resources, while conflicts involving the region's emblematic wildlands and wildlife are generated by short-sighted, politically driven, and often heavy-handed nineteenth-century practices, attitudes, and values. Do we really fully recognize how special this place is where we live, here in the Northern Rockies?

As we point out in our gift agreement, a preponderance of future residential developments are predicted to continue to occur within less than 50 kilometers (31 miles) from National Forests, National Parks, and Wildernesses, further intensifying the above concerns, forcing our iconic wildlife to make the most of ever diminishing habitat and with management solutions that are often estranged from science, society, and any sense of place.

Pattie and I were never "bleeding-heart" preservationists. But we believed a paramount question facing us in the twenty-first century is: How might our ever-expanding human populations live close to or amid the world's last remaining wild or natural places without, in fact, destroying those places and their biological resources?

Can higher education and the College of Forestry and Conservation really make a difference? We believe it can by assuming a leadership role in deciding the future spiritual, biological, and intellectual fate of the Northern Rockies. As the University President pointed out in his remarks, the college represents "an academic and research powerhouse."

Admittedly, conservation can be a "messy problem," but Pattie and I strongly believed applied research, education, and an enlightened public are key to society's unloosing the Gordian knot and for addressing long-standing intractable issues. I know, too, that can be a big order politically in a state that has failed to designate a single new Wilderness area in thirty years.

The University of Montana is well positioned to be a frontline leader in conservation—geographically, intellectually, and scientifically. Yellowstone National Park was the first of its kind in the world. Within this same landscape today, we can also be leaders in demonstrating to the world how to live in ecological and sustainable harmony with our wildlands and wildlife. It is toward that goal that Pattie and I are pledging this gift.

On another level, I know you must be wondering how a country boy who overcame his origins, together with a transformed Southern Belle, ever came up with the extra cash for this gift? I can only tell you, it was the old-fashioned way: strong work ethics, saving, and investing. That combined with a conservative lifestyle and our being indifferent consumers. Rather than material things, the wildflowers in the Tetons' alpine meadows, Yellowstone's wildlife, and each other, provided our joy and happiness.

As I was delivering my talk, looking around the room I noticed many in the audience were in tears, which made control of my emotional upwelling even more difficult.

Afterward, amid many congratulatory well-wishes and words of gratitude, we made our way to a room set aside for a beautifully prepared celebratory luncheon, complete with champagne and toasts performed for Pattie and me. But it was made even more memorable by two of the menu items—elk tenderloin and wild Montana huckleberries. No one had informed the chef that those were two of Pattie's favorite foods. It was one of those astonishing slack-jawed coincidences.

I felt Pattie's close presence. Together we had contributed a lasting legacy toward the preservation of wild lands and wildlife in the Northern Rockies through education and science.

Other memorials or events that would also come to bear Pattie's name as part of her legacy were The Murie Center's Pattie Layser Writer-in-Residence and the Pattie Layser Mary's Nipple Mountain Challenge. The Murie Center's Pattie Layser Writer-in-Residence program at Moose, Wyoming, is intended to assist writers in promoting the value of wilderness, wildlife, and nature within our society in perpetuity. The program would come to be taken over by Jackson Hole's Teton Science School. The Pattie Layser Mary's Nipple Mountain Challenge is an annual ski event hosted by Grand Targhee Resort to raise money for St. John's Hospital Oncology Department for breast cancer victims.

The Layser family farmstead at Pine Creek was deeded by Pattie and me to become a part of Pennsylvania's Tiadaghton State Forest, a portion of which will be managed as State Forest Wilderness Area and a part as roadless streamside public recreational lands.

A weekend set aside for women to learn fly casting and fishing at Pennsylvania's Pine Creek has been named as the Pattie Bell Layser Women's Fly Fishing Event by an Orvis fishing guide and friend.

In the Winter 2013–14 issue of *Teton Valley Magazine,* a magazine to which Pattie had been a frequent contributor, the editor eulogized her with the following words: 'Farewell to a woman of truly uncommon character—one of our longest-serving contributors—one who loved any weather the Tetons could throw at her . . . or caress her with.'

Any legacy Pattie and I may create stems from gratitude. We were deeply grateful for our relationship, each other, and the wildlands, wildlife, and lifestyle that the Northern Rockies afforded us. What we wish to leave behind is a contribution toward those wild landscapes continuing to exist into perpetuity for the enjoyment of future generations.

Pattie *and* Earle
September 18, 1993

PART I

THE SPRINGTIME OF OUR LIVES

CHAPTER 1

PROVIDENCE

You cannot connect the dots looking forward; you can only connect them looking backwards. So you have to trust that the dots will somehow connect in your future. You have to trust in something. your gut, destiny, life, karma, whatever.

— Steve Jobs

Someone once said, "When you get to the end, you begin to think about the beginning." It is true. My mind frequently involuntarily transports me back through time, vividly replaying and reflecting on our lives and time together. Ours is truly a love story; it is our story, Earle's and Pattie's.

There were many critical junctures in my life which led me to Pattie. Had she or I decided any of them differently, it is unlikely we would have ever found each other. Were these junctures coincidences? Perhaps, but what were the odds?

Still, whatever individual actions our free will appears to decide toward a purpose or future, it is generally only afterward that we "connect the dots" and wonder was it instead providence or destiny that shaped our lives.

In the late 1980s, I was a career employee with the USDA Forest Service in central Oregon. As a white, 50-year-old male, my chances for any immediate advancement dead-ended when the agency mandated diversity of its workforce goals. I had a good life and friends in Oregon. The prudent thing to do was to continue on there, and coast with my ample and secure civil service salary.

But being restless and unsatisfied, I chose instead to take an early retirement from my federal Forest Service career. At the time I still had a youthful head of hair without any frosting of grey. Healthy, strong, and fit, I wanted to create a new and more rewarding life while time and energy remained.

My decision to leave the Forest Service was not the result of a midlife crisis. Something or someone was mysteriously beckoning me to return to the Yellowstone-Teton region, a place I knew from having worked in Jackson Hole years earlier. Something or some part of my life there remained unfinished. My dreams sought reality. Free will set fate in motion.

After a retirement party held at the Juniper Country Club near Bend in January 1990, I put my furnishings in storage and drove my newly purchased blue four-by-four Toyota pickup to Jackson Hole. In my mind, I was returning there for the open space, wildlife, wilderness, endless skiing, and the mountains and mountain town lifestyle—things that were a big and important part of my identity—to begin a new life. That was the plan, as far as it went. Little did I realize this new life would become a journey of the heart.

I moved into a poorly heated, dilapidated cabin in funky Wilson, Wyoming, in Jackson Hole. It was twenty below zero, with snow piled high around the shack. An icicle hung from the cabin's showerhead. I thought of it as an adventure, a new beginning, not a hardship.

I was fortunate to have found any rental at all in midwinter. The valley's itinerant population of skiers and service workers had already settled in for the season, taking up the few available lodgings. The next morning, my new truck would not start. The extreme cold was an impressive force. It stirred my imagination, stimulating some whimsical doggerel:

> Arctic winds blow with incessant frigid force
> and in whirlwinds lit with surreal light,
> lend to snowstorms all their might.
> Then follows a clear and star-lighted night

when temperatures settle out of sight.
By dawn the shrunken mercury has congealed,
and the cold's power is revealed.
Glittering from frost so intense,
ice crystals stand erect in magnetic suspense.
In the dawn's glowing light,
those tiny prisms will a fiery blaze ignite,
in mockery of the past cold night.

From the town of Wilson, named after its nineteenth-century polygamist Mormon founder, I had ready access to Teton Pass and Grand Teton National Park for backcountry skiing. Nora's Fish Creek Inn restaurant and the renowned Stage Coach Bar in Wilson provided for my social life. The public library housed in the old log building on King Street in the town of Jackson supplemented my literary needs. I breakfasted with the locals, read books, danced with the Sunday regulars, and skied. I felt relaxed and unburdened; it was where I belonged.

I dropped a résumé off at a local engineering firm to do environmental consulting work, which almost immediately netted me part-time work and extra income to supplement my small retirement. I named my independent environmental consulting business Land Management Services.

Foremost, though, was skiing, which I practiced daily in all its forms, locations, and conditions because, you might say, tongue in cheek, perfecting the sport and lifestyle required practice. The various forms of skiing included downhill, backcountry, freestyle and classic cross-country. Unlike today, there were comparatively few backcountry or extreme skiers at the 8,431-foot elevation Teton Pass. Picture a quiet world encased in four to five feet of loose powder snow. On one route, I would ski south from the pass summit, finding and breaking trail along the interconnected ridges to Mount Elly, and then continue on to a glade-like bowl named Edelweiss. In my telemark-turn descent, I knew enough to stay along the treed edges and ridges to avoid triggering an avalanche.

After reaching the bottom, I would have to climb back to the top of the pass. At the time, I did not own climbing skins or have benefit of today's modern equipment, so it was a significant workout switchbacking up, climbing by sidestepping, and using herringbone maneuvers in the deep snow. I felt young and strong; I reveled in the challenges of this silent adrenaline-filled world set within deep solitude. But in retrospect, skiing alone in the backcountry probably was not the wisest thing.

I also took road trips to explore the living desirability and skiing conditions at places like Bozeman, Gardiner, Cook City, and West Yellowstone, Montana. I was searching for something—adventure and newness, maybe. And for the first time in my life, I enjoyed the novelty of complete freedom, with no responsibility for anyone other than myself, no alarm clock or schedules. Feeling lonely or at loose ends never occurred to me; I only recall a sense of exhilaration as though at the beginning of a long-anticipated voyage.

I participated in Bozeman's 18-kilometer Jim Bridger Langlauf Series Viking Revenge classic cross-country ski race in Hyalite Canyon, where I won my age class. Unknown to me at the time, I was very close to finding Pattie during those Bozeman visits. The budget motel where I would crash in Bozeman was only several blocks from her gallery on Main Street.

When the snow began receding in April, I rented an inexpensive off-season condo at Teton Village in Jackson Hole. I extended my running routes from Teton Village into Grand Teton National Park following along Granite Creek Canyon. In early spring, there was no one else on the trails. Buttercups, fawn lilies, and bluebells colorfully lined the paths winding through the otherwise stark sagebrush. Granite Creek roared with snowmelt and mists rose from receding snow banks permeating the forest. It was exhilarating: a natural endorphin-induced intoxication some athletes call "runner's high," "flow," or being "in the zone," a focused and energized calm verging on euphoric.

Running on a mountain trail,
through the forest in dawn's early light,
dank from thundershowers of the night.
Running past trees bejeweled with water beads
on to where the trail leads.
Running where a drapery of morning mist is departing
like a great celestial curtain parting.
Running quietly on the spongy trail,
silent but for a mountain thrush
and the canyon cascade's rush.
Running with an easy rhythm,
past snow banks in shaded nooks,
from which glide small brooks.
Running through meadows
graced with buttercups and lilies glowing
and sparkling rivulets flowing.
Running in the forest
the simple joy of being—
a timeless eternal bonding
with the mountain morning!

On one of my forays, I visited the Greater Yellowstone Coalition's headquarters, a nonprofit conservation organization based in Bozeman. There the staff directed my attention to a Nature Conservancy advertisement for a Greater Yellowstone Ecosystem Coordinator position. I was not sure I wanted a salaried job but applied for the position with mixed feelings. As an independent consultant, I was doing just fine. Why would I want to tie myself down with a salaried job? On the other hand, I imagined the coordinator position would have me traveling around the Yellowstone region, interacting with agencies on resource management decisions and conservation issues, and getting paid a little for it, too! I envisioned it as a chance to contribute to wildland and wildlife conservation—an opportunity to give back.

In the job interview, I proposed my office be located in Jackson Hole. My interviewers were agreeable, but it turned out to be bait-and-switch. After hiring me, the Conservancy state directors did an immediate mid-stream change and, instead, insisted that I locate in Bozeman. Another fork in the road, a twist of fate, perhaps?

I took advantage of Bozeman's severely depressed real estate market to purchase a stunning log home on five acres located twenty minutes from downtown. It was situated north of the Springhill Community at 11832 Gee Norman Road, along the foothills of the Bridger Mountains overlooking the Gallatin Valley. The price, quality, and attractive setting, combined to make the property an exceptional investment.

I dedicated a room in my new home as an office space. I was the sole worker in an office of one. Unlike earlier in Wilson, the isolation began nagging at me. The frequent trips on the narrow winding road into Bozeman, where I knew no one, wore on me. Sure, I had guests, relatives, friends from outside the area, and Conservancy employees visiting frequently. They sometimes overnighted, came and went, but for the most part, I was alone and totally on my own. I did long solitary runs and bike rides on the neighborhood's unpaved roads, and hikes along the nearby Bridger Mountain slopes and summits.

One might dismiss what led me to locate in Bozeman as a series of unremarkable coincidences—a decision to take early retirement, acting on a persistent yearning to return to the Greater Yellowstone, applying for the Conservancy job, and their last-minute switch, requiring that I locate in Bozeman. But if you believe in providence, what happened next is undeniable testament.

I felt driven by what I interpreted as a desire to meet some new friends for socializing, skiing, hiking, cycling, dining, and meeting for after-work drinks or shows. Being single, I hoped to find friends of the opposite gender who would be interested in doing these activities with me.

At the time Bozeman's shopping district and businesses were

mostly confined to downtown Main Street. The store fronts ran parallel on each side of the street for four or five blocks. The outlying franchises, malls, and shopping center sprawl that characterize Bozeman today had yet to arrive.

The fifth day of April in 1991 is forever fixed in my mind. Not many people were about that morning; a blustery spring snow shower was swirling through downtown. I had the crazy idea to start at one end of Main Street and go door-to-door visiting each store—investigating the merchandise, finding any attention-grabbing places, meeting any interesting people, getting to know Bozeman better. Where could I have gotten that idea? What inspired the idea to conduct essentially a systematic search along Bozeman's Main Street?

I had not gone far before ducking into Quest Gallery and Gift Shop at 122 East Main Street. A whirlwind of blowing and swirling snow ushered me through the doorway. A very attractive, energetic young woman greeted me. She was wearing western boots, a brightly-patterned western skirt and blouse, dangling ear-rings and western turquoise jewelry, including a tasteful Concho belt. She was modeling items she sold in her store, but the way she wore them were an expression of her identity. An Elizabeth Taylor look-alike, she had the same height, weight, and hour-glass figure. Her mane of long dark hair was outrageously and magically thick and curly; her smile radiant. She was a delightfully, dauntingly gorgeous and charming person. I learned her name was Pattie; she was the gallery's owner.

Pattie retailed the works of a hundred consignment artists through her gallery. Her professionally displayed merchandise consisted of an eclectic mix of original paintings, pottery, jewelry, Indian artifact replicas, bronzes, carvings, and other art and craft items. Pattie could speak knowledgeably on any of it, and compellingly about the artists themselves, too.

She showed me craft and art pieces and talked with me about them, giving me the sales pitch and testing whether I might be a prospective customer. We made small talk, though I no longer recall what we talked about. No doubt we were hesitant and self-conscious, as people are when they first meet. Noting that she was not wearing a wedding ring, I wondered how this gorgeous person could be single. I investigated no more Main Street stores that day.

A day or two passed before I ventured back into Quest Gallery. When I did, Pattie appeared from the back of the shop, and walking toward me, cheerfully greeted me by name: "Hello Earle."

Closing my eyes now, I can still vividly recall the moment and hear her voice. The fact that she had remembered my name impressed upon me that maybe I was not viewed as just a potential customer. Her "Hello Earle" would resonate in my mind for the next twenty-two years and forever after. Like the lyrics from the song "Abracadabra," when I heard her call my name, "I lit up like a burning flame." The flame she lit will burn in me for her for the rest of my life.

While details of our conversation have faded, I recall that I offered to take her to lunch.

"I can't leave the store untended over lunchtime. Otherwise," she encouraged in her agreeably smiling and demure manner, "I would love to have lunch."

The next day I showed up at Quest Gallery just before noon with lunch for two, including chocolate-covered strawberries and a bottle of white wine. It was the beginning of a courtship and love affair that would lead to our marriage and a relationship that flamed unquenchably, until as we would vow, only death would cause us to part.

Our meeting on that snowy April day remains nothing less in my mind than a fortuitous miracle. It was a reunion of souls. Considering the combination of coincidences involved, some would say it was testament to the existence and workings of providence.

CHAPTER 2

THE DANCE BEGINS

What were the odds that we would find each other, this one remarkable woman and I, that our paths would meet and match as they had? What are the odds that we'd change from strangers to soul mates?

— Richard Bach, *One*

The courting of a lasting friendship is a sweet responsibility, the recompense of which is a gift of perennial blossoming throughout a marriage and a lifetime.

As it was, the next evening after work, we agreed to meet for drinks. Getting acquainted, sitting together in the semi-darkened lounge booth, both our antennas were inquisitively tuned to initial impressions. Conversation, banter, and laughter came easily. I do not remember any awkwardness. "Intrigued" perhaps best describes both our initial reactions.

Pattie made a remark that we would joke about forever after: "I think you are too young for me."

Maybe it was a polite and clever way of asking my age? She was surprised to learn I was nearly ten years older than she. As a sage advised, "Find an age you like and stick with it." In those years, I was managing to do just that. I was a model of health and fitness, appearing much more youthful than my chronological age. Both of us appeared younger in that way.

It was before e-mail, Twitter, Facebook or selfies. Handwritten notes, cards, love letters with flower petals enclosed, delivered roses, and telephone calls back and forth at all hours of the day and night followed in a passionate blizzard of interchange. All this was in addition to seeing each other on dates every day. It was a fulltime occupation. You might even have called it an obsession.

Infatuated, I nicknamed her "Pattie Cake" ("Patty cake, patty cake, baker's man, bake me a dozen as quick as you can . . .") and teased her about being Scarlett from *Gone with the Wind*. Somewhere she found commemorative postage stamps boldly entitled "Gone with the Wind," showing a scene of Rhett and Scarlett embracing, which she affixed to her letters to me. While Pattie was originally from Memphis, Tennessee, she had consciously worked to erase tell-tale Southern mannerisms and a Deep South accent. She was quite capable of turning it back on though, parodying the "y'all" and slurred syllables for effect whenever she wished.

Both of us saved correspondence from that time. On April 16, only a short time after our meeting and our first dates, I composed and mailed her a poem. I had it delivered to her door along with a red rose by a florist.

It was a long search—a Quest,
to find her somewhere in the West.
In a moment of fate, on a snowy April date,
I found her wearing beautiful brown curls.
When she mysteriously confided,
it was all apparently already decided.
To some this may seem fast, but we already had a past.
Our karma is fulfilled, and spirits again reunited;
we begin the long awaited timeless dance,
and the Quest is stilled.

Normally cautious, I had gone from intrigued to smitten in a short time. Somehow, I knew I had found the person I had been searching for — that one person that makes you feel whole.

In a letter postmarked April 19, Pattie responded:

I felt you thinking of me when I awoke. The rose was lovely, still smelling sweet—I knew I'd hear from you today. All day I chided myself for such silly but eager anticipation of going home to check the mailbox . . . And there wasn't a post card—there was a beautiful poem, a moving chronicle of recognition . . . a sentiment of serendipity and synchronicity.

Christopher Morley's verses kick off thoughts of your oneness with Nature . . . and my wondering if this poetry was what I would discover in you . . . wondering if you would introduce me to the most natural of worlds—the most foreign of worlds to me.

Born comrade of bird, beast and bee
And unselfconscious as the tree . . .
Elate explorer of each sense
Without dismay, without pretense . . .
Life's queer conundrums you accept.
Your strange Divinity still kept . . .
There were days, O tender elf
When you were poetry itself!

More than two decades later, after Pattie was gone, I discovered a note in her journal she had saved from that earlier time. The note, which Pattie wrote to herself, told me that she too had recognized that our meeting was something beyond the ordinary:

Angels at Work . . . When one sees a sign of serendipity, it's merely Angels hard at work. Earle has a strong sense of self. It's wonderful for him . . . and it is wonderful ("for me" was crossed out and "to see" inserted). It's kind of a nice, quiet nudge that says: truth is simple/life is good/I, too, can find my center. Chalk another up for guardian angels . . . nice the way they place someone in your path at fortuitous times . . . I value our fledgling friendship. The little I know of you, Earle, I like and respect.

Pattie's lovely personality and inner beauty graced everything she did. It even showed in her handwriting—a delightfully artistic Victorian-like script with bold flourishes, sweeps, and swirls. I believe a person's handwriting tells a lot about them. When she wrote to me, she would always draw the Chinese Taoist yin-yang symbol ☯ on the back of her envelopes or in place of a return address.

Yin, the female side and yang, the male, represent contrary forces which can be complementary, forming a dynamic in which the whole is greater than the parts. The concept can also refer to opposing forces that require balancing to optimize overall results. For Pattie and me, the yin-yang symbol represented the power of us together versus that of two separate individuals standing alone.

Fittingly, too, some say, projecting energy through a symbol is a means to cast a spell. Needless to say, Pattie's yin-yang symbol worked. I was captivated, spellbound. Beginning with our meeting that snowy April day, our relationship would grow into an uncommonly deep and intimate bonding, becoming an authentic, meaningful, and passionate journey.

Perhaps considered old-fashioned and "straight" in today's world, our relationship was fueled by exceptional closeness, intimacy, and deep passion. Love and mutual attraction cascaded us along with the force of a mountain avalanche. It would continue for as long as each of us lived and beyond: an unending spiritual journey, forever lasting.

Our lives together would come to bear witness to Helen Keller's observation: "The best and most beautiful things in the world cannot be seen or even touched. They must be felt with the heart."

CHAPTER 3

DISPARATE BACKGROUNDS

In magnetism, opposite poles attract and like poles repel . . . thus satisfying the principle of yin and yang . . . I have known a lot of people who often marry people like themselves; some of those marriages last while others break up. I married a girl twenty-nine years ago, who was in perception and reality entirely opposite of me.

— Abdullah Ahmad

When searching for a prospective mate or a person to date, it is common wisdom, and generally advisable, to select someone with whom you appear to have much in common. On the surface, Pattie and I came from vastly different backgrounds. How could it ever possibly have worked?

In *Shadows on the Grass*, author Isak Dinesen eloquently addresses this question: "In order to form and make up a Unity, in particular a creative Unity, the individual components must be of a different nature... two homogenous units will never be capable of forming a whole..."

When Pattie and I first met, we were without a doubt "of a different nature."

Both of us were also more than casually familiar with the single's social merry-go-round of the era and experience had taught us to be guardedly cautious. I had been unmarried for nine years and Pattie for eight when we met. Both of us were wary of the intense, but generally brief and empty affairs that so often characterized dating and relationships in those years.

When dating someone, it was a learned practice to be cautious and distrustful initially, always on guard—watchful for signs of offensive behavior, boredom, mistrust, or character flaws—and to keep one foot out the door, ready to "split" just in case. Those behaviors were even more pronounced or prevalent in and about resort towns, where a significant segment of the population was transient—always on the move, footloose, looking for a good time, unemployed or underemployed, responsibility phobic and perennially single.

Many puzzled about those things for us in the beginning of our relationship. Yet it turned out we were a match made in paradise. And, for us it only became better the longer we were together. Over relatively short time, we grew together chimera like, becoming EarleandPattie or PattieandEarle; where one ended and the other began, you could not be sure.

We proved that disparate backgrounds can actually contribute to making an interesting, compelling and strong pairing, when combined with maturity, mutual attraction, respect, honesty, open hearts, educated minds, reciprocity, patience and willingness to work in concert. Whew! Admittedly, it was a lot to ask for or expect. Like Pattie's yin and yang, it turned out that we balanced and complemented each other in many ways, from a healthy lust to deep affection. We respected each other; and both of us sought to live up to the high regard with which we viewed one another.

Epitomizing that sentiment in a 1995 Valentine Pattie had written:

> Happy Valentine's, Earle! A Western man and a Southern lady might appear a mismatch but, h…m…m… you suit me perfectly. I love you and all the many things we enjoy together. My luck in life had always been about average— until I met you. Love you dearly, Pattie. We're a mismatch made in heaven!

Earle's History

I had grown up on a farm in a mountainous and remote rural area of Pennsylvania known as Pine Creek, near a place called Cedar Run, population maybe twenty-four. Fishing and hunting not only served for subsistence, it was also the sole source of recreation and entertainment. The unspoiled natural settings, clean mountain streams, and abundant wildlife made it a wonderful place for a boy to grow up.

But to say jobs were "scarce" implies there were some; it is more accurate to state there were none. The day after high school graduation, a group of classmates and I enlisted in the United States Navy.

I served in faraway places in the Pacific. On late-night shipboard watches, a friend told me tales about fighting wildfires in the Rocky Mountains and smoke-jumping in Missoula, Montana. Another buddy frequently spoke about his former summer job with the U.S. Forest Service; living in backcountry tent camps in north Idaho, doing blister rust-control work, eradicating *Ribes,* the alternate host for a disease affecting valuable white pine trees.

My father, too, had worked in Johnson County, Wyoming, wrangling cattle on the Powder River and herding sheep in the Big Horn Mountains, not long after the Johnson County Cattle War in the early part of the twentieth century. I had listened to his reminiscences my entire growing up. He had wanted to become a forester. But instead, when he returned to the East, he became entrapped by family obligations that dictated the course of his life.

After my military tour, I drove my 1957 Chevy from Pennsylvania to Missoula, Montana, and matriculated in forestry. Elements of the Old West still persisted. Cowboys, loggers and Native Americans walked the streets in Missoula; silver dollars were still in circulation. I labored in sawmills at night and seasonal forestry jobs in summer to pay for college. And I satisfied my goal to become a smokejumper.

In my sophomore year, I met and married an attractive nineteen-year-old girl, who, in contrast to me, had never lacked for anything growing up. Her father had been a medical doctor in Hollywood, California. She had gone to debutante school, had been her high school class president and valedictorian, and she drove a car her parents had given her that was newer than mine.

She related to the pseudo sophistication of big cities and pop culture, and I to nature and the outdoors. Our relationship was based on social media messages and clichés, youthful exuberance, and the idealism of inexperience. We were trendy and with-it. It was, after all, the revolutionary 1960s. We were married in a small fundamentalist church, to which we had no other connection, in Hamilton, Montana.

Nine months later, we had our first child. Through both of us working, and my scholarship awards and the GI Bill, I was able to go on to graduate school, earning a Master of Science degree at Syracuse, New York. I obtained a career position with the USDA Forest Service, and worked throughout the western United States in national forest administration. My career was promising; my advancement rapid. I received prestigious awards for my contributions. Our two sons were athletic and academic achievers. We were admired as a model family. Then it all nightmarishly came apart.

To abbreviate what was a distressfully difficult time, let me say this: people change, and character deficits surface. Rather than growing together, we grew apart. My ex-wife became ruinously addicted to alcohol. Her favorite thing in life became Black Russians, a cocktail made of Kahlua and vodka.

She secreted bottles of liquor around the house, hiding them in the washing machine, the garbage cans, in the back of closets—never facing the world honestly. Her artifice became more convenient than truth. Boozing, cigarettes, diet pop, and bulimia became more important than anything else in her life—more than family and children, and least of all, our marriage, my career, or me.

She disparaged it all. She rationalized her alcohol problem by becoming a combative soldier for militant feminism. Melodramatically expert at "blame and shame," men, especially authority figures, became her dastardly enemies. After sixteen years of marriage, the last few of which were hell on earth, I sued for divorce. To demonstrate her disrespect for "the system," she did not bother to appear at the proceedings, and she swore not to want any part of child-rearing responsibilities. I was awarded full legal custody of our then teenage boys. Only the financial settlement amount I would agree to engaged her interest.

Pattie's History

Pattie was born second of four daughters in Memphis, Tennessee. Her father, who had been an Army Air Force tail gunner in World War II, was an attorney for Memphis Power and Light. In an unpublished memoir, Pattie wrote: "I was born in the big city, but grew up provincial, a sheltered and protected hothouse flower of the Deep South. The fenced backyard of a quarter-acre lot in the suburbs effectively contained azaleas and roses and my life experiences."

Pattie graduated second in her high school class, demurring to be first, and was voted "most likely to succeed." She was crowned in pageants and awarded a scholarship at Rhodes College in Memphis, where she graduated with distinction.

After college graduation, in a large formal wedding, she married a law student. Later she wrote: "Life became living in cities and vacationing in larger ones . . . we took a few trips, doing what we knew to do. We celebrated the Great Indoors at highly polished places boasting four-star cuisine and garden tours for the wives."

They also attended formal Washington, DC functions in Pattie's husband's role as a junior liaison for Whitehouse communications. At one function, former Alabama Governor George Wallace singled Pattie out, complimenting her beauty.

A few years later, at age twenty-five, Pattie faced death. She was struck down by a ruptured cerebral aneurism from which survival was a rarity back then. She was flight lifted to Birmingham, Alabama, where a skilled surgeon saved her life. In those days, rest, not physical therapy, was prescribed. She lay in a hospital bed until atrophied muscles no longer held her joints in place. She was carried out of the hospital when she returned home. The near-death experience forever changed her outlook on life.

Attending a business conference at Jackson Lake Lodge near Moran, Wyoming, her father and mother had thrilled at the sight of the scenic Tetons. To encourage Pattie's convalescence, her family arranged a novel vacation for her to spend part of a summer at the Triangle-X Guest Ranch in Grand Teton National Park. There she learned to ride horseback and fell in love with the Tetons. It was a deeply fundamental change from her previous life, a new beginning and destiny. In memoir notes she wrote: "I boarded the plane to leave, lugging an endless, bottomless ache for the Tetons with me."

Pattie had an opportunity to move west to Big Timber, Montana, to work for Western artist Jack Hines and portraiture artist Jessica Zemsky, who mentored her art interests. She also became friends with Western writer Spike Van Cleve at the Lazy K Bar Ranch. And she even owned her own horse.

The Crazy Mountain Range beckoned on the horizon, but she never ventured there. It was the West, but not the Teton Mountains she cherished. However, she learned and evolved from her association with down-to-earth, small-town, authentic Western folks. It was a foreign new life and a lifetime away from the Deep South. Pattie successfully became what author Gretel Ehrlich, *Solace of Open Spaces*, called a "culture straddler."

Pattie discovered her husband lying to her about several matters. He blamed her for not having children; but it turned out, he was the one unable to father a child. He was sedentary and lacked ambition. Unable to find work, he secretly relied on his parents for livelihood. The intimacy Pattie wanted in her marriage was absent. In the end, she lost all respect for her husband and divorced him. In the process, he further alienated her by being adversarial and pettily contesting their settlement. In time, Pattie moved to Bozeman, Montana, bought a home on South Tracy Avenue, and independently opened Quest Gallery and Gift Shop on Main Street.

CHAPTER 4

THE SPRINGTIME OF COURTSHIP

Yes, the Earth speaks, but only to those who can hear with their hearts. It speaks in a thousand, thousand small ways, but like our lovers and families and friends, it often sends messages without words. For you see, the Earth speaks in the language of love.

— Steve Van Matre, *The Earth Speaks*

Outside in the Outdoors

In her journal notes, Pattie penned: "When Earle walked into my gallery, I took his hand and together we walked into the outside."

The imagery in that line is beautiful. One's imagination choreographs what is left unsaid. But Pattie's lovely reference does not explain just how major a role outdoor activities and authentic encounters with nature played throughout our dating, courtship, and relationship.

It is said that being in love opens us to better communion with nature and the landscape of our lives. As author Diane Ackerman writes, "By loving a person and nature at the same time, the passion for both is heightened." Both of those observations came into play for us.

The outdoors and nature became the playing fields where together our souls danced and celebrated. To paraphrase Isaiah 55:12, it was as if the mountains and the hills broke forth into singing before us, and all the trees of the field clapped their hands, happily welcoming us as a couple. We heard the Earth speaking, and for us, it truly resonated in the language of love.

Albert Einstein once said, "There are two ways to live your life: One is as though nothing is a miracle. The other is as though everything is a miracle." For Pattie, it was all an enchanting miracle. She possessed a contagious innocent joy and enthusiasm for life and an uncomplaining and uncomplicated desire to experience and try everything. It was uplifting and a pure delight to be with her. As the reader will later discover, there was also a *raison d'être* behind Pattie's uncommon receptivity.

People have told me, "You were lucky to have been with Pattie." While I agree that luck and lust played a part, it went much deeper. Our coming together like two tightly orbiting stars, and the profound and loving relationship we created, was never just "luck." Both of us had earlier opportunities to be with others, but were not satisfied. We were searching for that one special person, reluctant to be entrapped into settling for less. And we both delighted in making our relationship meaningful and lasting.

We had the experience and intelligence necessary to envision an idea of what it was we wanted. When we met, we were both mature and smart enough to recognize the possibility of old-fashioned fulfillment as a couple. Our courtship and bonding reflected emotional maturity, interpersonal communication skills, reciprocity and unselfishness. One might ask, was it luck, free will, or destiny? Very little of it, in my opinion, was "luck." To the question of, "Are you there for me?" the response from both of us grew to be a resounding, "Yes, always."

Many couples appear *not* to build a relationship based upon growing together as one, but rather settle for establishing precisely defined and inviolate boundaries. Instead of passion and romance, they are dutiful and concerned with comfort, forming sort of a business partnership. Over time, a fondness for one another and desire for security characterizes the relationship, not action, passion, romance, intimacy, or necessarily enduring love. Neither of us were the sort to capitulate or compromise, settle for comfort and inviolate boundaries, or for distorted images of romance and love.

Maybe, too, some of the people, who categorized what Pattie and I enjoyed as "luck," were envious and making a sour-grapes statement about their own personal dissatisfaction, disappointment, or mediocrity with their partner or marriage. Successful, fulfilling, lasting relationships and marriages are rarely simply luck.

In *The Book of Love,* the thirteenth-century poet, Rumi, noted: "A thousand half-loves must be forsaken to take one whole heart home." Some knowingly or unknowingly, it seems, settle for Rumi's "half-loves."

Because of Pattie's gentle gracious personality and her attractiveness, there was a tendency by some to mistakenly categorize her as a "Southern Fluff." Nothing was farther from the truth. Once, at a Bozeman gathering, one of her acquaintances came up to me and snidely remarked, "If you think you are going to make a 'mountain woman' out of her, good luck." In the Northern Rockies, so-called "mountain women" were independent women who could keep up with or surpass athletic men in outdoor activities or sports of the region, such as hiking, climbing, backpacking, kayaking, or skiing.

Over time, Pattie proved the acquaintance wrong. Whatever Pattie lacked at first in physical endurance and skill, she made up for with an unpretentious and happy enthusiasm. When we first met, I had a routine of running a seven-mile gravel road loop out at Gee Norman Road, north of Bozeman. I gave Pattie my mountain bike to ride while I ran. I was sorely put off when she was challenged to keep up with me on the hills, even with the bike. I wanted a companion who could share outdoor activities with me, and believed we each needed the stamina to be each other's mate. It was a testing of our fledgling relationship.

Years later, Pattie would sometimes kiddingly chide me because, as she termed it, I "almost dumped her" over the incident. But other aspects of our budding friendship gave me pause. I asked myself what was truly important at that stage in life. What do you want? What really matters to you? I concluded that continuing to get to know each other was paramount and much too lovely to give up so soon, just to preserve my fitness snobbery. I sacrificed some of my preconceived ideas in order to encourage and accommodate her—a nascent sign of potential commitment.

Making a deliberate effort to curb any elitist tendency, I suggested instead that we do some beginning run-walk intervals together. Not reluctant, though maybe curious, Pattie viewed it as a novelty. She excelled and had fun with it. Significantly, she was not inclined to try to compensate by complaining or holding me responsible for any of her personal physical difficulties or challenges. Pattie had moxie and never lacked ability, only opportunity and experience.

I never again confused trading Pattie's smiling and happy enthusiasm for any preconceived ideas about outdoor skill levels. She gently taught me it was worthwhile and rewarding to patiently wait, help, or further explain. The lesson carried over in my life into helping others, too. Eventually, I no longer had to wait for Pattie. In fact, at times, she would later be required to wait for me. We helped each other; over time we became a close team, empowering each other.

When we first met, Pattie had an established routine of walking after work: following paths along Bozeman Creek, climbing the foothills along the edges of town. They were not short strolls, but long ramblings. Intrigued, I suggested that we try some hikes in the nearby mountains instead: all new experiences for her.

Among those earliest hikes near Bozeman, I recall, were Storm Castle Mountain along the Gallatin River, where, on south slopes, we were attacked by a bazillion ticks; Sacagawea Peak, at 9,665-feet elevation, the highest peak in the Bridger Mountains, where we shared the alpine summit with mountain goats; and the steep twelve-mile round trip up Cascade Creek following alongside the tumbling cascades and waterfalls to Lava Lake in the Spanish Peaks Wilderness.

In Jackson Hole, we postholed up the switchbacks on the late spring snowpack to the still frozen Amphitheater Lake in Grand Teton National Park, where we kicked steps up the steep corn-snow embankments and glissaded back down. And later, on another memorable outing in the forest along the north end of the Gallatin Range, we surprised two different black bears that were foraging on buffalo berry. Not to be outdone by the bruins, it was on this hike that Pattie delighted in her first taste of wild huckleberries.

I have never forgotten Pattie's surprised expression of pleasure at her first taste of huckleberries, a tart and aromatic wild fruit. Introduced to the forest's proverbial wild bounty, she became an avid berry gatherer.

The hikes we went on might be considered relatively strenuous. Back then I was little inclined to stop much or go slow. I know Pattie must have hurt at times, but she neither complained nor blamed me for any difficulties or discomfort she experienced. Never complaining, she pushed herself to keep up and gradually became stronger because she had discovered a new-found enjoyment in the physical exertion, and delight in the mountains and the varied beauty of nature. For us it was Nature romantically represented by a capital N—a goddess in a flowing garment of mountain landscapes, wildflowers, waterfalls, bears, warblers and colorful butterflies.

Sometime around then, Pattie sent me a beautiful card illustrated with a delightful scene of an Indian woman walking among wildflowers, butterflies, birds, and forest animals, in which she had written:

> This card entitles bearer to the companionship of one becurled, novice hiker for a four to eight mile walk . . . to be used at bearer's discretion. In a postscript at the bottom she added: "Offer optimistically presented with no expiration date, but how about redeeming it in this lifetime. ☯

Pattie had a mountain bike of sorts, and we peddled the roads south of Bozeman, which, in those simpler times, had little traffic. We would ride up toward and to Hyalite Basin. I led her on her first off-road biking experience. She was elated riding the trail, zipping through the tree-lined riparian corridor, from Nash Road down Bozeman Creek.

"Why didn't someone tell me about this before!" she exclaimed.

We went fly fishing—again, another novel experience for Pattie—at Sixteen Mile Creek, near where a scene in Hollywood's *A River Runs Through It* would later be filmed. I had discovered a beautiful pool there earlier that supported an abundance of wild trout. When fly hatches magically appeared over the water at dusk, the fish came alive, erupting into classic surface feeding. And there was never anyone else around. It was breathtakingly idyllic.

Fly casting was an art that I had learned and accomplished with metronome precision as a child. Catching trout on artificial flies at the Sixteen Mile Creek site was impressively easy. Pattie was captivated.

Forever after that, Pattie would embarrass me by telling others how she was fascinated by my casting. "Watching the artful beauty of Earle's fly casting made me want to be able to do that, too." I bought her a fly rod outfit, and she began learning by practicing casting on a lawn.

As a child, Pattie had had happy family outings fishing at children's ponds in Memphis. Fishing in all forms was something she comfortably identified with as being a fun activity.

On our first challenging backcountry trip together, we were out for over four days. Back then I owned a 17-foot Kevlar Old Town canoe. Setting out before dawn, we canoed from Mary's Bay on Yellowstone Lake, paddling twenty-some miles deep into the furthermost wilderness reaches of the lake's South Arm to the mouth of Chipmunk Creek. It was a major wilderness outing.

The expansive surface of Yellowstone Lake can be mesmerizingly glass-like at times; at other times, a tempest of wind-driven swells and huge waves, making it intimidating and dangerous in an open canoe. Pattie was not the least fearful or apprehensive, but was instead exhilarated. She later wrote: "That day I caught my first cutthroat trout and drifted past a bull moose feeding along the lake's edge."

Pattie caught not just her "first cutthroat trout" that day, but literally dozens as she figured out how to spin cast from the canoe as I paddled. At one spot, on a far-reach of the lake, she hooked up with beautiful, deeply-colored sixteen-to-eighteen-inch native cutthroat every cast. As she reeled the struggling fish in, I was kept busy netting, unhooking, and returning them to the lake.

Drifting directionless in the wind while she fished, I pleaded, "Okay, Pattie, we've got to go on now."

"Wait, just one more cast," she'd say. And then, the lure would go sailing out into the lake again, and within a few cranks of the reel, another cutthroat would be hooked and giving fight.

We camped lakeside in a meadow at Chipmunk Creek, where I gathered some of the abundant elk thistle shoots. An edible wild plant resembling broccoli stalks, it supplemented our dinner. Forever after, Pattie delighted in a private joke. Putting on an innocent expression, she would tell people: "On our first camping trip, Earle collected and cooked *thistle* for our dinner."

"What?"

Those people she selectively chose to tell this story were unable even to imagine her sleeping in a tent on the ground. The thought of the poor dear having to eat thistle mortified them (even though they didn't have a clue what it was). Pattie would barely refrain from a giggle at the horrified expressions directed at me and my fumbling attempts to explain about edible wild plants.

On our return across Yellowstone Lake, we camped on the southern tip of the Promontory. We intended to wait until dawn to return across the yawning expanse of the lake's Southeast Arm—a time of day when the potentially unruly lake would be the calmest.

I have a self-timed photograph showing us at dusk sitting in a cloud of smoke from a smudge fire trying to keep swarms of voracious mosquitoes at bay. Both of us are peering through the smoky haze and clouds of mosquitoes directly into the camera with funny dazed-looking expressions. Whenever that photograph surfaced over the years, it was like an inside joke for us and never failed to make us laugh.

Fourteen years later, Pattie gave me a twelve-by-fourteen-inch anniversary card. It pictured a canoe pulled up on a gravel beach of a large lake, with a camp fire burning on the shore and heavy forest surrounding the wilderness scene, while a full-moon glowed on the water. When I view the card now among our mementoes, my mind immediately and movingly takes me back in time to our first Yellowstone Lake canoe trip. It is a cliché, but it really does seem like only yesterday. Our first backcountry canoe trip together on Yellowstone Lake remained among the many cherished and vivid memories buried deep in our hearts.

As I mentioned earlier, I was very much into skiing in those years—all kinds. In Oregon, I had won the classic ten-kilometer Crater Lake wilderness ski race three years in a row. I was a Nordic ski instructor at Grand Targhee Resort for a season, too. But it wasn't just about the skiing; it was also about being outside in the beauty of winter.

So, of course, when winter rolled around, I began teaching Pattie to ski. She owned a pair of waxless cross-country skis that had hardly ever been used. Later, she would refer to them as her "clunkers." They still hang in our Alta garage, part of her history. Instead I gave her a pair of light narrow racing skis to use. Because they can be more difficult to learn with, racing skis are generally not recommended for beginners. But Pattie easily overcame the difficulties and became proficient on them—lightness and speed vs. slow-moving clunkers.

We frequently cross-country skied near Bozeman at Brackett Creek in the Bridger Mountains. Later, in our back-and-forth between Alta or Jackson Hole, we would stop off at the renowned Rendezvous Ski Track in West Yellowstone, Montana, where Olympians trained; and in Jackson Hole, we regularly did the ten-mile round trip along Cottonwood Creek out to Jenny Lake and beyond, skiing on the frozen snow-covered lake; and, at times, a greater distance, over to Timber Island and along the river break terraces in Grand Teton National Park, where it would generally require that I break trail in the deep loose snow.

Those beautiful settings replete with wildlife became some of our favorite places for cross-country skiing. They could be challenging ski tours for anyone. But what was backcountry and solitude then has today been transformed into high-traffic front and side country through the advent of technology, improved equipment, trail grooming, and more and more people. It is as if the Yellowstone Ecosystem today is assumed to have unlimited capacity to accommodate ever increasing visitation and recreation uses—growing human population pressure exacted on fragile landscapes and environments.

In 1990, Teton County, Wyoming had a population of 11, 200. Twenty years later, the population surpassed 21,300—a 91 percent increase. The rapidly growing number of people has continued, not only among the resident and transient population, but also in the seasonal tourist visitations to Yellowstone and Grand Teton National Parks. Both parks had increases of about one million visitors annually over the above time period—an increase by one-third for Yellowstone and a doubling for Teton Park. In 2014 alone, ten-million people visited Wyoming, the attraction being Yellowstone, the Tetons, and cowboys. A massive magnet, Yellowstone region's biodiversity and wild places attract people from worldwide—from the worldwide population of over seven billion and exponentially growing. The numbers of people also clashes philosophically and irreconcilably with our cherished notion that wildernesses should be places with minimal human presence.

But up through the early 1990s, in winter especially, it seemed Pattie and I had much of what was *then* considered outlying areas to ourselves—clean unbroken sparkling snow and backcountry solitude in an incredibly spectacular setting beneath the Teton Mountains and elsewhere, too.

I have a photograph of Pattie covered by hoar frost after our skiing around Timber Island breaking trail in sub-zero temperatures. Whoever imagined she was a Southern Fluff was way wrong. We took Pattie's friend—the one who had warned me about trying to make her into a mountain woman—to Brackett Creek skiing. The friend struggled, hard pressed to keep up with Pattie.

We went to the Ski Swap at Bozeman, an annual ski town event. A whole new and exciting world of colorful equipment, gear, clothing, and possibilities appeared spread out before Pattie. We outfitted her with her first downhill equipment.

I began teaching her lift skiing at Montana's Big Sky and Wyoming's Grand Targhee Resort. Characterized by exceptional deep powder snow, Targhee's slogan was "Snow from Heaven, Not from Hoses." There was less grooming of runs than today, more skiing powder and crud.

The first time I took Pattie to the top of Fred's Mountain at Targhee was probably terrifying for her. She did not say anything—only gave me an anxious questioning smile. We started down with me below her giving instructions. On this occasion, the ski run was hard-packed and frozen. Pattie fell and slid down the slope into me, knocking me down.

She uttered one word, "Help." Entangled together, with Pattie clutching onto me, we slid for a long distance down the steep slope beneath the chairlift. Riding up the lift together in later years, we frequently recalled the incident, joking about providing local entertainment for those riding on the lift above us that day.

Early in our relationship, we made a mid-winter road trip to Banff in Alberta, Canada, driving late into the night in a snow storm after first stopping off to visit with a friend at Great Falls, Montana. We stayed in a wonderfully intimate lodge in Banff with snow piled high around it. Under a romantic full moon with looming peaks, we went cross-country skiing down the frozen length of Lake Louise. We spent the days downhill skiing at one of the large resorts.

Conditions at the resort ski runs were icy and difficult. Pattie joined up with a guided beginners group that was supposed to introduce novice skiers to the resort's easier slopes. Later, I took a series of lifts up to what was named "Top of the World"—the highest and most challenging point on the mountain resort—and there was Pattie.

Alarmed, I blurted out, "What are you doing up here? What kind of guide would take a terrified beginners' group to the summit and then desert them?" I wondered aloud. Pattie just laughed uneasily.

I took a photograph of her standing next to the sign saying "Top of the World." Then I helped her work her way down the steep and icy terrain. I have often told the story over the years of discovering Pattie at the Top of the World. Friends would look over at Pattie disbelieving and she would laugh. While it was amusing in retrospect, it was nearly calamitous at the time.

At some point, I proudly described Pattie's learning to ski to her father, who had lived his entire life in the South and had a deeply ingrained Southerner's aversion to cold and snow. He looked aghast, exclaiming: "Who ever heard of learning to ski at age forty?" But Pattie did. Not just "bunny slopes" either; she learned to competently ski deep powder and Black Diamond terrain and to cross-country tour on "skinny skis"— light weight racing skis.

Inside in the Indoors

Someone once said, "All life is chemistry." If the *Wow!* of our initial attraction was in part stimulated by pheromones, then our high-energy pairing was additionally supercharged with neurological rocket fuel: euphoria inducing pheromones, endorphins and adrenaline, stimulated by both physical activities and our mutual attraction to one another. It was subsequently further powered, some might say *over stimulated*, by lusty drenchings of phenylethylamine, the so-called naturally occurring "love drug" and oxytocin, the naturally stimulated "trust hormone," which plays a role in bonding. Together, we generated some powerful natural chemistry. Borrowing author Ellen Meloy's phrasing from *The Anthropology of Turquoise*, it was "un-unrequited love."

In a relatively short time we were deeply in love. There's no mistaking it: the "divine madness," the "ultimate oneness." How did we know? We didn't. But it appeared to have all the hallmarks: mutual attraction, trust, honesty, joy, passion, intimacy, and commitment. We were there for each other, devoted companions. But as most couples invariably do, we later encountered some bumps we had to work through, which I'll explain later.

On Mother's Day, we went to a buffet at the historic Gallatin Gateway Inn near Bozeman. It was an extravagant "dinner date." Among other things, in an impressive "all you can eat" table array, they served a large whole-poached salmon and champagne. Both Pattie and I had dressed for the occasion—she in a form-fitting fashionable dress (she could wear a four, but size two, you might say, showed off the dress better); and me, in slacks, casual sports coat, and my dress cowboy boots. It was a beautiful and memorable spring day, the kind when one's spirit sings.

Unabashedly touching, holding hands, glowing at one another, caressing with our eyes: our being in love was obvious to others, too. Both Pattie and I had thick, curly hair—"caressable plumage . . . the fetish of love," as Diane Ackerman dubs it. I used to joke that when our heads touched, we stuck together like Velcro. As we were leaving, we overheard a woman, who had been observing us, comment: "They even look like brother and sister." The remark served to reinforce our infatuation.

We frequently attended the old Main Street movie theaters in Bozeman and rented home movies. Some of Pattie's "chick-flick" romantic favorites at the time, which she could not wait to have me watch with her, were *When Harry Met Sally* and *Sleepless in Seattle*.

At times, we would go down to Chico Hot Springs at Pray, Montana, and have an elaborate breakfast. Afterward, we'd drive into Yellowstone Park and walk to the Boiling River's confluence with the Gardiner River. After changing into our bathing suits along the riverbank in the sagebrush, we would soak in the sensually warm water. I recall it sometimes blowing snow, while we enfolded ourselves in the river's delightful warmth. Again, it seemed we mostly had the Boiling

River intimately to ourselves, especially on cold and snowy days.

Pattie published stories profiling her gallery artists in the *Bozeman Chronicle*. The articles were of a quality that could have been and, in fact, later were published by art magazines, such as *Southwestern Art*. As an example, Pattie wrote:

> Anyone seeing Beth Ann Loftin in a downtown coffee shop in Bozeman, Montana, would appreciate her contemporary flair. But pulling into her driveway, past her corral, and past her cat, a different Beth emerges. Frequent laughter punctuates an afternoon's discussion of passions that have shaped this artist's life—especially her love of family and horses . . . Her sketches and oils of these equine companions visually map her life.

Pattie boasted a large stable of loyal consignment artists and was responsible for giving many aspiring artists and craftsmen their start; and they were all eager to claim her as a friend.

When Pattie held artist showings in her gallery, I would help her set up for the occasions, doing strictly only what I was told. I knew when to stay out of her way. More than just business, the Art Walks were Bozeman social events that attracted a gathering of celebrities, friends and prospective customers. As always there was also a rag-tag contingent who wandered in off the street attracted by the free wine and food. Good naturedly, Pattie laughed about the latter, but wisely kept an experienced eye peeled for shoplifters.

Billing itself as "the capitol of the western art world," Great Falls, Montana, annually hosts Western Art Week in conjunction with the C.M. Russell Museum. Considered the largest art show in the country, Western Art Week draws over one hundred and forty artists. Pattie generally attended to network with artists and other gallery owners looking for business connections for her gallery. When I attended the show with her, it seemed Pattie knew nearly all the western artists, and many gallery owners, too, including those from Jackson Hole.

Pattie was hardwired into the business community. At one point, she was voted "Bozeman's Retailer of the Year." Understandably, she conscientiously and proudly put her gallery business first over all things in those years. It was her baby. But her willingness to devote significant time, thoughtfulness, and energy to *us* on top of everything else made it apparent that from the beginning she highly regarded our relationship, too.

Shakespeare said, "Music is the food of love." Music can be seductive, and most courtships have been associated with memorable music—tunes that nostalgically and intensely summon those moments filled with passionate feelings, closeness, and getting to know one another. Hearing those songs can transport one back to happy, fun-filled moments which were jam-packed with energy and mutual attraction, bringing to mind the intense and intimate feelings associated with falling in love.

We enjoyed eclectic tastes in music. However, a lot of our early Bozeman dating was to the rhythms of local Western sounds. You might say, we wore suits and dresses by day, and jeans and boots by night.

We shared a fondness for the romance of the Old West. When Pattie and I first met, there was still a strong Western element to living in Montana and Wyoming; we were both into it. You do not find it as much anymore; much of the West has been homogenized into Anywhere, USA. The Millennial generation mostly dresses in nondescript "casual" clothing manufactured in Third World countries or outdoor wear by Patagonia and similar brands.

When we met, both of us commonly dressed Western in well-fitted Levi jeans, large showy belt buckles, Western embroidered blouses, snap button ox-yoke shirts, tooled leather belts, Justin and Tony Lama boots, turquoise and leather. Pattie wore her jeans "Texas style," tucked into her boots. She knew the authentic way to wear Western jewelry, how to tie and wear neckerchiefs—the buckaroo square knot—and even about such Western esoterica as stampede straps. Imagine all that for a Southern girl.

We attended rodeos together at Cody, Livingston, and Three Forks. At the Three Forks, Montana, rodeo we sat up next to the arena opposite the bucking chutes, so that the riders came out of the chutes directly toward the stands, enveloping everyone in a cloud of dust, dirt, noise, and mayhem.

On her way to work, Pattie would sometimes take me to breakfast at the last remaining old-time cowboy restaurant on Bozeman's Main Street, just down and across the way from her gallery, a place where faded and broken-down ranch hands, cowboys, and the semi-homeless would drift in for their morning coffee.

It was perhaps a side to Pattie that few others ever knew or saw—a good looking Southern woman who unaffectedly greeted all kinds of people. It certainly impressed me. I admired that she was an attractive and educated woman who unpretentiously related to all kinds of people, from celebrities to common working-class folk. That was something you might not commonly expect from a well-educated, gorgeous-looking Southern girl who had grown up in the race- and class-conscious Deep South.

Pattie and I followed the popular Bozeman group known as *Montana Rose* around the Gallatin Valley. Claudia Williams was Montana Rose, and her band played Western swing and rock. It was said that their music "had been forged in the crucible of cowboy bars throughout the Rocky Mountain West." I guarantee that if you were out with Pattie and listening to that group, you would have wanted to dance. It was just as songwriter and poet Leonard Cohen's lyrics describe: "dance me to your beauty with a burning violin." And dance we did when Claudia belted out her signature songs: "Montana Rose" and "He'd Never Lie," and "We're Talking Tears."

I choked up when years later I found a *Montana Rose* tape in the car after Pattie was gone. She had been playing it in the last days that she was still able to drive. I assumed she had been recalling those early years and the good times we had enjoyed.

Pattie was not experienced with Western swing when we first met, but she enthusiastically worked at learning. While we would practice in her living room, we never became really accomplished like some. Still it was not too long before we were doing moves like the *cuddle, pretzel,* and *window*. We got reasonably good at the two-step, too. A hallmark of the two-step is supposed to be smoothness. But Pattie jokingly used to call it doing the "bouncy-bouncy," referring to our own particular style.

Don't get me wrong. We did not hang out in cowboy bars much, but we did blow off steam and have a lot of fun with it on occasion. It was a diversion. We had the energy to stay out late, and still get up early for work the next day. Neither one of us were ever big drinkers. That would not have worked for me after my experiences with my first wife's drinking problem.

We discovered Stacey's Old Faithful Bar at Gallatin Gateway, advertised as "Where the West is still the West." A rustic cowboy honky-tonk with live music, it had character. They advertised what they termed "real Western dancing." We enjoyed some boot-scootin' good times at Stacey's. I can still see Pattie's flushed and smiling face. She would want to dance all night. I have a birthday card from those early years. Yellowing with age, it is illustrated with a Pattie look-alike curly headed girl on the front intently writing a salutation. On the inside of the card Pattie had written:

> Humming as I write this missive (a medley Happy B-day to you and W. Houston's "I'll Always Love You"), excited to be helping you welcome in another glorious year. Let's do this together every year! Today and always, Happy Birthday! I love you ~ Pattie

Pattie would frequently hum or sing the lyrics to me from Whitney Houston's song, "I Will Always Love You" after its 1992 debut.

If we were in Jackson Hole on Sunday evenings, we would drop in on the Stage Coach Bar in Wilson. The Stage Coach band played there on Sundays from 7:00 to 10:00 p.m. I called it "Jay Hess's Sunday Night Services," referring to the owner who was always present among his customers. We would dance to a few songs and then head for home across Teton Pass.

Among other tunes, the Stagecoach Band played was the music of a group known as *Sawmill Creek, the Wild Western Windblown Band.* Sawmill Creek had a dedicated local following and frequently entertained at the Cowboy Bar in Jackson. The lyrics they composed and compellingly sang were about that special part of the world—Jackson Hole and Wyoming: "Next week we'll be in Jackson Hole . . . Lord, don't you know it's a good town."

The Stagecoach Band also played Canadian cowboy artist Ian Tyson's songs. "Katie and the Navajo Rug" was among Pattie's Tyson favorites. In later years, whenever we passed by the Stage Coach in Wilson on Sunday evenings, Pattie would always playfully sing a few stanzas of *Katie* to me: "Aye, aye, aye Katie, Whatever became of the rug and you?"

And, in later years, Dan Seals and Maria Osmond's "Meet me in Montana" uncannily reminded us of our courtship and years together in Bozeman: "I wanna see the mountains in your eyes . . . meet me underneath that big Montana sky."

What I would not give today for Pattie and me to be able to meet underneath that big Montana sky again, just one more time.

The Art of Love Letters

Writing letters longhand may be impossibly passé, but I feel sorry for couples today who rely solely on electronic communication. Compared with letters composed with pen, paper, individual handwriting, and imaginative sketches, which one can preserve forever, social media seems impersonal and transitory. What are you going to do, save your computer's hard drive? Store your electronic messages and selfies in "the Cloud"? I suppose you can print out the messages and file them in other than an electronic folder, but it hardly seems romantic.

Pattie and I both grew up in the era before the Internet and electronic mail when handwritten letters were valued. Letter writing was an art and love letters . . . ah, they were the ultimate art form. Some early handwritten exchanges in our relationship are reproduced here from the original letters. They were written and posted while I was out of town on work projects or in Alta, and sometimes when we were both in town, too:

May 1991

Dearest Pattie,

Thanks for your thoughtful and loving call this early morning. I'm getting ready to go out the door. It is 7:30 am, so you are right, I am behind schedule . . . already?

I'll be thinking of you and looking forward to being with you upon my return. The closeness we have shared has been a real joy! I want our relationship to continue to grow and deepen. Please know I care a great deal for you in this short time we've known one another. With much love and many kisses—Earle

I had put tulip petals in with the letter. The petals were preserved in the envelope along with the letter when I reopened it more than twenty-two years later.

May 23, 1991

My Dearest Pattie Love,

I'm hoping this letter precedes me back to Bozeman, but in either case, I look forward to your embrace, kisses, love-making, and sweet self.

Do you think love letters are silly? I hope not because I'm about to write you a real gushy one! Obviously, if you can't tell, I'm flying in the clouds—you know, the "Cloud 9" syndrome!

You're on my mind constantly and your presence travels with me everywhere. It's good you are not here; otherwise I'd be passionately attacking you. I feel like I'm missing something important—almost grieving—by being apart from you for even this short time. What kind of web have we woven?

Pattie, it has been <u>very</u> nice for me—this getting to know you and spending time with you. You no doubt have heard the line, "I'd like to explore a relationship with you." Well, this isn't a line; I want a relationship with <u>you</u>. I believe it can only deepen and grow between us, if we allow it.

There are other ways to get endorphins than through exercise. One of those is "being in love," and since I've met you, I've been on the nicest high. There is a nice balance of lust and tenderness between us. In some relationships, it is either one or the other, not both. I feel a loving tender closeness for you, curly-locks, which readily goes back and forth between tenderness and lust and desire. I look forward to the deepening of emotions and feelings towards each other continuing. It can only get better in all ways.

True, it has been "fast," as they say. But I see nothing wrong with that. Perhaps going "slow" is not the nature of either one of us. I only know it has been very nice and want more. I like the way you are seeking to live life. I want to be a partner, friend, companion, and lover for you in your quest. I believe we both have a great deal to offer each other.

I consider myself fortunate to have met you, and that we have a chance to seek our destiny together; to learn where the potential we appear to have together will lead; to attempt to direct our fates together.

I don't want this impassioned letter to be "scary" for you.

You have more than met me halfway up until now, and I trust my expression of deep feelings will not put you off. My desire is that you'll receive this letter and words in the loving manner they are intended; and that you'll reciprocate and complement these loving feelings in like manner that they are conveyed and intended. With care—bubbling with love and lust for you—Earle

May 30, 1991

Dearest Darling Earle ~

(Clearly, I can't abide love letters!)

If I haven't been shouting from the rooftops, it's because I've felt this placid acceptance that magic was in motion—and it couldn't be shoved, crammed, or coaxed into a neatly understandable box.

It swept away self-consciousness and tickled us with lust <u>and</u> tenderness from the beginning. At the moment we met, at the first dusting of moonbeams and rays of love, "our spirits began the dance."

I keep remembering, reading Joseph Campbell's ideas about Eros, Agape and Amor. He believed that with Amor, there is a kind of seizure that comes from the meeting of the eyes—the sudden recognition of our identity in the person; seeing aspects of the same being; being jolted into recognizing your soul's counterpart in the other person.

A person can want this, but they can't will it—and if that's what this is, it's delicious. I fervently hope that for once I can suspend judgment and just go with the flow. I'm so happy you want to go with me!

Unless we get zapped with an "aha" of a totally different sort, I, too, would like to be a partner, friend, companion, and lover with you. It's exciting and happy making and I look forward to what else we will discover.

I suppose the only things your love arrows couldn't pierce would be my shields of fear (—but I think the shields I haven't dropped have huge tears that an archer could take advantage of!).

So, my sweet love, I'll be waiting here with open arms and open heart—trying to keep the bubble bath hot and the Hagen Daz cold. Looking forward to some sweet—and some outrageous—lovemaking—Love, Pattie

CHAPTER 5

EARLY TRAVELS

Travel is more than the seeing of sights; it is a change that goes on, deep and permanent, in the ideas of living.
— Miriam Ritter Beard

There is a special knack or art to road trips. The key is cramming a lot into a short time at relatively little cost. Epic or otherwise, the romance of the road generally entails mileage (often many miles, possibly at all hours) and serendipitous encounters with local culture, attractions, and problem-solving situations. Assuring economic efficiency means bringing food in coolers and sleeping bags. Most important is a reliable and safe vehicle. A road trip represents maximum flexibility infused with energy and novelty compared to the pace of a prearranged AAA family excursion. Our road trips were all pretty much before cell and iPhones or GPS and required knowledge of geography and map-reading skills.

When I first met Pattie, I was driving my blue V-6 Toyota four-by-four pickup. It was like a miniature tank: indestructible, able to go anywhere. Pattie named the truck "Old Blue—reliable and true."

Hard to believe anyone would be sentimental about an old pickup truck, but Old Blue piled up a lot of memories associated with it over the years. It had a camper shell or topper. I had a mattress that just fit the truck bed, which I used when doing field work. Pattie and I also used it on road trips. We would drive late into the night, pull off into the desert, forest, or streamside, and thrill to waking up somewhere hundreds of miles distant with the fresh smells and sounds of morning dawning in a new or natural setting. Pattie would then exclaim, *Carpe diem!*

An abundance of public land made it possible. It gave us freedom and flexibility not having to worry about finding stuffy and expensive motel room accommodations. We would get up at first light and freshen up a bit with cold water; Pattie would then take her comb and brush into the truck cab and adeptly fix her hair at the mirror. She would look terrific without taking a lot of time. Then we would be back on the road or onto a trail in minutes. Amazing for a Southern Belle!

In a 1991 card showing teepees and deer under a star-lighted sky, Pattie had written:

> Dear Wapiti-man—Did I tell you today how very special you are to me? Every time I see this card, I think of camping with you and creeping into your tipi. You're the one I like to greet the sun with; you're the one I like to see the stars with. I love you, Earle.—Pattie.

She had artfully drawn a yin-yang symbol ☯ on the front of the card's envelope.

A small package arrived just before I was leaving for several days of field work. Inside was a packet of night-glow (phosphorescent) stars and solar features, depicting the night sky, generally used to affix to a child's bedroom ceiling. Included was a card, the front of which pictured children dancing under the stars, and a Chekov quote:

> "We shall find peace. We shall hear the angels. We shall see the sky sparkling with diamonds." On the back of the card Pattie had written: "For the ceiling of your truck camper . . . Please know that I hover close. Whenever you strike out solo, you'll know you are not alone—just look up and I'll be there!—Pattie."

I applied the stars and planets to the inside of the camper shell ceiling, and thereafter, whenever I, or Pattie and I, lay in the back of the truck at night, we would look up and see those stars glowing above us—our galaxy. They stayed attached for all the many years we drove Old Blue, reminding us always of the closeness we shared and places we had traveled and camped, going back to our earliest years together.

That first summer we took whirlwind road trips to Glacier National Park and southern Utah. In Glacier, on the trail to Grinnell Glacier, we saw six different bears. We camped along Cutbank Creek, where an owl provided an intimate serenade throughout the night. In southern Utah, we visited and day hiked in Arches, Bryce, Capitol Reef, and Zion National Parks, and in Goblin State Park. We slept out along the Colorado River above Moab and in the desert.

From the Mormon outpost of Escalante, we backpacked down the Escalante River for several miles. It was Pattie's first backpacking experience. Along the river bottom, we camped beneath a large red sandstone amphitheater or grotto. A full moon illuminated the surrounding canyon walls that were streaked with desert varnish. Anthropomorphic pictograph figures painted on the grotto walls lent mystery to the site, which was set in deep silence except for crickets droning. You could almost feel the presence of the ancient Anasazi, the spirit guardians of the river canyon's entrance.

Pattie never forgot that desert camp spot within the massive sandy-floored grotto. It captured her imagination. Over the years, she would talk about her fascination with that outing anytime someone mentioned southern Utah.

But I think her favorite thing in Utah was the Green River Watermelon Festival. By chance, we arrived on the right days for the festival. Her favorite fruit, I learned, was watermelon. In later years, Pattie hung an attractive and colorful framed picture in our kitchen showing a pile of watermelons, accompanied by a quote from Mark Twain:

> The true southern watermelon is a boon apart, and not to be mentioned with commoner things. It is chief of this world's luxuries, king by the grace of God over all the fruits

of the earth. When one has tasted it, he knows what the angels eat. It was not a Southern watermelon that Eve took; we know it because she repented.

On another occasion, in early summer, Pattie dropped a friend and me off near the top of a couloir in Montana's Beartooth Mountains. After walking a short way to the sheer edge and putting on our skis, my friend and I leaped into the near vertical ravine that was filled with corn snow and, making hop turns, we skied down the long narrow fissure. Pattie drove Old Blue down the highway switchbacks to meet us near the bottom. Flushed with adrenaline, we went back up and did it again.

When Pattie's birthday approached, I asked her what she wanted. With a serious, but self-conscious look, she told me, "I'd like a *promise ring*." I suppose that is as close to saying engagement ring as one can get while still hedging a bit. A promise ring symbolizes a person's commitment to taking the relationship to a higher level. I probably said little at the time, but began looking. Other than my first wife's wedding ring, when we were still immature kids, I had never bought any woman a ring.

I did not intend to get a customary diamond ring, but wanted it to be more imaginative or personal: something special and fitting *our* relationship. I found the perfect ring. It was made with a Yogo sapphire—a type of sapphire found nowhere else but in Montana. It radiated the intense blue color of a Montana sky. Pattie wore it always, for the rest of her life.

The card I chose to accompany the ring depicted a settler woman collecting wildflowers on the prairie with a ground-tied horse beside her. In it, I wrote the following note:

August 14, 1991

My Dearest Pattie,

You are my most precious love. Please let this white gold

and rare Montana sapphire ring symbolize the blazon of passion and love we've come to know and share.

This blue-purple sapphire is found nowhere else but from one location in Montana. Likewise, I know in my heart, I could search the world, but there is only one place to find the love of my life, and that is here with you. Both the sapphire and a love like you are rare.

I hope you'll accept this birthday gift as a token and symbol of my love. Your acceptance represents our heartfelt promise, binding us together out of a mutual desire, to continue to love, to share happiness in each other, and to grow together.

May all the love, smiles, and the gentle understanding that you've brought into our lives and others' come back to you to make this day very special! Happy Birthday—I love you.—Earle

PS. At age 42 you are in your "prime"—what a lovely, sexy person you are!

In autumn of 1991, in a card illustrated with a Native American man and woman with a blanket wrapped around them while standing in a field of flowers, Pattie wrote:

Dearest Earle—

It's lovely to think back over the last months . . . the laughter we've shared; the beautiful places we've seen together; the frustrating moments of each trying to understand—trying to make a good thing better; the moments of tenderness and passion.

You've cast rays of warmth and caring throughout my life—how lucky I am to have stepped into your glow. I hope to reflect back some of that sunshine. But as nice as the memories are, even greater is my excitement and anticipation of the times to come.

I look forward to seeing your Pennsylvania home place. I can't wait to spend our first Christmas together. I foresee many happy days of loving, learning, and growing.

Happy 6-month Anniversary! I love you—Pattie.

At the time, I also owned and was maintaining what had once been the family farm in the mountains near Cedar Run, Pennsylvania. A remote heavily-forested setting for the East, it had been passed down to me. It was an exceptionally beautiful spot.

We commonly referred to it as "Pine Creek," after the large stream bordering the property. Creek was a misnomer, the stream was 180-feet wide at places with long deep pools interspersed with rollicking fast-flowing riffles and rapids. Based on water volume alone, it should have been named a river. Native Americans had in fact called it *Tiadaghton*, roughly translated as the River of Pines. Beginning from our first autumn together, Pattie and I seasonally spent cherished time there together—fishing and canoeing, hiking and cycling, visiting family and friends, and watching wildlife. Deer and black bear often wandered through the yard. Eventually, Pattie came to genuinely love our time at Pine Creek, and I deeded her co-ownership in this mountain property.

Over the years, our seasonal arrival on Pine Creek was invariably met with a perennial question from the proprietors of the nearby general store and post office. The standard enquiry regardless of our reliable biannual appearances and lengthy stays over the years was: "How long ya in for?" In their minds, the daily coming and going of people and the passage of the seasons all blurred together. All nonresidents were assumed to be "going to hunting camps." As longtime second home owners with a family history of residency going back to 1947, it took Pattie and me years to achieve a vaguely different status in their minds. That status only came about slowly, as did any changes in this deeply rural setting.

When Pattie and I met, I was involved in independent business endeavors—natural resources consulting and real estate investments. Before meeting Pattie, besides the Gee Norman property, I had also bought two contiguous building lots in Targhee Towne at Alta, Wyoming. There were only a few residences existing in the large subdivision at that time, structures that had originally belonged to and were used by famed mountain climber Paul Petzoldt, mostly it was farming fields.

The building lots I purchased offered direct views of the iconic Three Peaks of the Tetons, called *Les Trois Tetons* by early nineteenth century French-Iroquois trappers. The location was additionally attractive to me because it was close to Grand Targhee Ski and Summer Resort as well as Jackson Hole.

I had contracted to build a recreation residence there around the time Pattie and I met. My initial intention was for it to be an investment, a spec-house. But also, in the back of my mind, I wanted to have a place next to Jackson Hole, the Teton Mountains, and Grand Targhee Ski Resort.

Viewable through the windows of the home I had constructed were the looming Teton Peaks—the Grand, Middle Teton, and Mount Owen. The peaks were commonly embossed with pink alpenglow or a glowing full-moon silhouetting the Grand. The roof design of the house I had constructed formed three peaks mimicking the mountains. Eventually, we would move there and the iconic mountain scene would become part of our everyday lives. But at first, it was a second home from which to enjoy the Teton Mountains, skiing, and proximity to Jackson Hole.

In the meantime, I left the Nature Conservancy. The job as it had turned out was a disappointment. It lacked realistic opportunity to contribute much that was lasting or meaningful. While the Yellowstone region fairly boiled with critical resource management and conservation issues, the Conservancy's newly appointed state directors at the time ducked and dodged anything that potentially smacked of controversy or that might have spotlighted attention on them.

Inconsistent with the organization's general reputation, the Conservancy's inexperienced Greater Yellowstone state directors at the time simply did not have the desire or knowledge to engage in the region's complex natural resource policy issues. Playing it cautious, avoiding both controversy and substance, they concentrated instead on collecting their donors' well-intended contributions. The amounts that they took in were generally proportional to the distress well-meaning supporters felt from the region's unabated and escalating conflicts over natural resources and the continuing heated public debates over conservation issues.

I sold, or "flipped," as it has been termed, my Gee Norman property for a nice profit. But now I was seriously conflicted about leaving the Bozeman area. I entered a notation in my journal: "I don't want to leave Pattie to move [to Alta]. She has been very lovely to be with in so many ways."

Instead, because of Pattie and the importance of our growing relationship to me, I chose to purchase another more modest home located on one acre at Springhill Lane in order to retain a place of residence in Bozeman. The depressed Bozeman real estate market was on the rebound; it was lucky timing for me. This Springhill property was sometime later also easily marketed, yielding another substantial capital gain.

As our relationship deepened, though, I was caught between locations—Jackson Hole, Bozeman, and Alta. Pattie had quickly become such a significant part of my life that I decided to maintain two places of residence: one in Bozeman and the other under construction at Alta. Pattie had her home on South Tracy Street, too. Along with the Pine Creek property, we did not lack for real estate and residences.

Our first Christmas together, we spent at Pattie's house in Bozeman. Pattie's business required her to work right up to and including Christmas Eve. It was her busiest time. People constantly wandered in for last minute shopping for gifts, and she enjoyed assisting them in selecting appropriate gift items. The season and people coming and going in her gallery was very festive. Pattie made an effort to make it that way, too, with her cheerfulness and artful decorations and displays.

One of the gifts Pattie gave me that Christmas was *Edible Flowers*, a beautiful recipe book that resides on our Alta kitchen shelf yet today. Inside the book is a folded card where Pattie had written: "All we really need is . . . a vegetable garden for our health, a flower garden for our souls, and love growing in our hearts. Merry 1st Christmas, my Sugar Blossom! Love, Pattie."

For both of us, Santa had put zip-together sleeping bags under the tree—to use on our road trips in Old Blue. We made use of those sleeping bags, zipping them together for the next twenty-two years. They still reside on their closet shelf in our Alta home, patiently waiting to be pulled out for our next road trip.

CHAPTER 6

RELATIONSHIP SPEED BUMPS

It is quite clear that between love and understanding there is a very close link . . . He who loves understands, and he who understands loves. One who feels understood feels loved, and one who feels loved feels sure of being understood.

— Paul Tournier, *To Understand Each Other*

Like the moon, relationships go through phases. It can be tricky. After the "honeymoon phase," even with a magnetic love attachment burning hotly and believed to be gloriously written in the stars, mundane issues may begin to elbow their uninvited way into the glow.

As someone once said, "Love lets us do our finest dance." And there was no question that Pattie and I enjoyed an exceptionally deep romantic attachment. Our initial courtship phase of dating was adrenaline-charged, full of lust, and remarkably fun-filled. Unfortunately, life is never just wine and roses. Unlike young people who enter into their first serious relationship unscarred and with a clean slate, many later-in-life adults can bring past experiences and issues—so called "baggage" and "demons"—along to the table. One is acutely aware of all that can go wrong.

Building a relationship to the next level necessitates that both parties hold that objective in common. And, to be lasting, it requires more than just physical attraction. For starters, it generally will take knowledge and experience, honesty, trust, communication skills, understanding, and a nurturing compassion and commitment to helping each other through the invariable difficulties.

All that can be a lot to expect. It is never 100 percent easy. It can become involved and complicated, and no longer all fun-filled. And it can be risky—emotionally damaging, scary, or hurtful. What if it turns out to be one-sided? What if one of us misconstrued our own or the other's feelings? What if, in spite of it all, one of us falls out of love? What if a hidden character flaw emerges and the relationship fails? What if . . .? Some who have been burned tend to be overly tentative, even apprehensive, and want to keep one foot out the door, just in case.

A Jackson Hole columnist recently gave singles the following advice: "Making anyone or anything outside yourself the source of your happiness is a recipe for disappointment and disempowerment. . . . It places your happiness at the mercy of other people's moods, behaviors, and unforeseen life events." No doubt this is good cautionary advice for singles in mountain resort towns, but it is also a cynical dismissal of the rewards of love and the potential empowerment of meaningful relationships, too.

Both Pattie and I possessed strong communication skills and a stubborn, albeit cautious, old-fashioned belief in love; otherwise, it is unlikely we would have ever gotten to where we did. Still, we were careful. What we did not want was Lola Haskins's nightmarish description of a destructive relationship in her poem, "Love," which has been slightly modified here:

> They try it on . . .
> decide it doesn't fit
> and start to take it off.
> Their skin comes off, too.

Yes, even for us, serious challenges to maintaining and growing our relationship emerged and came into play. While not on all fronts, our challenges involved work goals and commitments, juggling schedules, giving up personal time to meet the other person's needs, differences in values and priorities, and finances. We also had to deal with what

Pattie termed "summoning one's hidden demons." By that she meant the ingrained insecurities, fears, and projections of negativity resulting from one's history of past hurts, criticisms, or failed relationships—the "baggage" mature adults inadvertently bring along with them to a new relationship. It all required patient understanding and the desire on both our parts to deal with it.

When two people are as much in love as Pattie and I were, you would think it would have all been easy sailing. But budding and even ecstatic love relationships can hit speed bumps that slow things down or even derail them. The bumps began surfacing about six to eight months into the relationship. We struggled between the extremes of bliss and mired in misery. At such times we went through an emotional up and down and push and pull to get unstuck and back on track: back and forth difficulties, yin versus yang.

Late night phone calls followed by six-to-eight-page letters written in the wee hours of the morning—earnest, plaintive, pleading, wherein one or the other of us tried to right wrongs or explain and justify themselves, all the while professing the deepest love. It was an emotional balancing act. Sound familiar? Even the heavenly marriage of the Greek gods, Zeus and Hera, had difficulties at times, too.

Pattie had saved over forty letters of mine from 1992 alone, and half a dozen cards that had been included with flower deliveries. I have an equal number of letters and cards from her from that time, too. Rereading our letters and notes from those times, I relive the wide swings: sad and hurt feelings back-to-back with ecstatic joy-filled rapture. We rode an emotional roller coaster at times: painful and exhausting on the downside; intense and wildly exhilarating on the upside. But the bottom line was that the rewards invariably outweighed the strife.

As we worked through it all, we made solid progress toward a stable relationship. While it did not always seem like it at the time, we developed strong trust and solid interactive problem- solving skills. We came to know each other well and learned to laugh at our foibles as we built an honest, authentic, strong, and loving relationship foundation. Looking back, it is interesting how closely we adopted precepts that Sue Johnson discloses in *Hold Me Tight* about relationships and love— especially the fact that "a secure connection to a loved one can be empowering."

Part of our balancing act was successfully finding the time and energy to be with each other despite our full and demanding schedules. I had five major and widely geographically separated consulting projects under contract and was having a post-and-beam house custom-built in Alta, which was a four-hour drive from Bozeman. I had a half-dozen different contractors simultaneously working on the Alta house. Pattie's gallery occupied her six days a week, ten hours a day. There were also evening artist showings, Art Walk events, and window displays for her to prepare for and set up. Good part-time employees were rare and difficult for her to find, and they required significant training time.

In addition, because we were spending time on rivers and lakes canoeing, Pattie had started taking evening swimming lessons to improve her ability in the water. And all our hiking and skiing had brought attention to a painful bunion problem, for which she was trying to decide on treatment. It seemed a recipe for self-induced stress.

My schedule did not leave much or any unoccupied or down time. Reading my journal notes, what seemed to bother me the most was the irony that I had retired in order to be free from a regular full-time work routine, particularly, to be able to travel. Instead, I was starting to feel tied down and on overload.

Relationships can take a lot of time, commitment and sacrifice. It seemed as though our relationship and my work projects were holding me back, though from what? I felt time was slipping away . . . time for what? Did those feelings have any validity? I struggled with sorting out the turn the direction of my life seemed to have taken. And Pattie's priority was running her gallery business, which required her full time attention and then some. The self-created stress was off the charts for both of us. Little wonder if we tended to overreact to any perceived affronts or to the slightest suggestion of not being understood.

Our letters from the time reflect the difficulties. We wanted it all—full-time relationship, full-time work, and round-the-clock play and fun. There were not enough hours in the day. It was not always easy. But it was never dull. People who later knew us and the easy closeness we shared would never have guessed that in the beginning, we sometimes struggled with our relationship's direction and meaning.

I would love to have Pattie here with me to read back through old letters and notes from those times. I am certain she would have substantial insights and perspective, which I may be overlooking. I know we would no doubt tease each other and laugh about how silly we were in some respects and in hindsight.

In retrospect, how overly cautious and trivial some of our upsets seem now, knowing how sweetly our lives came together. But at the time, it was a necessary part of sorting it all out—making sure we were not just infatuated with love itself; or God forbid, that one of us did not have a hidden character quirk, nightmarishly waiting to surface at some point.

On one occasion, just before I walked through the door at Pattie's house, one of her closest single friends had been spreading seeds of doubt and discouraging our relationship. Who knows what might have been said or suggested? I imagine the bomb was dropped in the concerned context that she "didn't want to see Pattie getting hurt." Whatever it was, it had been an effective broadside shot at our nascent relationship. Appearing distraught and visibly upset, "confused," as she put it, and feeling like she was "not measuring up," Pattie told me she did not want to see me anymore. I was left speechless and pleading, trying to figure out what had happened. I went home and wrote what grew into a series of letters back and forth to each other trying to sort it out.

December 5, 1991

It's hard for me to see the dreams and love we shared so easily shelved. To learn that where only a short time ago we shared a vision, there are now only differences and division . . . I cannot accept as true either . . . to have been so in love, and then have the one I love and care for suddenly instead profess in its place 'confusion.'

What became of the resolution and trust in love you so devotedly declared . . .? You seemed so sure and determined, and so happy in love that I believed and trusted in you and us. The love I offered you was never conditional. Why do you suddenly think you must 'measure up' in some way?

I do not know what the 'demons' are you keep referring to, but they are destroying something very nice, very precious, and very special to me (which is or was us). You are hurting yourself, you are hurting me, and you are hurting us. Please, please stop. I can only think of and remember the good times and nice things we shared, and have only wanted to give you (and us) more of those times to remember forever—Earle

After we had seen each other again, Pattie wrote:

Sunday a.m. Undated

You just left. I feel warm, secure, loving and loved. What are the differences? Euphoria or devastation—all with my same Beloved. One moment's poison dart is the next moment's cupid's arrow piercing my heart. So sensitive. Maybe this letter points to some of those fragile areas, ripe for confusion and misunderstanding. Do I expect Norman Rockwell all the time? (Worse yet, Hallmark greeting card?!!) I believe there are subtle cues that activate your fears and walls— and I responded with fear rather than open heart. And vice versa. I want to work with you toward loving empathy, in lieu of self-defense. Love you—Pattie

I responded on March 26, 1992:

My Dearest Love,

These questions are on my mind this morning: Are we caught in between? Do we want to try to continue to have a relationship if we can't get beyond the level we are at? What is going on? Why?

Don't get me wrong, the loving is, when we are together, the sweetest I've ever known! It is so good! But if I suggest a trip or something new and different, where we will share fun times and build an even deeper attachment, it backfires for some reason, raising concerns about your gallery, money issues, and crossed-up communication. I'm made to feel I've done something wrong or been inconsiderate. It leaves me feeling like our relationship is a second priority. It appears you want to limit or control the relationship, to keep it where it's at for now—come home from work, eat, and go to bed. How do we get beyond this impasse???

Our disagreements sadden me. They destroy and eat away something that has been so precious to me—our love. I'd like for us to be all we can be, and to enjoy life _together_ to its fullest. I only ask that we keep on track, try to remember how important our love is, too, and not put it second to day-to-day things. It deserves more than that in my mind. Please go back to the questions I listed at the beginning, Pattie. I'm on the edge of feeling defeated, and I really need your help and reassurance to make this work. I still feel you and I have so much potential. People who see us together always support that view, too.—Earle

The next day, March 27, I wrote again at 4:00 a.m.

Dear Pattie—

It's raining. I lay awake thinking. Trying to put my finger on what started this riff between us. I finally realized it was because you can't beat me at scrabble—no?

Actually, I found myself wondering why I felt so contrite yesterday—why was I taking on responsibility again for something I really couldn't fix (by myself) or didn't start.

My crime was to enthusiastically bubble about a great travel deal I found . . . [Then] I walked into a buzz saw. You know the things you said really cut. They hurt. I know you were feeling insecure and overloaded, but why dump on me that way? I didn't deserve to be treated that way, and I don't deserve the treatment I'm getting from you now. Yes, I couldn't sleep thinking about it. I was furious when I called you at 2 a.m—not about money but that you would treat me that way. Yes, I said "you're crazy if you think this is only about money . . ."

I think you are right when you said (confided) that our relationship is bringing up old issues for you. I don't think you're being honest with me or [with] yourself at times. The issues that come up are not all my fault. [I] may be inept at dealing with them, but they are not even about you and me. And you are taking it out on us, why?

I find myself apologizing, fighting to keep our relationship intact, trying harder, etc. I see you pulling back. I think you have been unduly hard on me, yourself, and us. What is it all about, Pattie? I love you and miss you. Your happy smile, bouncy curls and self are things I will never forget— nor your precious loving.—Earle

Pattie replied:

Undated

Earle, I need to talk with you. And perhaps there are some things you're trying to say that I'm not hearing. Hence my perceptions or misperceptions that are troubling to me. Don't misunderstand me. I want to know how you feel. But if something I'm doing is hard for you or hurtful or insensitive, it deserves its own time to be brought up and resolved. It clouds the discussion if it's brought up "in defense" (when none is needed) or to attack (when none is needed). If I feel hurt or confused or insecure, that's not "ragging." Another mind-set is possible: I love you dearly Pattie, what's going on with you? What's making you upset? There's no doubt I love you. But you can't say that if that's not what you feel. Help me clarify all this.

Help—I want us both in sync. My goal for us—my heartfelt desire is ever-increasing love, understanding, knowledge, growth, communication—higher, higher, HIGHER!! Love, Pattie

Pattie followed up with another note:

Tuesday nite

Where are you, Sweetie? I thought it was very sad to go to bed last night without harmony reestablished. It is truly hurtful and confusing that you would let another whole day go by without making contact; without trying to connect. You know I see our "differences" as just that— differences—spawned by a common desire. A "grievance" is a stalemate—but gradually going towards resolving a difference is caring, nurturing—and could be exciting when you feel the good unleashed.

Being individual and different is good. Being <u>stuck </u>and covering the same ground—not having an idea of how to reach middle ground and <u>starting</u> to do that—that mires couples down.

Startling revelations sent to you with hopefulness and love.

Remember the dream is Real—Love, Pattie

Pattie wrote again:

Undated, 3:30 a.m. Thursday

Hi—Breakthrough . . . Breakthrough. I just had an "aha" experience. I'm sorry I get so shrill and loud and matter-of-fact (controlling) when we are having our "misunderstandings." I suddenly realize that you wouldn't react the way you do if you weren't hurting also. You don't try to torture me anymore than I want to hurt you. I'm excited. Are we getting somewhere? Progress! Major Break Through (?)!

If you've ever had a similar frustrated, semi-hysterical response to your chilling, unresponsive quiet (controlling)— as I have had to my matter-of-fact (controlling)—then perhaps it's time for us to learn together a more effective way to discuss sensitive issues. Let's do it. Love, Coach/ Cheerleader

On April 1, 1992, I wrote on a card in which I enclosed with flowers:

April fool, my little fox with the curly locks.
How can it be that you are not here with me?
We both know in our hearts,
We are big fools to be apart.

On April 2, 1992, after more continuation of our relationship's uncertainty, I composed and mailed Pattie a list of affirmations. I entitled it the Magna Charta for our relationship. Rather than criticize her, I accepted the full blame for any of our misunderstandings:

Dearest Pattie:

I hope you will accept my most sincere apology for the upset in our relationship. In retrospect, the fault and responsibility are entirely 100% mine. I am truly sorry. Our relationship is <u>very</u> important to me. I honor and cherish what you have given me and what we have shared. I have been very proud to be with you; being your lover has been heavenly.

I very much want this relationship. I want the relationship to be fun for us. I do not want to be "right," dead right. I want you more than I need to be "right." I will work with you to transform this relationship into what we both truly want. I will not pull back when confronted with problem solving or your wonderful closeness. My intentions are to have a loving, committed, and lasting relationship with you. I will support and help you, within my abilities, in your life's endeavors.

I want to be your lover and mate; I would like you to want to be mine. I concede to your power for you to end this relationship; but entreat instead, for you to empower it and us. I'll do what I can within my power and abilities to make you feel secure, not threatened, and happy. You are a special and precious person to me. I promise to love and cherish you always.—Earle

PS. Can you promise me the same things? Please keep this letter in case we ever need it as a reminder.

On the fifth of April, 1992, Pattie sent a card celebrating the anniversary of our first year together. In it she had written:

Happy Anniversary, Darling. What a year! (She had drawn an up and down pattern in which she had asterisked the tops with "Thank You," and the bottoms with the question, "Can we do better?!") Obviously, from the Magna Charta, your thoughts are the loftier. I'd love for the graphic depiction of our next year—and rest of time together—to show us climbing ever higher—higher, better, and out of sight!!!

I love you.—Pattie

I sent Pattie a Charlie Brown cartoon showing Linus insecurely sucking his thumb, while he and Lucy are having an argument. Lucy says, "Oh yeah? Well you always. . . ." Then Linus replies, "Don't say 'always'! Nothing in this life is for 'always.'" To which Lucy retorts: "Every now and then, once in a while you drive me crazy." It sort of reminded me of us at the time.

On April 28, 1992, we met halfway between Alta and Bozeman at Island Park, Idaho, and canoed the Henry's Fork River. We danced the two-step in a riverside meadow filled with glacier lilies to music played on the truck's sound system. The lyrics from one of those songs, "Have I Told You Lately that I Love You?" were words we would frequently repeat to each other over the years.

I had brought dinner and wine in a cooler. And then we slept in the back of Old Blue in our zipped together sleeping bags. In the morning, we each headed home in opposite directions. The day afterward, in a letter to Pattie, I included a detailed colored sketch of a glacier lily, labeled *Erythronium grandiflorum*. I enclosed dried glacier lilies in the envelope with the letter I had written:

Hi Sweet Lips,

Precious love, I've been thinking of you, as usual. But don't feel that the frequency with which you occupy my thoughts makes it commonplace. It is much more. From deep inside me the yearning thoughts for you seep day and night into my brain and leave me restless and seemingly incomplete without your presence. The desire for your touch, your smile, your embrace is with me constantly . . . You have captured my heart and all my love. I only wait until we are together once again and our spirits dance as one!

Thanks, my love, for the time together on the Henry's Fork and at Island Park. The gopher mound two-step at dusk memory somehow remains very much with me, as does the whole time with you—especially, breaking in our new sleeping bags!!!

Love you and look forward to being with you again soon.— Earle

PS. I got your card! You don't have to worry about me keeping a "cozy corner in my heart for you." You occupy my entire heart!—E

Resolving disagreements, problem solving, testing and exploring our compatibility for making a life together was an essential part of it all. Solid trust was required to put our lives and future on the line and into each other's hands—to let go and open ourselves to total vulnerability. Some may say, "What for, why bother? It sounds like work." The reward for us developed into one of the most meaningful things in life: an exceptionally deep and caring loving bond and all the pleasures it conveyed.

In a journal entry from that time, I had written:

Packing to move to the new house in Alta . . . I don't want to leave Pattie to move down there. She has been lovely to be with in so many ways. She is so tied to her business in Bozeman though. I don't see how she will find the will or flexibility to change her situation . . . I don't want to live in Bozeman forever, but I don't want to lose Pattie either.

I wrote from Alta:

May 11, 1992

Dear Luscious Love—

It's 6 a.m. and I've been awake awhile, thinking of you while the wind whistles and beats about. Funny how I can sleep cuddled with you for 9–10 hours at a whack, but alone I put off going to bed and then wake up before dawn. After we've been together for a few days, I go thru withdrawal, like a junkie. I'm hooked on and miss the closeness with you and your love.

I built a fire in the woodstove this morning—the temperature in the house read 50 degrees. It is chilly—I miss your warmth, being here all alone. Thanks for the wonderful time the past four days. You recalled that at this time last year, I said I was "smitten" with you. You're right, I was. I still am but it has grown to being deeply in love with you. I'm certain that my love for you has the potential to grow and mature each year, so that it only gets better. I hope you share those sentiments.

On to my favorite musings: Why am I in Alta, when you my love are in Bozeman? Let me recount the reasons: financial, business, travel, recreation and Jackson Hole ambiance. Those are a few of the reasons I picked this area to live. It appeared to most closely offer the lifestyle I wanted. Ah, but those are all left-brained field marshal reasons. I didn't figure on falling in love with someone in Bozeman and how that factored into the equation—that is a matter of the heart. Our relationship obviously has become a most important facet of my life and I treasure it. I'm hopeful that a solution to our situation will emerge, given time and as our love continues to grow.

I'm looking forward to Saturday and being able to be with you again my love. Until then, please know I'm thinking loving thoughts of you and of us together.

My Love Always, Earle

Another of my journal entries from July 9, 1992 reads:

Long-distance relationship (from Alta) has its difficulties
and expense. Time and money I (we) could be spending
on travel/trips elsewhere, instead of on the road between
Alta and Bozeman. And then there's my time hanging
around Bozeman when I get there (while Pattie is at work).
But my relationship with Pattie has been and is a pleasant
plus in my life.

Looking back at those journal remarks, I realize I was a master of
understatement regarding the rewards of our relationship: a "pleasant
plus in my life." Indeed?

Taking it slow has its place, certainly. But forgive my restraint.
She was my muse and the love of my life; she brought a wonderful
sense of meaning to my life. Only over unaccountable time do the
heavens perfectly align to arrange true love—soul love of this kind.
And then one must somehow have the wisdom to be able to recognize
what is at hand when it magically presents. Ah, but that is the difficulty
and mystery—avoiding negativity and knowing and trusting. Being
egotistically and narcissistically driven, so many are inclined to
misjudge or misconstrue.

The upsets began to be less frequent, less difficult. Commitment,
communication, trust, and understanding continued to grow and
deepen. Pattie voluntarily began sharing the commute between Alta
and Bozeman. She purchased a low-mileage 1991 Subaru AWD
station wagon to use to travel back and forth to Alta and also to be
able to haul large paintings. At my urging, she had sold a vintage
black Corvette that her ex-husband had given her in their divorce
settlement, which had sat unused in her garage for years. The low-
slung rear-wheel drive Corvette was not a safe or practical vehicle to
use in Montana's winter. Its sale helped pay for the Subaru. In a way,
the Corvette's sale and the Subaru purchase were symbolic of Pattie's
changed new life and lifestyle.

The commute back and forth between Alta, Wyoming and Bozeman, Montana, became an accepted part of our relationship. We ended up taking turns, making the normally four-hour trip in all kinds of hours, weather, and road conditions—blowing and drifting snow, icy and snowpack road surface, subzero temperatures, and, at times, with black bear, bighorn sheep, elk, moose, and bison on the roadway. Anything to spend precious time together.

It was an uncommon commute. The highway from West Yellowstone to Bozeman cut through the southwest corner of Yellowstone National Park along the headwaters of the Gallatin River. Wintering elk and bison concentrated there. It was extremely hazardous to drive at night because of animals on the roadway. Invariably, truckers would go sailing through at night, leaving dead elk in their wake. Often by the time we would come along, a gathering of ravens and eagles were gorging on the roadside carcass. Weighted down from the engorgement, flapping along in front of the windshield, they would labor to get airborne. Meanwhile, coyotes, with teeth bared, grudgingly skulked from the roadside banquet when our vehicles approached.

Before the Montana Grazing Association insisted on destroying all the buffalo outside the park, wintering bison drifted down the Madison River and hung out all along the highway around West Yellowstone. They were as indifferent to road traffic there as they were in the park. One had to drive at a careful crawl to circumnavigate the lumbering beasts. But it was something that made us smile, not get angry.

On one occasion, returning to Alta from Bozeman in a snow storm, I got as far as Ashton, Idaho, at nine o'clock at night. In the blowing snow and darkness, my headlights illuminated the local Sheriff's Deputy erecting a Road Closed sign and barrier. It was not uncommon for drifting snow to make the road impassable on the stretch between Ashton to Tetonia. Snowplows operated when they got around to it. Recognizing I was not local, the deputy came over and snarled into my rolled-down window, "The road is CLOSED," as if my arrival had somehow threatened his authority, or he thought I intended to run his blockade.

I could have stayed in a motel in Ashton, which at the time had a place creepily named the "Bates Motel" after the 1987 psycho thriller television film. But even though I was less than an hour from Alta, I turned around in the dark and snow and drove back to Bozeman to spend the precious hours with Pattie.

When I arrived back in Ashton around noon the next day, the barrier was down, the road had been plowed, and I made it on through piled high drifts to Alta.

In winter, the road was mostly devoid of any other traffic. Traveling alone, Pattie was once pulled over by a highway patrolman on a stretch north of Ashton. The road surface had intermittent bare spots mingled with ice patches. Approaching on the driver's side in a cautious manner, the patrolman questioned her: "I saw you weaving across your lane, what's going on? Have you been drinking, or are you tired and falling asleep?"

Pattie smiled back. "No, my boyfriend told me to keep a wheel on dry pavement, wherever I can."

One of the patrolman's eyebrows rose expressively, "Good idea," he said.

In the spring, the extensive roadside meadows along the highway around Island Park became resplendent wildflower gardens. Stands of blue camas, marsh marigold, and mariposa lily flooded the vast wet meadows with scenic hues of blue and lavender, inset at places with yellow mule's ears.

Pond's Lodge in Island Park and Ernie's in West Yellowstone were favorite stops en route. Ernie made and sold over-sized cookies; Pond's specialty was chicken noodle soup. In later years, anytime we drove the Bozeman-Alta route, out of habit, we would stop at those places, saying "Let's split a cookie at Ernie's." It nostalgically reminded us of the intensity and fun of our early years.

It is an understatement to say, we both got to know the road between Bozeman and Alta really well and all the places in between. Having one or the other of us walk through the door into each other's arms was always a powerfully anticipated and passionate reuniting, even if we had been apart for only a few days.

What can I say about a gorgeous woman who would share such a commute? I acknowledge that I was a very fortunate guy. We were both very much in love. In later years, whenever we were in Bozeman, we would always drive past Pattie's house on South Tracy, reconnecting again with our first years together—exquisitely sentimental journeys down lovers' memory lane.

On an undated post card from that time, Pattie had written:

Do you have any idea how many Brahma-topped blue Toyota p/u's cruise through town when you're desperately missing your honey? It's a mean tease. The weekend was lovely! Love you, Pattie.

There was nothing Pattie and I would not share with each other. We had no secrets. Our issues became the equivalent of dirty dinnerware left over from past parties and times, left for us to do the kitchen duty. Cleaning up, we disposed of the past's leftovers, which we each carried around, and scrubbed clean all the leftover dishes and old soiled linens that needed attention. We exorcised the demons of doubt. Working together we cooked up a recipe that was wholly our own and served it to one another on clean platters. It only became sweeter and more delicious with passing time.

The exceptional life we designed together was truly and richly seasoned with love and mutual respect. A heightened sense of intimacy emerged from our building and sharing mutual dreams. And more than just fun, through our intense engagement of outdoor activities together, nature and the glorious natural beauty of the Yellowstone-Teton region became the physical and emotional setting for our rebirth, renewal, and ever growing love.

CHAPTER 7

FIRST INTERNATIONAL TRAVEL AND MARRIAGE PROPOSAL

Years from now you will be more disappointed by the things that you didn't do. So throw off your bowlines. Sail away from safe harbor. Catch the wind in your sails. Explore. Dream. Discover.

— Mark Twain

In January, 1993, I arranged a tropical getaway to Cabo San Lucas in Baja, Mexico. Although we had made road trips to Canada, throughout the western United States, and cross-country to the East Coast, this trip was really our maiden voyage for international travel together. Pattie was at first somewhat unsure, dubious about taking time from her gallery work and the expense of such travel. It was counter to her conservative nature and work ethic at the time.

A new resort hotel was offering a deeply discounted five-day package including airfares. The developers were busy in Cabo. New concrete walls sprouting thickets of rebar and structures plated with colorful tile trimming were springing up everywhere. But relative to today, the developments were still in their infancy. Just north of the city of Cabo the beaches were pristine and totally empty.

After checking in at the new, immaculate and plush resort hotel, Pattie and I walked out onto a second floor veranda. We overlooked tropical plantings, a pool lined with palms, and vibrantly tiled patios, beyond which lay clean sandy beach with the turquoise Sea of Cortez stretching to the horizon. The temperature was agreeably warm and pleasant. We had the entire place to ourselves. Pattie stood there thoughtfully viewing the setting; then half to herself and half to me, she murmured, "I could get used to this."

Our hotel was located several miles north of the fishing and resort community of Cabo. We found great places to snorkel at St. Maries and Los Barriles beaches, which we had all to ourselves.

I have a photograph someone took of us, sitting close together on a patio in Cabo overlooking the fishing boat docks—composed, smiling, neatly dressed, margaritas on the table in front of us—a lively sombreroed and brightly sequined mariachi band behind us, serenading us about *el amor*. The photograph is part of a framed montage that hangs on our kitchen wall in Alta. When I look at it, again, it seems like no time has passed. It is easy to remember the image itself, but I am reminded of the actual place and moment. How confident, young, attractive, and happily assured and in love we both appeared.

We arranged to go out on a marlin fishing charter. Unfortunately, Pattie developed a touch of Montezuma's revenge, as did the other two people who were supposed to share the charter with us. The boat was paid for in advance, so I was the only one who went out on the fishing excursion.

The boat captain and deck hand spoke only Spanish; I spoke only English. At sea, the captain located several marlins by their shark-like tail fins as they cruised along near the surface. The magnificent fish's glowing iridescence as it rode the swells is something I have never forgotten. After observing the creature's incredible beauty, this gringo had absolutely no enthusiasm for killing them, much to the disgust of the fishing boat captain.

At dusk, on our last evening, Pattie and I went to dinner at a restaurant located on the white sand beachfront. They graciously set up a special table for us on the beach, literally *in* the water's edge. Not only in Mexico but everywhere we traveled in our early years, it seemed people went out of their way to pay special attention to us as a couple.

We took off our shoes and warm waves lapped gently over our feet. The lights from the restaurant reflected around us on the water. The setting was as dreamily romantic as it gets, south of the border *romantico*, with our neurotransmitters firing, the moment buried deeply into our beings, a soul memory. We ordered champagne and lobster. They served us two huge cooked lobsters resting on a large platter of garnishing and our coupe glasses were filled repeatedly.

We toasted one another and the proposition of marriage came up. I think Pattie had expected me to use the occasion to propose marriage in a Norman Rockwell manner, down on one knee. The setting begged for it. I disappointed her, and I am sorry now.

I was still conflicted. Yes, I wanted it. But the thought made me hyperventilate. Vestiges of old demons reawakened and did a knee-jerk tap dance in my brain. I guess in spite of it all a part of me was still leery. The legal systems favored women at the time. I had seen too many friends' marriages unravel, leaving the men financially ruined, taken to the cleaners.

So that memorable evening on the beach under the stars, with reflected lights dancing on waves and warm water playing around our bare feet, and with champagne flowing, we shyly and gently came to a joint tentative agreement to marry, but did not dwell or obsess on the seriousness of what we had decided just then.

On Valentine's Day, I sent Pattie a card showing a heart scratched into the sand on a beach containing the words, "I love you." Inside the card I had written: "Pattie—from the warm sands of Baja to the snow on the Tetons, the message is the same—I love you. Happy Valentine's Day! Earle."

In February 25, 1993, I sent another card from Alta, and on it I had written:

Dearest Love,

Snow crystals are blowing about on this brightly lighted, sunny afternoon. Amid the sparkling splendor, I reflect on our love and loving you, the promise of our future, and how you have brought a happiness and joy into my being. I feel that my expressions of love for you are inadequate and too infrequent . . . I want to tell you once again, how very much I love you. I look forward to the years ahead and a life together—together for all time.—Earle

CHAPTER 8

ENGAGEMENT

All books are complex tomes of relationship, connection, and seduction, and this is the world we enter when we give and get them ourselves.

— Malcolm Bradbury, *The Courtship Dance*

Books can sometimes be given in place of writing or conveying complex communication and thoughts. In the *History of Love*, author Diane Ackerman points out one way lovers can blend their hearts is by sharing sympathetic authors and words. Pattie somehow was attuned to that idea. She gave me a beautifully illustrated little book by Mary Engel, *A Good Marriage*. Its simple unpretentious messages totally reflected both of our philosophies and what we wanted, beginning with a line from the first page: "There is no lovelier, friendly, and charming relationship, companion, or company than a good marriage."

In an enclosed separate letter, Pattie had penned in longhand: "In the moments we share there is light. I know that beneath the manmade chaos of the world, there is a Creation of perfection and an unending well of love, that the pleasure, the excitement, the hope and the completeness I feel with you is but a microcosm of all that is there for people at their best."

Simple as it sounds, our decision and our commitment to marry further improved our relationship. It lifted it to a new level and reduced the tension of uncertainty, strengthening our bond. I'm sure it would not work that way for everyone, but it did for Pattie and me.

I no longer felt like we were marking time. We were both agreed and committed to the goal of making a life and future together. Knowing where we were ultimately headed, and particularly because it appeared to be something we *both* wanted, a lot of uncomfortable uncertainty and tension went away—well, almost anyway.

My Valentine to Pattie in 1993 showed a Victorian-dressed woman set within a heart-shaped bower of flowers who was coyly remarking:

> Oh love of mine,
> I'm here to say,
> My heart doth pound.
> In that special way for you,
> I crave both day and night . . .
> Let's hop in the bed and make some hay!

Beneath the card's ribald message, I had added, "Yeah!!!" I had also written a message inside:

Pattie, You are a very special person to me
my lover,
my friend,
my life's dream.
May we always be together and happily in love!
You hold the door key to my house . . . oops, I mean to my heart!
—Earle

On March 27, 1993, Pattie wrote:

Dearest Love:

You sounded as if you needed some reassurance, so I'm hoping customers will think that I am typing something of critical importance to the world of business. I'm sitting here at my desk, looking at the photo of the two of us at Hyalite and at your card showing the two little kids skipping off to the beach, sand buckets in tow.

We have had a lot of good times—and I am happily confident that there are to be many more funny, wonderful, playful, thoroughly delightful times together. So Sweet Precious, I say—

Come live with me and be my Love,
And we will all the pleasures prove,
That hills and valleys, dales and fields,
Or woods or steepy mountain yields.
—Marlowe in 1570/Pattie in 1993

And I kiss your toes, and kiss your nose
and every inch in-between.
Does this help to make it all better?! I love you mightily.
—Love, Pattie

Because it so closely expressed our sentiments for our life together, we often quoted Marlowe's verse to each other over the years. I unconsciously associated the lovely flower-nymph who lived in the mountain woods, and to whom the gallant proposal was made, with Pattie. In later years, we had a fairyland scene framed along with the verse. It sat on Pattie's desk where it still resides today.

We were continuing to make the long Bozeman to Alta commute, coordinating it with Pattie's business schedule and mine. We could not sleep when we weren't together. When we were with each other, we generally stayed up all night, too.

On April 8, 1993, Pattie wrote:

Hi Precious Love—I think I'm going to lobby for a reduction of paperwork in this marriage thing. Sheesh!! My schoolgirl employee called about my "dress code"— get them while they are young and malleable (employees, not wives; we of the "seasoned" variety are better. Trust me on this one.) Did you read about the last couple in the Becoming Partners book? Their marriage encountered many crises and they just kept emerging stronger, continuing to grow, and becoming more individual and more united. I don't want crises, but I do want all that last part. I Love you, Earle.

My journal is bursting with entries from that spring. We packed a lot of living into that point in time. In the high water month of May, 1993, we canoed 120 miles of the Green River in Utah through Canyon Lands National Park, from Crystal Geyser at Green River, Utah, to Spanish Bar on the Colorado River. We did it in five days on the river. It was all Class I water, meaning little current and few riffles or waves, so it required a lot of paddling. Pattie was fond of pointing out the guidebook recommended taking twelve or more days.

The isolation and solitude in the deep gorge made for a true wilderness experience. We saw no one else the entire time. We explored the history of the canyon with its abandoned homesteads, old outlaw cabins, ancient rock art, and Anasazi and Fremont cultural sites; the spectacular red rock formations and spring flowers; and the unusual wildlife, such as lizards, scorpions, kangaroo rats, canyon wrens with their evocative song, fast-moving racer snakes, and on the river, lots of beaver who were more curious about us than afraid.

Rattling pots and pans awoke us one night. In the darkness, something attempted to scratch its way up the outside of our tent. Pattie startled awake said, "What was that?"

Zipping open the tent fly and turning on the flashlight revealed an invasion of small scurrying and hopping long-tailed rodents scattering from our campsite. Maybe we had left dirty dishes out. "We've been overrun by a family of kangaroo rats!" I exclaimed.

When the Green River joined with the Colorado, we continued down the powerful Colorado in our open 17-foot canoe to Spanish Bar. On the Bar, a large flat riverside outcropping of rock, we spread out our gear and clothing to air and dry in the sun. It looked like a disorganized yard sale. A jet boat had been prearranged to meet us there and transport us and our canoe back to Moab, Utah. With Pattie in the bow of the canoe, it had all made for indelible memories and a lifetime of conversation topics.

Later in May, we hiked the buttes behind Kelly Warm Springs in Jackson Hole. It was a magnificent spring day with the reemergence of green on the landscape, wildflowers on south exposures, remnant snow banks on the north, and the grandeur of the still snow-covered Teton Mountains as a backdrop. We surprised a large and very vocal band of elk close up, which thrilled Pattie, and encountered a half-dozen bison, seven deer, and an inquisitive red fox. We found shed moose and mule deer antlers. Our hearts sang; it was gloriously springtime in Jackson Hole.

W. Somerset Maugham said, "Sometimes a man hits upon a place to which he mysteriously feels that he belongs." Both Pattie and I felt that way about Jackson Hole and the Tetons—we both believed not only that we belonged there, but also that we belonged there with each other.

Around that time, one of Pattie's acquaintances married a Native American, and we were invited to attend the outdoor sunrise wedding. We were required to be at the site in pre-dawn darkness. Buffalo robes and other accoutrements lay scattered around on the sagebrush. It was a clear morning. Chanting and drumming began as daylight began to glow in the eastern sky. Guests were positioned to look toward the hill top ceremonial site, with the morning sky backlighting it and the couple. After a while, the rising sun became too intense a background to view. A marriage of backlit shadows was accomplished within a haloed fire-ball, amid a crescendo of shrill chanting and drumming.

In July, we traveled to Talkeetna, Alaska, where we tent camped on the edge of town. Talkeetna was one of my favorite places in Alaska. It was still a relatively remote Alaskan village, a bush community. In 1984 while residing in Alaska, I had won a citizen's cross-country ski race in Talkeetna and was awarded a Fairview Inn mug. The Fairview's claim to fame is that when President Warren Harding visited in 1923, he died from food poisoning after dining at the Inn. Jackson Hole and Talkeetna have a strong connection with each other through the mountaineering and adventuring community. Climbs on Denali are staged out of Talkeetna.

On this trip, a friend in Anchorage loaned us the use of his coveted 1970s vintage Volkswagen van that was rigged à la hippiedom for sleeping and camping. Top speed for the bus was maybe 45 mph. The impatient drivers that got behind us assumed we were the last vestiges of flower children. We were slowing traffic on Alaska's only major highway, Route 1. The signaled expressions of resentment were creatively graphic. Redneck road rage! We smiled and waved back. Flower power was not admired by Alaskans.

In Homer, we were walking along what is called the Spit, when the driver of a passing pickup called out, "Pattie?!"

Small world. It was one of Pattie's acquaintances from Bozeman. He and his wife lived and worked in Alaska in the summer doing commercial fishing.

Backing his vehicle up to talk, he exclaimed: "I would recognize that hair anywhere."

We fished the Talkeetna and Susitna Rivers for king salmon. When Pattie caught a forty-pound salmon in the swift river current, I was afraid the powerful fish was going to drag her back out to sea with it.

There were no other women on the rivers. It was a world of macho bearded Alaskan guides. Pattie was a star attraction. Fishermen and grisly guides gallantly rushed to help her, making sure she hooked up with the monstrous salmon, but did not get swept away by the surging fish or strong river currents in the process.

In our Alta kitchen photomontage, there is a picture of Pattie and me standing in the forecastle of a jet boat, each of us holding up an impressive 35–40-pound king salmon. The fish were more than half as long as Pattie.

We froze and packed whole king salmon and sockeye salmon that we caught on the Kenai River into large Styrofoam boxes, shipping them through as checked luggage to Idaho Falls, Idaho, which is something probably no longer possible with the airline luggage requirements nowadays.

In between our travel and everything else we managed to have going on, I continued with my environmental consulting business, Pattie operated her gallery, and we still commuted back and forth between Bozeman and Alta. It took a lot of energy; we had a lot of it! I have a journal entry from that time noting that I "mowed our Alta lawn on June 22 in an unseasonal snowstorm."

Pattie used full and part-time employees to run her gallery when she wasn't there. It was frustrating for her and not very satisfactory. Pattie had outstanding skills for engaging customers and knowledgably promoting her gallery's merchandise. Salaried or hourly wage employees were not always motivated to work in that manner. I know the business's bottom line sometimes suffered without Pattie being present to assist potential customers.

But she was rock solid and happily upbeat about our upcoming marriage. Pattie was the most loving and considerate person I had ever known. In our ever continuing correspondence in between our times together, she quoted Shakespeare to me:

So, to end this missive on a classical timeless note, I give you Shakespeare:

Let me not to the marriage of true minds
Admit impediments. Love is not love
Which alters when alternation finds,
Or bends with the remover to remove:
Oh, no! It is an ever-fixed mark.
That looks on tempests and is never shaken;
It is the star to every wand'ring bark,

Whose worth's unknown, although his height be taken.
Love's not Time's fool, through rosy lips & cheeks
Within his bending sickle's compass come;
Love alters not with his brief hours and weeks,
But bears it out even to the edge of doom:
If this be error and upon me proved,
I never writ, nor no man ever loved.
—And we know he writ—and we know I love you—Pattie

On April 9, 1993, I sent Pattie a card with Cupid pictured on the front, pointing at himself as if to ask, "Who, me?" Inside I had written:

Dearest Love—

Just wanted to make sure you received proper congratulations on your wedding engagement! Thanks for the last lovely three days. While a lot time was spent on the road, it was nevertheless fun. I bounced along in my truck on my return from Bozeman amid spring snow squalls with good, happy thoughts about us and how everything appears to be turning out so well. I'm excited for us!

I had a call from Debbie (in Pennsylvania). I told her about our engagement. So now you can be sure everyone back there will know. Looks like Cupid was right on target.

Born to love you, Earle

The choice of a marriage partner is momentous, it can be life transforming. The act of marriage itself is one of trust and optimism. Our engagement provoked soap opera behaviors and drama among family, friends, and acquaintances. For many, it seemed, second marriages were particularly damned and not to be trusted. I am not suggesting couples ignore sage advice, but one's judgment and confidence can certainly be tested by the naysayers.

We received more than our share of negativity from perennially single cynics and other skeptics. Many simply advised us against marriage. "Why ruin a good thing by getting married, follow the way nowadays," they said, "be partners instead of spouses." Others told us, "It won't work; marriage doesn't work," or that it would require "miserable putting up with unwanted things," or "when you marry, you lose." They meant nothing personal.

While some of the advice was near comical and good natured, there were others for whom the prospect of our marriage was incredibly threatening, provoking extreme jealousy and ugly nastiness.

My adult children dropped the bombshell to their mother: "Guess what? Dad's getting married!" My younger son added, "Yeah, I visited them and she cooked the best southern fried chicken for dinner. Even packed a lunch for me to take when I was leaving."

Nearly hysterical, my ex-wife, who I had not seen or heard from for a decade, suddenly took it upon herself to try to discourage Pattie. She repeatedly phoned my mother, who ignored her frantic demand for Pattie's address. In a venomous letter to me, my feminist ex referred to Pattie as a "doormat."

In spite of Pattie's warm kindness to the younger son, my ex was able to enlist him to her cause. He wrote: "You are with that other woman, while my real mother is living [elsewhere]." Considering that he was normally intelligent, it was odd he did not realize his mother had been the one who had chosen to leave without him and live elsewhere.

Even after Pattie and I had been married for years, my younger son remained devotedly poisoned by his mother and would not recognize Pattie as my wife. Instead, he continued to refer to Pattie as "my girlfriend." In spite of it, much to her credit, almost approaching saintliness, Pattie was always smilingly gracious and kind toward him, the magnanimity of which was totally lost on him.

My own mother did not attend our wedding. We assumed it was her advanced age and the rigors involved with traveling from Pennsylvania. A half-sister of mine sent us a nondescript card on which she simply signed her name. A nephew and his wife sent us a tiny potted curio-cactus. We kept the cactus alive all these years on our kitchen window sill. Shortly after we received the cactus, though, the nephew and his wife divorced. So maybe subconsciously it had said more about the thorny nature of their union than of ours.

Pattie's stepmother arranged a get-away trip for us to meet them in Reno, Nevada. Pattie and I had fun. But at the time, I was unaware of the subterfuge and disingenuous motive behind her stepmother wanting to get us to Reno. Pattie clued me in afterward. Her stepmother had thought she could manipulate us into a sleazy "quickie wedding." It was funny, but insulting, too. In the stepmother's judgment, it didn't make any difference that we were engaged. Because we had been living together without benefit of matrimony, we were destined to burn in hell.

Conversely, a niece of mine wrote to Pattie: "We so enjoyed getting to know you. I've told my mother and sister and brother how terrific you are and how lucky Earle is to have such a sweet companion—such a good relationship."

It turned out that our marriage was the precious gift of a lifetime to each other. It "worked" delightfully and was never "work." Neither of us felt coerced; we both wanted it. It was not "luck." There was never taking the other for granted, immature negativity, games, making the other out a fool, pointless tasks, or demands on each other to give up things in order to prove our love. We were vigilant not to do hurtful, careless, petty, or stupid things to each other.

CHAPTER 9

MOUNTAIN TOP WEDDING

The couples that are "meant to be" are the ones who go through everything that is meant to tear them apart and come out even stronger than they were before.

— Anonymous

I postal mailed Pattie a cartoon with a little boy asking his mother: "Why do they call it Holy Macaroni, Mom?"

We set an early autumn date for the wedding—September 18—a time when Pattie's busy summer work season normally slacked off. Then we began looking in the Yellowstone-Teton region for a special place to hold the ceremony. That search proved to be a major undertaking in itself, but figuring everything out—the planning—was part of the fun.

For a place to hold the wedding, we considered and visited Chico Hot Springs and another small resort lodge in Paradise Valley, Montana; the chapel at Big Sky that looks out on Lone Mountain, Montana; a church in Jackson; the Granary at Spring Hill in Jackson with its impressive view of the Tetons; and the Heart Six and Turpin Meadows Guest Ranches in Buffalo Valley near Moran, Wyoming. We finally decided on the perfect spot for our outdoor wedding: the top of Signal Mountain in Grand Teton National Park, a truly dramatic and spectacular setting with the Teton Mountains cloaked in their autumn splendor for background!

Jackson Hole's weather can be unpredictable in September, but we were willing to risk it. The top of Signal Mountain had road access and a singular scenic setting. On one side, the view takes in Jackson Lake and the Snake River with the Teton Range panoramically providing a dramatic mountain backdrop; and in the opposite direction, the Leidy Peak highlands and the confluence of the Snake and Buffalo Fork Rivers. The road corridor to the site would be brightly lined with gorgeous autumn colors. The location was symbolic of our connection to the Tetons, and we were willing to take our chances on the weather.

We decided we would do all our own planning: arranging any catering, music, making all other preparations, and holding the reception afterward at our house in Alta. We planned to hire a local young woman to work at serving the guests in our home during the reception.

We made a big personal investment in the arrangements. Looking back, the rituals involved with our doing everything ourselves made it more special and memorable. Where everything is catered and traditional, the bride and groom generally may not put much sweat equity or thought into the details themselves. Consequently, they may not acquire all the memories Pattie and I did. Our approach was totally hands on, reflecting our commitment, personalities, and lifestyle.

We had a sepia-toned photograph made of us dressed in nineteenth-century period clothing at a shop located just off the Square in Jackson. I am sitting with long coattails, top hat and cane, with Pattie standing beside me in an old-fashioned hat and lacey bodice gown, her hand resting on my shoulder. We used the photograph for the front of our customized wedding invitation. Pattie picked, pressed and dried wildflowers, and in each invitation she included a special touch—her dried wildflowers.

Our wedding rings were custom made and very special to us. My wedding band was crafted by a jeweler in Whitefish, Montana, one of Pattie's consignment artists. He forged an emblematic scene of the three Teton peaks, with forest in the foreground and a full moon represented by a diamond inset above the mountains. Pattie was also acquainted with a ninety-year-old jeweler in Bozeman. She and he together designed a one-of-a-kind ring with antique-appearing fine-filigree inset with rubies and a center diamond. People always remarked on the uniqueness of our rings. Wedding rings are important and symbolic. A circle without beginning or end, they symbolize eternity.

After much searching, Pattie found a beautiful vintage lacy-white wedding dress and early twentieth-century high lace-top shoes at an antique clothing store in Laurel, Montana. A perfect fit, they no doubt had once belonged to a frontier Montana woman who had cherished them. I was not allowed to see Pattie wearing them until the day of the wedding.

At the reception in our Alta home after the wedding, among other things, we planned to serve one of the large Alaskan king salmon we had caught that spring. It would take up one whole kitchen counter space. The owner and chef at the Royal Wolf restaurant in Driggs at the time cheerfully agreed to help. He had the only oven in the valley big enough to bake the monstrous fish whole.

Our wedding cake, a gorgeous three-tiered carrot cake, was made to order by a person in Jackson who specialized in baking fancy cakes. A few days before the wedding, we made a special trip over to Jackson to pick it up. I remember Pattie protectively holding the large cake in her lap as we carefully and elatedly negotiated the highway across Teton Pass back to Alta with it.

We arranged for Jackson Hole musicians Shelly and Kelly, who were friends, to provide music on the mountain top as people gathered. Among the songs they played and sang was Van Morrison's "Have I Told You Lately" with its memorable lines: "there's a love that's divine and it's yours and mine… give thanks and pray."

Another love ballad they played that morning, "Could I Have this Dance for the Rest of My Life," would become our signature song. When a bride and groom get married they generally begin the marriage with a slow dance. "Could I Have this Dance" was our wedding slow dance song. In the years afterward, whenever we attended a Jackson Hole function where Shelly and Kelly were providing the music, they would play *our* song when they saw us in the audience. Then Pattie and

I would get up and dance—close and slow—tenderly remembering those early years and our wedding morning on Signal Mountain.

We found a civil judge in Jackson Hole who specialized in outdoor weddings to conduct our services. Only in Jackson Hole would there likely be such a person. Pattie called him "The Marrying Man," and years later she would write and publish an article about him in Jackson Hole's *A Grand Wedding* magazine.

A small gathering of thirty or more friends surrounded us on the mountain top, in addition to our wedding party. My older son Brett performed admirably in his role as best man. At the time, he was an elite fighter pilot for the Marine Corps. In his dress uniform, he appeared to be our honor guard. Pattie's sisters, Donna and Lisa, were maids of honor; and Pattie's niece and goddaughter, Evelyn, served as our flower girl. Two different friends videotaped the wedding. Another couple, one of them, a professional Jackson Hole wildlife photographer, took rolls of film of us and everyone else in attendance.

I will always remember Pattie in her beautiful lacey dress and antique high buckle shoes, smiling as she walked down the mountain top path toward me. Holding a bouquet and two long-stemmed roses, she came to where the official and I waited. Then I took her hand. She was unforgettably beautiful.

It was stormy and snowing right up until only a few hours before the ceremony. Then it began clearing off. Snow-covered mountains dramatically peeked out from beneath clouds and the weather lifted like celestial curtains parting before us. The sun broke through and shafts of light descended and shone on us as we said our vows we had personally composed. It was a dramatic and unforgettable moment. Everyone remarked, "Wasn't that something . . . the clearing off, the sunlight? It was a good omen!"

Included here is an excerpt from Pattie and Earle's Wedding Vows, September 18, 1993.

Conducting official:

This celebration is but the outward sign of an inner union of hearts, and as such marriage is the most tender of all relationships in life—a relationship of the spirit and soul, and of love and trust.

This couple comes together before you here today with love, and together they ask our support and blessing, as they begin their adventure into married life.

All peoples of the world recognize marriage, and there are many common themes in all wedding ceremonies. The ceremonies usually give advice: the do's and don'ts of the culture's collective wisdom, and a blessing or wish for the couple. With tremendous insight, and very simply, one Native American ceremony puts it this way: 'Now you will feel no rain, for each of you will be shelter for the other. Now you will feel no cold, for each of you will be warmth for the other. Now there is no more loneliness. Now you are two persons, but there is only one life before you. As you enter the days of your life together, may your days together be good and long upon the Earth.'

Happiness in marriage is having a mutual sense of values and objectives. It is standing together, facing the world together. It is forming a circle of love that gathers in the entire family. It is willingly doing things for each other, not in an attitude of duty or sacrifice, but in a spirit of joy. It is speaking words of appreciation and demonstrating gratitude in thoughtful ways. A relationship where the independence is equal, the dependence mutual, and the obligation reciprocal—not only marrying the right partner, but being the right partner.

Earle:

Let the mountains before us symbolize our love and marriage—solid, enduring beyond our lives, and with a beauty that fills the heart. With you I will love and be open to love, so that we can become the very best we can be. I will be your true friend and someone with whom to share your passions, dreams, and life for now and always.

Pattie:

From this day forward, I choose you to love; and I look forward to awakening each morning to another wonderful day loving you. I want to learn and grow by your side each day, and dream by your side each night. To go through life hand in hand.

I give you a white rose. It is a symbol of my promise to care for you, to nurture you, to support you, to be your true friend.

I give you a red rose. It is a passionate color and a symbol for the excitement I feel in anticipation of experiencing all of life with you.

With you I will love, and be open to love, so that we can become the very best we can be.

Conducting official:

May you both enter into the mystery which is awareness of another's presence; no more physical than spiritual. May your lives come together, like the waters of the two rivers joining in valley before us, flowing and joining in an eternity; forever sharing a future filled with triumphs, love, and laughter; and with a new beginning each and every day.

For as much as you Earle, and you Pattie, have consented together before friends and relatives, and in the presence of those witnesses, by the power vested in me by the State of Wyoming, I now pronounce you husband and wife. You may now kiss the bride.

The long-stemmed red and white roses Pattie gave me that day are pressed and dried. They still reside in my dresser drawer, folded into a newspaper page that announced our wedding.

While we were pronounced "husband and wife," as is customary, we never thought of ourselves as archetype spouses. Our marriage was not based on traditional roles intended for child rearing, physical security, or survival; rather, we viewed ourselves as equals entering into a spiritual partnership. After the ceremony, Pattie's father was beaming as he exclaimed: "That was the most beautiful wedding I have ever attended."

When we arrived at the house, everyone urged me to carry Pattie across the threshold, so I picked her up. We skidded across the threshold as the carpet underneath us slipped on the hardwood floor entry. The scene was captured in a funny photograph. Looking wild-eyed, we barely managed to remain upright. With Pattie in my arms, clutching around my neck, we skated through the doorway into married life.

At the reception at our Alta home, everyone raised glasses of champagne as my son, Brett, made a fine toast to us. Our two wine goblets were hand crafted by one of Pattie's artists. They stand side-by-side today yet on our kitchen shelf. The wedding reception also served another unannounced purpose. It was a celebratory house warming party, too.

Our well established routine of commuting between Bozeman and Alta resumed. On October 23, 1993, I wrote and mailed Pattie a note inside a card saying:

"My Dearest Love,

It's late my lovely wife, but my thoughts are of you and

our time together. This card says it very simply: 'The best times are our times together, us together always'—I Love You, Earle"

The day Pattie and I married on the top of Signal Mountain was a remarkably special experience. It will always remain the happiest day of my life. With our marriage came what I can only describe as a deep sense of peace.

CHAPTER 10

FRENCH POLYNESIAN HONEYMOON

All the willow winding paths . . .
This is what I give . . . This is what I ask you for,
Nothing More.
— Dan Fogelberg, *"Since You Asked"* (lyrics from one of the love songs played by Jackson Hole musicians Shelly and Kelly at Pattie and Earle's mountain top wedding).

Before our wedding day, Pattie presented me with a four-weight Loomis fly rod and a matching reel and line for a wedding gift. It was a top-of-the-line outfit, the finest, and the most expensive fly rod and reel I have ever owned. I did not ask for it. She explained to me it was something she wanted to do. Loomis rods, at the time were acclaimed as the most successful for casting competitions. I still use and treasure that precious fly rod yet today, remembering Pattie every time I uncase it.

Pattie had a knack for giving personal and thoughtful gifts for the sheer joy of giving. I had never experienced anything like it before or since. When I think back, all those caring gestures stand out as special. They cumulatively add up to a mountain of love.

Once in a long while, a great love presents us with a fairy tale . . . those words aptly preface and begin to describe our honeymoon. For Pattie's wedding gift, actually, for both of us, I arranged our honeymoon trip to distant and dreamy French Polynesia—a mythical place. Without exaggeration, a tome of hedonism, romance, and passion set amid a tropical paradise could be written about our South Sea Tahitian honeymoon experience alone.

Around 1960 when I was in the Navy, my ship visited Perth, Australia. Roger and Hammerstein's musical South Pacific was playing in a theater there. Five giggling Australian girls offered to escort me to see the show. I long ago forgot what the girls looked like, but I never forgot the movie. Being stationed in Hawaii and the South Pacific at the time, I strongly identified with it. When it came to arranging our honeymoon, I could not think of a more romantic place than the islands of French Polynesia—Bali Hai!

We delayed our honeymoon travel until January 1994, planning it for after Pattie's busy work season following the holiday. We flew on a French airliner from Los Angeles to Pape'ete on the island of Tahiti, and from there we took a hydrofoil ferry to the island Moorea. There we had accommodations for a week at an intimate hotel beautifully situated on spectacular Cook's Bay.

That was the only hotel reservation I had made in advance. For the rest of the three-week honeymoon, we planned to spend time on the islands of Bora Bora and Huahine, but we were not committed to any particular resort hotel reservations or plans. Our itinerary would be impromptu and in the moment.

While awaiting our flight Pattie journaled: "Los Angeles International is an introduction to exotica . . . a parade of Nations; a cacophony of foreign tongues. We people watch to the point of overload."

My travel journal entry noted a close encounter: "Flew Delta to LA . . . at 12:15 a.m.; next Corsair (French) airlines to Pepette, Tahiti, arriving at 7 a.m. We flew out of LA that early morning, luckily just hours ahead of a major earthquake—6.6 Richter scale." The earthquake had shut down all air travel for days afterward.

Every day we recorded happenings and our impressions—lasting, hauntingly beautiful impressions—together into the same journal.

We began journaling with Pattie writing appropriately on right-side pages; me, opposite on the left-side. Male and female brains are wired differently. At the time it was thought that men's brains perform tasks on the left side, women the right. It was an interesting contrast: right brain vs. left brain observations—yin-yang.

Pattie penned lovely descriptive and poetic imagery. I chronicled facts and literal observations, including sketches of features, such as the dramatic volcanic mountain skyline behind our hotel at Cook's Bay. Our honeymoon diary became a prized possession. We often got it out over the years and reread through it together.

Based on our experiences in keeping travel diaries, in 2008, Pattie wrote a piece entitled: "Once Upon a Time . . . Chronicling Lives Together" for the *Jackson Hole Grand Wedding Planner*, in which she described how a couple's journaling can provide an added dimension to lasting memories.

In our honeymoon journal, Pattie had written:

The entire island (Moorea) smells like a flower. It is several days before I can differentiate among the smells of mango and papaya, hibiscus and gardenias—so hot, so humid. This is the meaning of sultry. How sensuous is the slow, languid movement of island life. It will be indelibly imprinted on my senses. It is mine always—more than likely it always was. I just forgot.

The Tahitians we met were friendly beautiful people. The women's first task in the morning was to weave a crown of tiaré blossoms, a type of gardenia, into their hair. As Pattie had noted, the air was scented with flower blossoms, the sea was gin-clear, sensuous and warm, the beaches clean and absolutely litter free. It truly was heavenly—paradise found!

Away from the hotel on the more secluded beaches, uninhibited deeply-tanned French and Tahitian women went topless. There were few biting insects and no poisonous snakes. We required mosquito netting over the bed only in the jungle uplands on the island of Huahine. Instead of mail, there were freshly baked French baguettes delivered every morning to a mailbox-like structure for us. Fresh fruit was abundant and inexpensive; fallen ripe mangoes littered the dusty roadside, for anyone to gather up free of charge.

"Breakfast," I wrote in our journal, "was five pounds of fresh fruit each morning." Truly paradisiacal, it is little wonder Captain Bligh's crew mutinied in order to remain in this South Sea heaven on Earth; and French artist, Paul Gauguin, whiled away his last years creating abstract paintings of Tahitian maidens.

Pattie journaled: "I love the fruit, the flowers, the colors, the lushness, the splendor, the sound and movement of water. The Tahitians are rich people with so little money. How often does a place exceed your fantasies? Surpass your dreams?"

At the time, one unpaved road encircled the island of Moorea. To travel around the island, we rented bicycles and sometimes a motor scooter. Wearing a helmet, Pattie sat behind me, clutching me tightly. There was little vehicular traffic; there must have been some, but I do not remember it. A bus (a converted flat-bed truck with open-air sides and hammered together benches for seats) ran on an irregular schedule. Sometimes it showed up; other times it did not. The hotel also provided us the use of a small outrigger canoe, which, with our canoeing experience, we used to paddle out to the barrier reef at low tide and explore.

At a village gathering, we were invited to participate in netting fish from the bay. As the lengthy net was tightened into a smaller and smaller circle, some of the locals began plucking out small fish and snacking on them raw. A villager next to me bit the head off a fish, and holding out the choice remainder, offered to share it with me. Pattie would forever joke about it.

Dressed in pareus, simple colorful cloths, the Tahitian vahines began their day by weaving flower crowns into their hair—tiaré and hibiscus. Around midday everything shut down. In the languorous heat of the day, everyone retired for a nap. Mesmerizingly slow moving ceiling fans kept insects off and warm humidity laden tropical air circulating. Pattie wrote, "Mother Earth is personified in Tahiti" and "When I look into Earle's brown face with his dark hazel eyes and smiling face, I see myself smiling back."

A nearby resort hotel had Tahitian drumming and dancing. Late in the day, the primitive drumming would begin. Attracted by the throbbing tempo, we would seek out the source of the sounds. The dancers would invariably pull us into their wildly abandoned performances. In my mind there is no more suggestive dancing anywhere than that of French Polynesia's tamure. Afterward, the native dancers would blissfully drape us with shell necklaces, crowns woven from flowers, and flower-blossom leis.

We attended a pareu-tying demonstration. The pareu, a colorfully patterned cloth that Tahitians wear, can be used to dress in many ways, from casual to formal. An attractive and deeply-tanned French woman, who was married to a Tahitian man, performed the demonstration for the small number of us in attendance. Not at all self-conscious, for each tying variation, she would completely remove the pareu, under which she wore only a skimpy bikini bottom, and start over. Her husband also demonstrated how Tahitian men wore and tied a pareu. It involved much fewer variations.

While I was distracted, Pattie quickly became proficient in the many ways to tie and wear a pareu. Pattie would later use the same techniques she learned that day to wear the African kanga cloth. Today, Pattie's colorful pareus lay neatly folded on her closet shelf in our Alta home, where they patiently await our long overdue next trip to somewhere exotic and tropical.

To make our way to Bora Bora, I bought us passage on a freighter ship that sailed at night between the islands. We spread some of our clothing out on the main deck to lie on, but sleep was elusive. The rusting hulk rumbled along noisily all night, arriving at Bora Bora at daybreak early the next morning.

At dawn, approaching the docks, we, and everyone else, gathered sleepily but excited along the ship's rail. On shore, someone hoisted a flag and loudly blew a trumpet to announce the ship's arrival. The funky trumpeting announcing our arrival amused Pattie, becoming another of her favorite and frequently told stories.

We did not have lodging reservations. Trusting our *Lonely Planet* guidebook, we made our way by local transportation to a pension on the far side of the island. The Polynesian gods must have smiled upon us because we were able to rent a lovely bungalow that was situated only a few feet from the sea. While cooling sea breezes circulated through open windows, we could hear the waves splashing, it seemed, at the foot of our bed.

The setting for many Hollywood films and celebrity escapades, Bora Bora was at that time relatively more commercialized than other islands, but not much more. We again got around all over the island mostly by foot and bicycles. The bicycles did not have fenders, so when it misted rain, as it frequently did, we became mud splattered. A swim in the sea or the fresh water hoses provided at the hotels served to clean us up, much to the amusement of the Tahitian children who delighted in hosing us down.

We hiked a trail leading to a remote waterfall deep in the jungle. The cascade fell crashing from a tall and verdant cliff. Pattie described it as "water cascading from heaven." We had it all to ourselves and swam nude in the plunge pool, amid tropical mists and a gentle warm rain. Pattie recorded, "It was the stuff of dreams and cherished memories."

On another occasion, we went on a snorkeling and boating tour. In an outboard motor- powered canoe, a Tahitian guide took a half-dozen of us to a small palm-tree covered atoll, called a motu, where we had a picnic lunch. One of the clients, an attractive young French woman, wore only the briefest of a bikini bottom.

When the guide chummed the clear water with pieces of fish, it morphed into a tropical aquarium teeming with vividly colorful fish. It was an amazing and delightful underwater celebration and perfect for snorkeling—until five-to six-foot-long reef sharks showed up and ruined the party for us. At another spot, we swam with curious manta rays that gently hovered close to us. We circumnavigated the entire island of Bora Bora in the outboard motor powered canoe before the day was over, sightseeing, exploring the barrier reefs, snorkeling, and swimming. We tanned nearly as brown as the Tahitians.

After our time on Bora Bora, we traveled to the island of Big Huahine. We had made no lodging reservations there either. On a bulletin board at Fare's waterfront dock, there was a hand-written advertisement for lodging and a phone number. I called the number from a pay phone at the dock. After some back and forth language difficulty, a twelve-year-old boy, who spoke some English, was put on the phone. He translated to someone on the other end of the phone connection that we were on our honeymoon.

Shortly afterward, the boy and his mother arrived in an automobile to take us to their place, the Chez Bellevue. The property boasted a special honeymooner's hilltop bungalow overlooking a large expanse of lush jungle, beyond which lay the turquoise sea. Our host had strewn the bed with fresh flowers; the mosquito netting was pink. Racing across the walls and ceiling, in contrast to the pink netting, were all sizes of green geckos, who shared the bungalow with us. We had found Shangri-La!

Privately owned and operated by a Tahitian family, the property had several other thatched-roof guest bungalows that were surrounded by fruit tree orchards, orchids and other tropical flowers, a swimming pool, and a cozy restaurant and dining area. As Pattie recorded in our journal, "We had discovered the quintessential honeymoon spot and bungalow."

We were invited to help ourselves to all the ripe fruit we wanted. There were only three other guests besides us—two gay Frenchmen and a starlet-like French woman whose only activity was sunbathing.

The owners also operated a fish farm below the resort along the coast, and sold fish commercially. Their restaurant, needless to say, served fresh fish du jour.

A large Tahitian woman employee, who weighed more than Pattie and I combined, announced she would be my "Tahitian wife" and took us to collect papaya. With a twelve-foot pole, the woman knocked the football-sized papaya loose from the tree using one hand, and deftly caught the falling fruit before they hit the ground with her free hand. Pattie used to jokingly threaten me that if I ever misbehaved, she would turn me over to my "Tahitian wife."

When the time came to return to the island of Tahiti, Pattie emotionally threw her leis from the back of the ferry boat into the sea. She had heard that if your flowers floated back to shore you would return one day.

On the day of our departure, Tahitian dancers and drummers were performing in the airport. They hung flower leis on us and hugged us. By then we were tanned nearly as golden brown as they were. In a moving departure, we reluctantly said our goodbyes: "*Maruru, Tahiti*, Thank-you, Tahiti."

Sometime afterward, Pattie composed a poem and presented it to me. She had written it on pale-blue stationery with a flowery background. She wrote, "I dedicate this poem to Earle—my husband, my lover, my friend . . . the man who made these memories with me."

Tahitian Honeymoon

Mango and papaya, tiare blossoms, and gardenias,
Voluptuous vulnerability in an aromatic haze.
Sea waters undulating . . . Lorelei . . . Lorelei,
The rhythm of the Siren's song filling our days.
Thermal persuasion; snaking towards my love,
Red-hot fusion as the noon sun peaks.
Yin and Yang in succulent symbiosis;
The beatific balance a lover seeks.

Passion's crescendo beneath a veiling of net,
Taunting . . . echoing . . . geckos in our midst.
Waterfalls thundering with a guttural roar,
Native drums synchronous with hearts as we kissed.
Flowers pressed into recumbent fecundity,
Sun-zapped lovers stretched out in repose.
A fan swirls passion into lasting love,
The love surpassing what dreams suppose.
Entwined with another, no longer separate,
The heart responds in exquisite measure.
Hearing silent laughter; crying unshed tears,
His pain, my heartache; his joy, my pleasure.
I love you, Earle—Pattie

It is said that "True love and memories are not of mind and body, but those that remain forever written on the soul." Our time together in French Polynesia was deeply and forever imprinted on us—warm tropical seas, the scent of flowers, unspoiled verdant jungle, gentle friendly people, and passionate love. It all melded and combined in our hearts and minds with a deep affection for each other and became a part of who we were. These were truly memories written on our souls.

The soul seeks eternity, and in Tahiti we had found it—boundless and timeless beauty combined with experiences that approached the metaphysical. We had always planned to return to Tahiti, *someday*.

PART II

SUMMERTIME AND THE LIVING IS EASY

CHAPTER 11

PATTIE SELLS HER GALLERY AND HOME

The fact is unalterable that a fellow mortal whose nature you are acquainted solely through brief entrances and exits of the imaginative weeks called courtship, when seen in the continuity of married companionship, may be disclosed as something better or worse than what you have preconceived, but will certainly not appear altogether the same.

— George Eliot, *Middlemarch*

After our South Seas honeymoon, we settled back into our long-distance relationship, commuting between Bozeman and Alta. Pattie ran her gallery, and I traveled throughout the western states doing environmental consulting projects. It had become a well-established routine for us.

Now, however, memories of our time in the South Sea Islands were seared into both our brains and souls forever. Vivid images from our time in Tahiti played like Tahitian drumming in our minds. We were passionately in love, which only continued to grow and deepen. In author George Eliot's words, our lives together had "disclosed as something even better than what we had preconceived."

When we celebrated our first wedding anniversary, we were apparently not attuned to number one being the "paper anniversary." Instead, we happily uncorked the traditional bottle of champagne. We had saved and frozen half the top layer of our wedding cake. For years on our anniversary we made it a practice to have a small piece of wedding cake along with our wine.

Hard to believe another year had rolled around so quickly. I had not remembered the passage of time being so rapid when I was younger. With Pattie and me, I always felt time was rocketing on fast forward. There was a prescient feeling that time was fleeting and to make the most of it.

We gave each other cards in which we had lovingly penned personalized messages. Rereading those cards, I note that wishing ourselves "many more years" together was a repeated theme from the first.

My anniversary card to Pattie showed a spectacular and colorful mountain scene. On it I wrote:

9/18/94

My Dearest Love,
On this our first anniversary, I reaffirm my love for you.
It has been a lovely first year, Pattie, and I look forward to many more with you!
I love you for all time—Happy Anniversary.
I love you, Pattie—Earle

Pattie wrote on her card that year:

Earle, my husband—

The day would mean little, had the year not been grand. The year was GRAND. Happy First Anniversary, My Darling! My Lover!! My Friend !!! I look forward to sharing all the years ahead with you. I love you dearly—P ☯.

May our hearts always be young and our dreams live forever. To my One & Only, Forever! I love you, Earle—Pattie

Looking out our Alta window at 11,106-foot Table Mountain,

we could feel it beckoning to us. The summit appeared deceptively close. In early summer, we set out on the fifteen-mile round trip to climb it for the first time, following the route up the North Fork of Teton Canyon. Snowmelt water roared down the canyon defile. Three different log crossings greeted us en route, rushing water nearly lapping over them. Pattie sat down and slid across, rather than wing-walk. A slip would have been disastrous. Above 9,500-feet elevation, the trail was lost, still buried beneath snow. We began climbing on snowpack, on the upper steep slopes, kicking footholds.

The return descent into the North Fork bottom was fast and relatively easy where we glissaded down snow-covered slopes. I even hiked back up one stretch just to be able to slide back down again. Where rivulets issued from beneath the melting snow, dense stands of Lewis's monkey flower, bluebells, lovage and columbine were already in full blossom. We encountered no one else all day. That is no longer possible nowadays. It has become a very popular hike.

When we were nearly back to the parking lot, I asked Pattie, "How are you doing?"

"My legs feel like they've been put on backwards," she grimaced.

In the first week of July, 1995, we made another trip to Alaska's Kenai Peninsula. Tent camping, we fished for salmon. We also returned to our favorite bush community—Talkeetna. And we also used the opportunity to visit Denali National Park, too. The village of Talkeetna had begun to undergo major change. Large commercial lodges were in the process of being constructed—the relentless march of industrial scale tourism.

We always had a great time in Alaska. In our years together, we made six or more different trips there. On one occasion, we were in Talkeetna on Pattie's birthday, where we had an intimate candlelight celebration dinner and cake served with a single birthday candle at one of the newly built log resort hotels.

On August 12, 1995 I wrote in my diary: "Pattie is the most

supportive and loving person I have ever known. . . . Many times I wish we had met earlier so that we could have had our own family. Pattie my love, we came together late in life . . . I love you, my friend and lover."

In a card marking our second wedding anniversary, Pattie had written:

18th September, 1995

To my lover, Earle:

Your love is the sun that melts the winters into spring. Another four seasons with you! What a lovely year; such lovely loving.

Putting our year in the photo album was the perfect way to herald our anniversary. The smiles brought by our memories were just as wonderful the second time.

I treasure our past. I look forward to our future, and I love you more on Sept. 18, 1995, than the mighty love I felt towards you September 18, 1993. It's wonderfully amazing.

So deep/so true. Happy Second Anniversary—Pattie

That autumn the tall shrubs along the road into Teton Canyon near our Alta home bore a particularly heavy crop of chokecherries. Driving toward the canyon early one morning, after an impressively hard frost had turned meadows and tree leaves golden yellow and the chokecherry bushes scarlet, we surprised a large black bear feeding on the wild cherries.

I struggled to put the encounter into prose. A version eventually ended up being published in a poetry anthology. Pattie used to tease me about my attempts to craft the chokecherry bear verse. What I ineptly created, though, was more than a forced free rhyme; it represents an indelible memory of that beautiful autumn morning riding in Old Blue with Pattie on the way to the Teton Canyon trailhead.

The Chokecherry Bear

At the canyon mouth in the fall,
stand cottonwoods bright yellow and tall,
they surround meadows of golden brown,
that along the edge have a scarlet chokecherry hedge.
In the glowing meadow stands a great bear,
with chokecherry stained and matted hair.
With sunlight glistening on his shiny black mane,
and a quick turn of his head, the startled bruin fled.
Like the galloping of a mighty steed it sounded,
when across the emblazoned meadow he pounded
—jet black amid bright colors of yellow and red.

Pattie had become adept at outdoor wear—polypropylene, wool hats and socks, hiking boots, flannel, fleece, goose down, and Gore-Tex parkas, but she would also confess to me: "I like being a girl, too." This was reflected in her fondness for silk scarves, velvets, hair ribbons, jewelry, vintage and retro fashions, and especially her signature broad-brimmed hats. With an artistic eye for detail, she crafted the hats herself by adding a band of artificial flowers and berries, and cutting open and banding the top. The hole in the top provided a way for her long tresses to spill out and the hat to stay on.

This was not simply an attraction to "girly stuff." It went deeper. It was a reflection of her personality, her identity; she enjoyed her feminism and feminine things. And her personality colored her love of nature and humanity, too, translating into her adoration of spring's renewal, family, the newly born, and the glory of mountain wildflowers, delicate lace-winged Mayflies, the West's cerulean skies, and the blizzards of butterflies we would later encounter in rainforests of Africa. She had an exceptional capacity to appreciate everyday things through an imaginative view of the world and an artistic appreciation for beauty.

In February, 1996, we traveled to San Francisco, California, where I had made reservations for us to attend a live performance of *Phantom of the Opera* at the majestic landmark Orpheum Theater. It was an opportunity for Pattie to "be a girl." Dressing for the theater and city, Pattie appeared tastefully glamorous. She turned heads when we walked down the street. The trip registered as another unforgettable off-the-chart experience on the romance Richter scale. The theater and performance were truly grand. For years afterward, we played the music from *Phantom* in our Alta home, reliving our visit to the Bay Area.

We visited China Town as tourists do. Pattie posed for a tongue-in-cheek photo next to the live fish and frogs at a market. We also did our own walking tour of Haight-Ashbury, the epicenter for the 1960s social revolution. The excitement of the 1960s flower children had sadly wilted, gone to seed—becoming seedy, that is. There was a pathetic residual of homeless street people, druggies, and sleazy merchants, trying to reenact the glory days and cash in on people's nostalgia by selling them souvenirs.

At one place, we posed smiling for a photograph in front of a large planter of flowers in blossom. We were documenting our temporary reprieve from the piled high snow banks in Wyoming and Montana at that time of year.

Before we left on the San Francisco trip, Pattie had willed herself to list her gallery business with a Bozeman realtor. It was a difficult decision for her. The business was her baby, her identity and security, and for years before I came along, the sole source of her livelihood. To people who knew her, she was Quest Gallery and Gift Shop. When, we returned from San Francisco, the realtor had immediately called to announce he had a full price offer. It must have been a chilling moment for her.

Pattie rented her business space. So in actuality, she was selling a continuance of the lease, her inventory, a contact list of consignment artists, her gallery's well-established name, and a lot of good will and blue sky. In addition, she agreed to provide several weeks of transitional training and personal assistance for the new owner. A short time afterward, Pattie's home on South Tracy also sold.

Pattie and I sailed away on the sea of life together, no longer tethered or moored to the Bozeman business, or any imposed schedule, or particular location. In life, it is good to know which tethers will result in personal growth if slipped, and which ones could be destructive if removed. We were not rudderless; rather we were eager to continue to engage in creating our own new life script together.

Pattie's selling her gallery was a huge statement of confidence and trust in our marriage and future together. That trust was built on five years of a solid loving relationship that possessed all that lay at the heart of a successful marriage.

We moved everything to Alta, combining two households of furniture into our post-and-beam mountain home, and storing a significant remainder in the garage. The transition went amazingly easy. We also arranged for the construction of an addition onto our home—an extra bedroom, a sleeping loft, an office space for Pattie, and a basement laundry area and more storage space.

Nearly twenty years later, the garage still houses items from the Bozeman move that did not fit into the house, barely leaving enough room for a vehicle, even after the addition was built onto the original home. Pattie still had items from her mother's home. It is sometimes hard to let go of the things that marked stages in one's life and family items. At least it was for Pattie and me.

Pattie had been the editor of her college newspaper and a dual English and psychology major. She decided freelance writing and brokering art sales (for some of her consignment artists) was going to be her next career endeavor. She named her new business Paintbrush Trails. We obtained a word processor for her, and she set up office in our Alta home.

Pattie had an undeniable talent for interviewing and profiling people, and for writing about the area's upscale homes, travel, and art. Over the next sixteen or seventeen years, she wrote and published over a hundred stories for magazines and anthologies, some of which are referenced within these pages. As time passed, Pattie would legitimately entitle herself a conservation journalist, too.

The woman who purchased Pattie's gallery business on a whim had little knowledge of art or artists and no inclination to learn. She was also not inclined towards day-to-day hands-on involvement in retailing. In the end, she converted Pattie's art gallery into an unorganized space, merchandizing dusty furniture and semi-old antiques.

Pattie had thought Quest Gallery would continue to operate in Bozeman forever, a part of her legacy. She had deservedly taken immense pride in her gallery. When it was there no longer, she grieved. Whenever we returned to Bozeman and drove down Main Street past the gallery location, the nostalgia was bittersweet.

Strong memories were everywhere for Pattie and me in Bozeman. We used to enjoy visiting friends there and reminiscing about our early years together there. But so far, since Pattie's passing, I have been unable to bring myself to go back to Bozeman. The images of our joyful time together there, and the ghostly presence of Pattie everywhere are too dreadfully painful for me to manage. I am stricken by sadness and apprehensive at the thought of returning. Someday I may be able to revisit Bozeman again, but for now, the thought of being there without Pattie is simple unbearable.

CHAPTER 12

LIFE ON THE WEST SLOPE OF THE TETONS

The magnificent scenery of the valley is bounded on two sides by broken and picturesque ranges, and overlooked by that magnificent group of mountains, called the three Tetons . . . so pleasant a sight was it to the mountain men that camp was moved to it without delay.
— Mountain man, Joseph Meek, 1829.

There is a fancy literary device known as a *synecdoche* describing how a part may be made to represent the whole. Stretching the concept, for example, availability of world-class skiing may be an indicator of the presence of a type of lifestyle (or conversely the lifestyle may be indicative of the skiing availability).

For us, in the Greater Yellowstone, there were many such parts or indicators that defined our outdoor lifestyle and activities—dramatic mountain terrain (backpacking, hiking, climbing, scenery), clean rivers and lakes (canoeing, kayaking, fishing), mega fauna—elk, moose, bison (hunting, wildlife viewing, photography), large carnivores—grizzly bear, wolves, mountain lion (wildlife viewing, ecological integrity), self-sustaining populations of trout (fly fishing), serious winter and astounding snowstorms (skiing), wilderness (intact ecosystems, solitude, aesthetics, wildlife), small towns (friendly people with similar values and interests). Those natural features and associated activities were sacramental in defining our lives and lifestyle and sense of place.

We began our mountain town lifestyle together full-time in

Alta, Wyoming. Located on the west slope of the Teton Mountains at 6,640-feet elevation, our home was situated about five miles from the Jedediah Smith Wilderness and Grand Targhee Ski and Summer Resort. Considered to be among the great mountains of the world, we directly viewed the ever changing beauty of the Tetons' iconic three peaks from our home.

Adjoining the Idaho-Wyoming state border, Alta and surrounding area had a population of fewer than two people per square mile at the time. A part of Teton County, Wyoming, its residents today are included among those with the highest average-income in America, a figure skewed by outrageously wealthy residents of Jackson Hole.

Situated in Teton Valley, the service town for Alta is Driggs, Idaho, population 1,100 in 2000; 1,660-plus and growing (along with the significant canine population) by 2010. Like many small towns in the Intermountain West, Driggs was named after an early Mormon settler. We used to refer to it jokingly as "Dregs." Alta was also once a Mormon farming community where early day polygamists are rumored to have fled in order to escape prosecution. A polygamist colony of Mormon fundamentalists is believed to exist still in the northern part of Teton Valley.

If you meet one of the valley's Church of Jesus Christ of Latter-day Saints' matrons, the perennial question they will ask is: "How long have you lived here?" The query is a challenge, not a question. They want you to know that their families have been there for four generations or more. Their granddaddies were the original settlers who transformed and "civilized" the valley's landscape: cleared the aspen groves and plowed up the prairie (and otherwise despoiled natural habitats and diversity), excavated extensive irrigation systems (completely altering the valley's natural hydrology; cutting off native fish migrations and spawning), and killed off most of the once abundant wildlife (mostly absent from the valley floor today are wolves, bears, bison, elk, bighorn sheep, and sage grouse). The valley's Saints religiously refrain from consuming alcohol, but see no contradiction in growing vast amounts of barley and hops for commercial breweries.

Pattie and I constructed our own markers to judge our longevity in the valley. I admit ours also had a small town provincial tone. For example, we were here before:

- stop lights
- the Dream Catcher ski lift
- Fred's Outdoor Gear Shop burned to the ground
- the ski track was groomed in Teton Canyon
- the last four expansions of the grocery store
- more than one golf course existed
- there was a glut of fishing guides and dories everywhere on the streams

Similar to Jackson Hole, Teton Valley attracted like-minded outdoor people. It is no longer just an isolated backwater of fourth-generation Mormon farms and ranching. It is linked to Grand Targhee Ski and Summer Resort, out-the-door recreation opportunities, wildlands, and amenities provided by the Teton Mountains and nearby Yellowstone National Park. And with its nearby famed trout and boating waters, such as the Henry's Fork, the Snake, and Teton Rivers, Driggs ramped into a rapidly changing and growing mountain town. Like Jackson Hole, Teton Valley has become recognized as an outdoor recreation mecca.

The surrounding area referred to as the Greater Yellowstone, encompasses eighteen-million acres of contiguous National Forests and National Parks of which a significant portion is roadless backcountry and congressionally designated Wilderness. It contains some of the nation's most sublime and cherished landscapes and remaining diverse wildlife populations. We especially felt a strong kinship to the diversity of wildlife—an awe for the remaining wild landscapes.

For a town its size, Driggs had some unique amenities back then. While Jackson, Wyoming, had *Jackson Hole Magazine*, Teton Valley also boasted startup of a small publishing company, Powder Mountain Press, which around 1997 began publishing two magazines—*Teton Valley* and *Teton Home*.

On Driggs' Main Street, Dark Horse Books, a bookstore that brought in writers and artists for readings and shows, provided a connection to the latest literary works, aspiring artists, and writers. There were also fishing, ski, and bicycle shops. The valley even sported its own microbrewery, the Grand Teton Brewery. Locally famous at the time for its Huckleberry and Bitch Creek ales, the Grand Teton Brewery's devotees purchased beer by the "growler," half-gallon or larger jugs.

In 1994, one national magazine characterized Driggs as "a town which looks like a Norman Rockwell scene." In 2002, it was named the "Best Place in the U.S. to Live" by *Men's Journal*. Another article lauding its amenities and outdoor recreation opportunities appeared in *National Geographic* in 2003.

A trip to Jackson Hole requires about a thirty-mile drive over Teton Pass. There were always activities and events taking place on that side of the mountains—excellent restaurants, seminars, theaters, museums, concerts, workshops and Grand Teton National Park. The south and west entrances to Yellowstone National Park were close by also.

It was all very manageable. Pattie and I often talked about moving to the Jackson Hole side of the Tetons, but in those years, Alta seemed a less crowded up-and-coming place. While Jacksonites were complaining of traffic congestion in the summer tourist season, Driggs still did not even have a traffic light. Our side of the mountains received better snow for skiing, too, an annual average of 500 inches of deep, dry powder. Targhee Resort referred to as the "Ghee," got accolades annually in *Ski Magazine* for "Best Snow in the Nation." And nestled into the Teton range, the ski area's scenic backdrop was among the most spectacular anywhere.

Bottom line, we were simply having too much fun on the west

slope of the Tetons to take the time to sell our Alta home and buy, build, or remodel another on the Jackson Hole side of the mountains. The trip over and back from Jackson in Old Blue—four-wheeling in winter, deftly dodging and miraculously avoiding moose and deer on the roadway—was no more than a hiccup for us in those years, part of the adventure and lifestyle.

Author Ogla Moore Arnold wrote, "The Grand Teton may not be the highest mountain in the United States but it is certainly the most spectacular; a great hooked dagger that stabs eternally at the sky, shaped like the Matterhorn and towering nearly fourteen thousand feet into the air. It dominates the Teton Range and the mere sight of it chills the blood."

Viewable out our windows and from our backyard, the three Teton peaks, which included the Grand, provided the backdrop for our lives. We could watch the wind blowing contrails of snow off the Grand's summit from our living room or front yard and witness the evening alpenglow. We were full of vitality and oomph. For a wonderful fleeting time, the world was ours—the proverbial apple. It was enviably and wonderfully crisp. We never imagined some demon force would decide to take it all away from us.

In the 1990s, there was confidence that the country was in an age of rapid progress. Democracy and prosperity were expanding worldwide. The Bull Market in equities roared. The Dow climbed and our investments gleefully rose along with the economic tide. Locally, Grand Targhee Resort planned a major expansion. Housing and property values in Teton Valley sparked hot and bubbly.

We rode the good times tide, planning trips, upgrading furniture items, selling Pattie's Subaru and buying a recent model, pre-owned Toyota Four Runner—a daring move for us. In spite of the good economic times, we were hopelessly and conservatively frugal. We were children of parents who had suffered in the depression. We could have bought a larger home, upgraded to new top-of-the line sports equipment each year, driven prestigious vehicles, slept in the best hotels when traveling, instead we mostly chose to get by with our equipment, sleep in the back of an old truck, and live below our financial means. Some might have attributed this to a bias for Wendell Berry's *Back to the Land* agrarianism. But, for us, our richness was measured in terms of treasured experiences and our priceless relationship.

We were more than happy with our lives, lifestyle, and our comfortable post-and-beam Alta home. Passionately in love with each other, we celebrated the simple pleasures in life. For a wedding anniversary, inside a gorgeous large card illustrated with the portraits of two wolves, Pattie wrote:

Our 9th Happy Anniversary

Earle—

Flights into the heart [a sketched heart] of wild nature will always allow me sunlight at midnight, wildflowers mid-winter. Thank you.

There is only one happiness in life, to love and be loved by you!

All my love, Pattie

CHAPTER 13

SEASONAL TRADITIONS AND LIVELIHOOD

In the heart of the Rocky Mountains, on the broad, rugged summit of the continent, amid snow and ice, and dark shaggy forests, where great rivers take their rise, there is a region full of wonders, surpassing in wakeful exciting interest any other region yet discovered on the face of the globe.

— John Muir

Our life and lifestyle in the Northern Rockies had come together seamlessly. How good life was—to be in love, healthy, and fit on the west slope of the Tetons in Teton Valley, near Jackson Hole and within the Greater Yellowstone. Places that people get to visit once in a life time, we made our daily playgrounds.

Columnist David Brooks observed, "Creative people organize their lives according to repetitive, disciplined routines, thinking like artists but working like accountants." I do not confess to us having strict routines, and none of it was ever just routine, but Brooks' words applied to us. We adopted the seasonal patterns and rhythms of mountain living, traditions we came to hold dear. A reverence for the wild and the seasonal rhythms and cycles contributed to our sense of place. And within that context, we superimposed self-chosen routines "working like accountants." It underwrote our livelihood, provided identity, and allowed us to engage in our mountain living lifestyle in a creative way.

No doubt to some, it appeared we lived hedonistic lives of frivolity; and perhaps to urban dwellers we appeared to be both unsophisticated and even un-American as we neither participated in rat-race consumerism nor held nine-to-five jobs.

In an elastic manner, we organized our lives around those things that gave us enjoyment and pleasure and were spiritually and personally rewarding. Our time spent in the outdoors provided inspiration, recreation, and avocation, and was spiritually gratifying, too. We avoided the mind-numbing sham and drudgery, and being glued to strict schedules, desks, and cell and smart phones, which so many people unfortunately identify with work and economic endeavor in today's world.

By example, without being preachy, we were lifestyle proponents and practitioners of evolutionary biologist, E. O. Wilson's theories of biophilia. Essentially, we were living proof that the happiness and psychological well-being of each of us can in part be correlated to our relationship with nature. We were also believers that the love of nature is an inherent part of being human. Wilson said, "The natural world is still imbedded in our genes and cannot be eradicated."

The intensity of our love was made all the greater by the magnificent natural setting where we resided and participating together in many adrenaline enhancing fun-filled activities. The outdoor activities, in concert with traditions of our own making, further united Pattie and me. Our lives reflected both synchronicity and seasonal chronicity.

Summer

We tended to be reluctant to leave the region in summer because of all that it overwhelmingly offered. People travel long distances and from all over the world to vacation in the Tetons, Yellowstone, and surrounding area. We asked ourselves, why would we want to go anywhere else?

There was trekking and frolicking in the high-elevation Tetons amid the dazzlingly spectacular wildflower displays and alpine scenery, with unlimited backcountry hiking opportunity to explore: the Teton Crest, Alaska Basin, Meek's Pass, Death Canyon, Hurricane Pass, and Table Mountain. Those awesome wild landscapes were truly just outside our backdoor and right up Teton Canyon, one of the major gateways to the interior of the Tetons. It was all God's gardens!

On fifteen- to twenty-mile day hikes, we would drop off a second vehicle at a predetermined place, then drive to Teton Village and ride the tram to the 10,450-foot summit. From there we could readily access the Teton Crest Trail and beyond, past Housetop Mountain and Marion Lake, descending back down side canyons—Granite or Death Canyon—cooling off with a swim in Phelps Lake on the Jackson Hole side. Or from the Crest Trail we would drop down Game Creek or Fox Creek back into Teton Valley to where the second vehicle waited, essentially traversing across a large part of the Teton Range in a day.

Before today's pine bark beetle infestations, we came to know individual gnarly ancient whitebark pines along the high-elevation routes as esteemed old friends. They were trees that were more than a century old when the Pilgrims landed at Plymouth. The grating khaaa, khraaa call of the Clark's nutcracker busy collecting whitebark pine seed in late summer accompanied us everywhere in the alpine country.

We would effortlessly sling our canoe on top of Old Blue and be heading off to pristine waters in a matter of minutes. Lakes and streams played a big part in our lives. We spent time canoeing the unspoiled lakes nestled along the base of the Tetons — Jenny, String, Leigh, and Jackson Lakes, and lake-like Oxbow Bend. In Yellowstone Park we canoed Yellowstone, Lewis and Shoshone Lakes. We planned early morning canoeing on the lakes to observe wildlife and immerse ourselves in the solitude. We also paddled the nearby rivers: the Snake, Teton River, and Henry's Fork, where the gin-clear waters from mountain snowmelt cascaded down canyons and into those rivers flowing pure and clean.

A local legend claims that Owen Wister's character, the Virginian, took his schoolmarm bride to an island in Leigh Lake for a place to honeymoon. Leigh Lake is the third largest lake in Teton Park. The story captured Pattie's romantic imagination. But Leigh Lake has two islands. The largest, Mystic Island, at the north end of the lake, would logically seem to be the one of honeymoon fame. However, the small island at the south end near the boat ramp is the one actually named Honeymoon Island. When we canoed to the far island, before a more recent forest fire had burned over it, we found it covered in an unforgettable profusion of lavender-flowered wild hollyhocks, one of Pattie's favorite wildflowers. I wrote an article about our canoeing Teton National Park's Leigh Lake at dawn:

> Dawn glowed on the surrounding mountain setting, while across the mirror-like expanse of Leigh Lake the sky was celestially reflected. In the distance, like a mirage, Mystic Isle was slowly being transported toward us as we paddled. For a time, sky and lake converged and it was easy to drift into a dream-like illusion that we were canoeing through the sky.

We made frequent road trips to Yellowstone National Park, where one could hardly see or experience all the natural wonders in a life time. On other road trips and nearby overnights, we slept entwined in the back of Old Blue, waking up in gorgeous settings. Some of those spots included the Wind River Range's Square Top Mountain at the head of the Green River; Sheep Creek above the Elk Refuge or on Shadow Mountain directly viewing the glowing sunsets and sunrises on the Tetons; along the rushing North Fork of the Shoshone River; Ten Sleep Canyon in the Bighorn Mountains; and the secluded North Fork of the Powder River canyon. Sometimes we traveled as far as southern Utah making sorties into the desert and canyon lands.

I became involved in researching and writing about the numerous waterfalls in the Greater Yellowstone. At that time, before Rubenstein, Whittlesey, and Stevens published *The Guide to Yellowstone Waterfalls and Their Discovery*, many major waterfalls remained unnamed and unmapped in Yellowstone Park. My project required that Pattie and I hike and backpack into far reaches of the park—as if we needed a work reason to justify backpacking into the backcountry—visiting waterfalls and photographing the region's thunderous and magical waters.

An article I wrote on the area's streams and rivers began:

The Yellowstone Region is awash with undine blessings. The greatest concentration of sublimely pristine and wilderness waters remaining in the lower forty-eight states is found here . . . over 50 rivers arise from within the Yellowstone region—the headwaters of the mighty Colorado, Missouri, and Columbia. The Crow Indians aptly named the region Popo Agie, "the beginning of the waters."

Known as the "Cascade Corner" of Yellowstone, the Bechler Region with its pristine waters became one our favorite haunts, though only after the mosquitoes in the vast Bechler Meadows succumbed to late summer frost. Around every river bend surprising discoveries awaited us. It was all new and exhilarating to us. We revered the Bechler Region of the park. And the only people we infrequently encountered in late season were National Park Service employees.

Among the many waterfalls in the park that we stood before and photographed, enveloped in spray and mist and in mystery and awe, were spectacular and scenic Dunanda Falls, 150 feet, Union Falls, 250 feet (said by one early writer to be a waterfall that "pleased with delicate sublimity"), and Albright Falls, 260 feet.

In the Bechler, we bushwhacked through dense old-growth spruce forest with heavy understory, crawling over and under thick downfall and around swampy ground to find the remote Ouzel Falls, 230 feet (not to be confused with Ouzel Falls on the Gros Ventre River). All the while we were uneasy, wary, and alert for brother bear.

Compared to Lower Yellowstone Falls, 308 feet, those Bechler region waterfalls are among the highest in Yellowstone Park. Along the way, we enjoyed soaking in the hot springs at the Forks of the Bechler and on Boundary Creek, and reveled in the hidden and densely forested Bechler Canyon with its abundant chanterelle mushrooms and autumn colors. Parts of the Bechler Canyon are forested with Douglas fir as compared to most of the park's lodgepole pine, alpine fir and spruce. All the while in early autumn, bugling, grunting, and squealing elk serenaded us with their love songs. Pattie wrote about the Bechler region:

> The Bechler houses 21 of Yellowstone's waterfalls, many of those taller than 100' high. Heavy snowfall makes it most accessible from around late August through the second week of October. While swarms of mosquitoes are present in the late summer, autumn is remarkable for its beauty. Aspen leaves littering wetland pools are the western counterpoint of Monet's water lilies at Giverny.

We were conscience-stricken writing about the Bechler and publishing photographs showing its singular scenery. At that time, it was wonderfully off the map for most visitors to the park, and we selfishly wished to keep it that way. *Jackson Hole Magazine* published a photo essay of mine on some of the waterfalls, purposely confusing the waterfall locations and names to discourage people from visiting those backcountry locations—as if our conflicted and feeble efforts alone could have stanched or slowed the growing tide of humanity that would come to invade the backcountry.

For a few seasons, I also taught a short course on the Water Features and Waterfalls of Yellowstone Park for the Yellowstone Association, which involved guiding the course participants on day hikes to various waterfalls, mainly in the park's front or side country, such as Fall River's Terraced Falls, 140 feet, and Cascade Creek's sparkling cascades, 40 feet; or the park's other Cascade Creek's Grotto Pool and Crystal Falls, 129 feet. It also involved climbing down Uncle Tom's Stairway to view the 308-foot drop of Lower Lower Yellowstone Falls from below. At Crystal Falls, the class participants and I were made to pause when steaming fresh grizzly bear tracks in the trail indicated the bear was just ahead of us.

Then there was the incredible trout fishing! Pattie had become adept at fly casting and loved fishing the mountain streams for native trout. We had nearby favorite spots all to ourselves back then—the Henry's Fork Canyon, places along the Snake and Teton Rivers, and the west slope tributaries, such as our favorite, Bitch Creek.

We would often split up in the evening on a nearby favorite stream, Pattie fishing upstream, and me down. She would invariably stay on the stream until past dusk and then would have to make her way back in the dark, while I fretted and worried or finally went looking for her. But then I would hear her splashing along in the stream toward me. When we'd meet up in the near-darkness, she would breathlessly whisper about her wildlife encounters: a curious beaver that had followed her; a black bear on the opposite bank; meeting a bull moose close up eye-to-eye in a streamside willow thicket; and of course, she'd proudly show me the results of her fishing success.

In a drawer at our home, there is a paper tracing from 1994 of a nineteen-inch native cutthroat trout Pattie caught in Bitch Creek. Cutthroat trout are beautiful fish. Firm, orange-fleshed, with a vibrant slash of red below the gills, they are wild fish, native born in the headwater gravels of the west slope's rushing tributaries. They are also the great white sharks of the mountain streams—vicious predators. We mostly practiced catch-and-release with these readily caught beauties.

Pattie was passionate about huckleberry picking in the mountains and searching for chanterelle and morel mushrooms. Only once did we encounter a grizzly bear also engaged in berry harvesting. Parked along the upper part of Jack Pine Loop road in Teton Valley, I was walking on the road toward Old Blue when a young, maybe three-year-old, grizzly bear lumbered out of the forest and down the bank onto the road and stood there. Pattie was in the thick subalpine forest below the bear busily picking berries. "Pattie," I cautiously warned, "There's a grizzly bear up here on the road!" After a moment of stunned silence, Pattie thrashed through the brush and emerged onto the road beside me in record time. The startled bear loped off and disappeared into the forest.

Our closest confrontation with bruin was not with a grizzly but rather a black bear. We were sitting streamside on a log having lunch along the lower Lamar River in Yellowstone, when a gaunt black bear appeared downriver from us. He very deliberately began heading our way, apparently wanting to share our lunch. It was before everyone carried bear spray. When he got within fifteen feet, we became alarmed and stood up. I began waving my arms and yelling loudly. Showing no fear, the bear hesitated then veered off, eying us with sidelong glances.

As if the wild berries weren't enough, we also grew our own generous supply of strawberries and raspberries. We froze berries and mushrooms to last us throughout the winter.

There were so many beautiful places to see and things to do locally and within the region, it kept us excitedly and busily exploring and engaged constantly. In those years, summers in the Tetons and the surrounding Greater Yellowstone area were incomparably glorious. They reminded us of George Gershwin's song *Summertime*, a stanza of which Pattie would sing to me: "Summertime and the living is easy, fish are jumping..."

We were open to having children, but with the ages Pattie and I were, it had become unlikely. Pattie had nevertheless picked out a name for a girl just in case: Lacey.

"Lacey Layser?" I asked to be sure she wasn't just kidding.

"Yes," she replied seriously, then grinned.

When it didn't happen, we instead adopted an adorable little white puppy from the animal shelter. We had gone to the shelter looking for a German police dog or a Lab and came home with what appeared to be a poodle-cocker spaniel cross. Hmm?

We didn't pick him, he picked us. It was meant to be. We named him Benji, after the 1980s television dog, which he looked like. Pattie questioned, "Do you think he will be able to keep up with us hiking?"

I assured her with a nod of my head. "Yes, I think so."

In a later piece, "And Benji makes Three," Pattie wrote: "We were only going to the Shelter to look. Maybe they had a Lab or German Shepherd, a big dog strong enough for sharing outdoor fun. Benji walked out in front of us, dreadlocks to the floor, and like an English sheep dog, apparently no eyes . . . Love comes in unusual packages when you least expect it."

An intelligent twenty-five pounds of puppy energy, Benji fit into our family like a little dynamo. He chewed Pattie's biking helmet and ate part of the cork handle off her fly rod. Benji's keeping up was never an issue; it was the other way around. Could we keep up with him?

When we were hiking and would come upon ethereal-like flowering mountain meadows or gloriously sparkling snow patches at high elevation, and always in the blue cloud of violets growing in the lawn in the springtime at Pine Creek, too, Benji would run as fast as he could go in circles around us, a happy expression on his face. It was as if he recognized and was celebrating life and the beauty surrounding us. Pattie would encourage him, clapping her hands and shouting: "run, run, run!" She called it "doing joy circles." We were all doing "joy circles" back then.

Benji's nemeses were bears. Moose and elk he would growl at if they got too close, but a bear was different. He would go berserk barking and growling. One wondered how an otherwise friendly little dog could appear so ferocious.

Once we had Dry Ridge Outfitters do a drop camp for us in the head of Bitch Creek at Hidden Corral Basin. It is a place located at the northern end of the Teton Range where the Winegar Hole and Jedediah Smith Wildernesses adjoin. Our camping gear was taken in by horses and dropped off at a predetermined location and then picked up and taken out at an agreed upon date. That way we were able to hike into the camping site and do day hikes from our camp without carrying heavy packs. When we were in camp, Benji would frequently stare across the meadow at the surrounding dense forest growling and sometimes barking. The trail passed nearby our camp, and one morning there was a foot-long grizzly bear track in the dirt within thirty feet of our tent. The track had not been there the night before. I laid our bear spray canister inside the track with room to spare. After that we were more encouraging of Benji's warning growls.

On a late summer outing to a favorite fishing spot in the Henry's Fork Canyon, at dusk, on one particularly warm day, we observed three moose playing. I tried to capture the wonder we felt in prose. It was later published by the Henry's Fork Foundation:

Moose at Play

Deep flowing waters of the Henry's Fork, set within narrow canyon walls, normally moody and dark, sparkled warm and bright under relentless summer sun.

A chill descended, and abruptly the waters darkened when the sunlight sank below the canyon rim.

Like actors awaiting a cue, three moose emerged from the forest and unhesitatingly wading deep into the river, they began to swim.

As I watched, they randomly swam up and down the river, for no other purpose that I could tell, but simple joy and pleasure.

Then one by one, they emerged in a gangly moosely manner from the water, shook themselves dry, and quietly disappeared back into the forest.

Seeing them made me recall sultry evenings long ago when as children we too gathered at a swimming hole, enjoying summer's simple pleasures.

The frolicking moose beg the question: Do wild creatures have feelings? What would you say, after watching the

Henry's Fork moose at play?

In the mountains, we anxiously monitored the fireweed, calling it "summer's candle." When the last flowers at the top of the raceme finished blooming, it signaled the sweet sadness of another summer's passing. You can understand why we had mixed feelings about missing any precious summer days with time away.

Autumn

Summer's outdoor activities continued while weather permitted. We hiked in the mountains in the radiance of Indian summer. The beauty of aspen forest turned golden, burnished-colored understory, combined with hues of late season asters, goldenrod, goldeneye, wild hollyhocks, bright yellow dogbane leaves and bunches of startlingly blaze-orange mountain ash berries, glowed luminescent in the low-intensity autumn sunlight.

The arrival of the first dusting of snow on the mountains generally in mid-September and hard frosts foretold a melancholy end to summer — beauty tinged with sadness. The first covering of snow on the mountains, we called "termination dust"— summer employees terminated and snowbirds left the valley.

Sometimes we would stay out at the Darwin Ranch, considered the "most remote guest ranch in the lower forty-eight," where we had use of horses to ride amid elk bugling in the high country and the splendid autumn colors in the aspen and willow bottoms along the upper Gros Ventre River within the Gros Ventre Wilderness.

On sunny fall days, the fishing was at its best. Only one fly pattern was required—a grasshopper. We picked service berries by the bucketful and ran them through a juicer-steamer extracting the tasty dark-colored, antioxidant-rich juice, which could be kept fresh by freezing.

Every autumn, we cut our own firewood in the forest and hauled it home, requiring several trips with Old Blue. Working in the woods on frosty, and sometimes snow-covered, mornings, I considered firewood gathering a form of outdoor recreation. I'm not certain Pattie was necessarily convinced, but she uncomplainingly and voluntarily worked at my side. We were a team in all things.

We were grateful for the region's animated and splendid wildlife. We treasured all the animals, but did not believe eating game meat was a contradiction. Each fall, I hunted and harvested an elk, which provided us a year's supply of choice protein, unadulterated with chemicals and commercially fed hormones. I would leave at 4:00 a.m. and when I returned Pattie was always there waiting, eager to hear my stories, successful or not. Self-sufficiently, we did our own butchering and freezer wrapping, too.

One autumn outing, Pattie and I scouted a potential hunting spot in the northern part of Jackson Hole before the season opening. We flushed out an enormous bull elk at close range. Generally, I shot only raghorns, spikes, or cows—strictly a meat hunt. But seeing the trophy bull got us both stirred up. I proposed to hunt for the big bull.

On opening morning, I returned to the location where we had seen the huge bull. In the predawn gloom, elk were whistling and squealing all around me. Tension grew. But as it began to get light, the elk quieted down and drifted away. I was left with having to move quietly and slowly following in the direction of the last bugling.

Easing up on an opening, in the early light I could see a large bull chasing several cows around the brushy willow bottom about one-hundred yards from me. It was not the record bull Pattie and I had seen earlier, but it was still a mighty big bull!

Laying down behind a windfall and using a protruding root for a rifle rest, I fired a single shot. The bull elk disappeared. The cows ran off. I breathlessly hurried over to where I had last seen the animal when I had shot. There lay a seven-point elk, unmoving. Hooray! But then the work began, a six or seven-hundred pound animal is a major challenge for one man alone to field dress.

It really was not the prime bull we had observed; rather it was an old guy, a seven-point in rut: mangy, smelly, sex-hormone driven, and caked in wallow-mud infused with urine. Pattie named him "Jonah." We had a European mount—the acid bleached skull with antlers—made of Jonah, who has decorated our high-ceiling living room wall ever since. Pattie attached a Rudolph-like red bulb to his nose at Christmas and it remains there yet. But Jonah proved to be literally inedible—gamey tasting, impossibly tough, all tendons and ligaments.

After that, Pattie insisted I never shoot another bull. The Jonah experience provided us with a lot of jokes about trophy hunting and having to eat what you shoot. It is perfectly understandable why some people will tell you, they "don't like game meat." They probably tried eating a Jonah who was in rut.

Another autumn we traveled down to the Sweetwater country—high-elevation prairies lying along the west-side of the Wind River Mountains—to hunt antelope and camp in the high-elevation sagebrush desert. The Sweetwater used to be a wonderful place in autumn—few people around, huge open space, snow-capped Wind River Mountains in the background, crisp white-with-frost mornings, good trout fishing and abundant wildlife: deer, antelope, jackrabbits, sage grouse, and coyotes serenading at night. With the extensive oil and gas development in that area over recent decades, I do not know how much of all that remains.

At first light, we looked for and found an antelope buck with trophy-size horns and were successful in stalking and bagging the exceptional animal. We would later wonder why the meat verged on inedible, tasting like eating oddly sweet-smelling sagebrush? We figured it out, of course; again, the large buck was in rut. When he went down, his harem had gathered around and stood over him. Pattie witnessed the protective behavior of the doe antelope and began crying.

The doe antelope's sentient behavior and Pattie's reaction changed my attitude toward hunting forever. It was the last time I hunted antelope. We both loved seeing and experiencing animals in the wild.

Of the many ways to enjoy wildlife, why should I, or anyone else, want only to relate to them through hunting and killing them? After that a camera and photography became our primary "hunting" method.

But elk did remain our primary red-meat protein source. And after I filled my elk tag each autumn, we would generally travel to our second home in the mountains of Pennsylvania for a month's stay—delighting in the autumn colors, the abundance of acorns and hickory nuts, cycling and hiking through the fallen leaves, picking apples and wild cranberries, entertaining and visiting with family and friends. When we returned to Alta, winter would have begun.

Winter

Winter in the Tetons for us was special. While some chose to bolt from the area, fearing the cold and snow, Pattie and I embraced it. Deep unbroken dry-powder snow radiated and sparkled in the sunlight; spindrift swirled about, crystals glittering; alpenglow emblazoned the peaks; sundogs glowed low on the horizon. It was a beautiful time. Our hearts sang as one.

Pattie wrote:

Rambunctious winds. Dervishes of snowflakes whirl past our window, blowing horizontally but inching up the outside walls. On the television, the Weather Channel is reporting Alta, Wyoming as 'blanketed white.' High winds. Rollicking, frolicking runaway snow. Our snow forecast is upgraded to a 'dump!'

Targhee Ski Area opened in late-November. We developed a tradition of downhill skiing on Thanksgiving Day morning and then driving across the Pass to the historic Wort Hotel in Jackson for their groaning board Thanksgiving buffet—all you could eat king crab, oysters on the half shell, shrimp, in addition to traditional turkey and all the side dishes.

In our early years in the valley, cross-country ski track was not set in Teton Canyon or in the other drainages. We broke our own trails. If we wanted groomed course skiing, Grand Targhee Resort did prepare extensive track in Rick's Basin, and so did the Jackson Hole Ski Club at Trail Creek. We cross-country skied in all the nearby drainage canyons—Darby, South Leigh, North Leigh, Teton Canyon. There were few people then, much fewer people with dogs, and a lot of wildlife wintering in the lower canyons. We could always count on encountering moose in Teton Canyon.

Pattie wrote:

> I turn my skis on edge to push off quietly. Winter's solitude and beauty merge with my frosty breath and sweaty exertion, creating a private epiphany. I feel bound tensions unraveling, trapped emotions sprung; pure joy released. I have grabbed this intimacy from other days skiing, but each day's climax is a singular pleasure.

At other times, driving Old Blue across Teton Pass in four-wheel drive, we would breakfast in Jackson, and then go on to Teton Park and ski favorite places that were fabulously scenic, and in those days, notably devoid of people. We would tour out to Jenny Lake, around Timber Island, and sometimes along the ice-covered river at Oxbow Bend. Other times, we would ski up Shadow Mountain, or up Cache Creek and over the divide to Game Creek, too. Brooks Lake Lodge in the Absaroka Mountains was another desirable ski destination. It never got old for us. Those places have since evolved into front- or side-country, overrun with people and, outside of the park, their canine companions. Some of those places are now even mechanically groomed for the public's ease of skiing.

Pattie thrilled in our going out into the forest every year and cutting our own Christmas tree. She related my dragging it back, while on skis, to a Norman Rockwell scene, and always wanting to take photographs to preserve the moment. She delighted in artfully decorating the tree with her exceptional collection of prized and unique ornaments.

Stretching to reach the top branches from a step ladder, we went through a familiar litany every year: "Get off the ladder, Pattie. Please let me do that part."

With our wood stove glowing warmly, we would engage in a competition—trying to outdo each other in stacking presents for one another around the tree. Pattie's gifts always were professionally wrapped to perfection. I could not compete; mine were more like a guy's best attempts generally appear. I have never known anyone who delighted more in Christmas than Pattie, her joyful enthusiasm made the holiday an extra special and wonderful time of the year.

Having Grand Targhee Ski Resort literally out our door, just up the mountain, we lift skied and skied some more, selecting the best powder days to cruise Targhee's 2,200 vertical feet of scenic sweeping bowls and forested glades. We were frequently first in the lift line, skiing in the mornings before the powder snow had been broken or heavily tracked, making "first tracks' or "freshies." Skiing deep powder is a sensation like floating through your surroundings. It is exhilarating.

Mornings after tremendous snowstorm accumulations—called "powder dumps"—took place during the night, "the floating heads phenomenon" would occur on the ski hill. The only part of a skier you could see coming down the slope was a head; the rest of the person would be hidden up to the shoulders in the bottomless and billowing light powder snow. The excitement was contagious. Skiers would be shouting, yodeling, and laughing. We were all united in the incredible joy of the moment.

Returning home invigorated, we would have lunch and then catch up with any work assignments, house work and snow shoveling. On particularly frigid and wintery days, we would soak together in our over-sized tub while enjoying a favorite drink—Irish crème with brandy. Pure pleasure.

Sometimes, we would also go up to Big Sky Ski Resort in Montana to downhill ski. And, for a number of years, on Valentine's Day, the Alpenhof at Teton Village in Jackson Hole hosted a "local's sweetheart special," where for $150 we could get a one-night package that included a luxury fireplace room, breakfast and dinner for two at a four-star restaurant, and Jackson Hole ski area lift tickets, including a half-day ski lesson for both of us—an unheard of deal today.

In late winter, as the daylight hours lengthened, the snow surface transformed into a crust, encouraging freestyle skiing—skating with specialized skis across the frozen surface. The vast sagebrush flats in Teton Park would be snow covered and sealed with a thick icy crust. We called it "crust-cruising." The extensive rolling farmlands in Teton Valley also afforded excellent skate-skiing. One could speed along over the frozen surface with ease, often on gorgeous sunny days, covering long distances.

Towards spring, we sported "raccoon-eyes"—faces deeply tanned and wind burned, except where our goggles covered. We used to joke that when we took off our clothing, the contrast between our pale untanned bodies and that of our faces made it appear that our heads really belonged to some other body.

Beginning in March 1996, and continuing every year up to and including 2013, we made an annual trip to Cook City, Montana, to look for bears and wolves in the Lamar Valley in Yellowstone National Park. Our first time was with a Yellowstone Institute sponsored group. Over a three-day period, my journal notes record we observed: thirty-five coyotes, three wolves, two cougars, twelve bighorn sheep, hundreds of bison and elk, trumpeter swans and bald eagles, and an uncounted number of mule deer. Where else in the world could one do that? An annual "wolf-watching" trek became a late-winter tradition—joining the breath of our being with that of wild wolves.

We established a wolf-watching routine. Overnighting in Cook City, we would get up before dawn and proceed to search and scope from the roadway in the Lamar Valley. In the predawn, we would be dressed in ski hats and gloves, layered fleece, Gore-Tex, and Snowpac boots, and it was still difficult to stay warm, waiting, watching, and scoping the vast terrain. We generally always spotted wolves in the Lamar Valley on these wolf-watching trips. Mostly, they were dark specks far across the snowbound valley requiring use of our spotting scope to observe them and their behaviors. And we were not alone; there were plenty of other people out in the early morning hours watching, too. There was a type of enthusiastic camaraderie, especially during those years when the large Druid Pack ruled the valley.

In a published story I wrote:

We directed our scoping to a distant meadow over a half-mile away. Breathtakingly, a black wolf came into focus. It was curled up, catching a canine nap, not unlike a large dog. But this was not in any way a pet. It was a wild wolf. Something you could not have seen in Yellowstone as recently as a decade ago.

On our last wolf watching outing, in March 2013, we did not get up and out before dawn as in the past. We were there more or less on a sentimental journey, going through the motions. It was mid-morning by the time we drove through the Lamar Valley. Most wolf-watchers had folded up their scopes and cameras and gone home. Suddenly, just above where the Lamar River leaves the valley through the canyon five wolves appeared loping down the hillside toward us. Four came within forty yards and then turned and trotted up the river on the ice just below us. No scopes or binoculars were required.

One wolf sat down on the hillside opposite us and began howling. An impromptu mournful wailing, it symbolized the wolf's defiance in the face of all life's adversities. It was our last time wolf-watching. The howl would become the wolf's farewell salute to us, a final parting serenade.

When conditions allowed, after snow plows opened the roads in Teton Park, generally beginning in April, dressed for cold morning temperatures, for years we would cycle out to String Lake and Jenny Lake, and beyond. High banks of snow still lined the roadsides, no motorized vehicular traffic was allowed. And on weekday mornings, no one else would be about. We had the whole park on those mornings magically to ourselves.

One early April morning in 1997, we were cycling the park when two wolves crossed the road directly in front of Pattie. This was the first official sighting of wolves in Teton Park following their reintroduction to Yellowstone National Park two years earlier. Pattie wrote and published a story about her sighting and experience in "A Chance Encounter" in *Teton Valley Magazine.*

Sometimes, in late winter, we would fly to Austin, Texas, to visit Pattie's sister, Donna, and her nieces, to whom Pattie was godmother. After we tired of Austin's Central Market, lunch at the historic Driskill Hotel, and the frantic rush of the city, we would drive south along the Gulf Coast to Port Mansfield; a remote fishing community located on the Laguna Madre near the southern tip of Padre Island. There we enjoyed some of the finest, relatively undiscovered, salt water fishing remaining anywhere—redfish, drum, speckled sea trout, sheepshead, flounder. Along the way, en route, we would also stop off at San Antonio to enjoy a cocktail at the popular River Walk.

We remained at Alta relishing the spring skiing until Targhee Resort closed around mid-April. Spring was skiing variable powder dustings, corn snow, and slop, often under sunny skies. Locals would congenially gather on the decks to bask in the sun, socialize, and enjoy a beer afterwards. Everybody knew everybody.

The ski area's closing generally coincided with the elk in Jackson Hole beginning their annual migration, drifting back north following the snow line. The valley's eight thousand or so elk do not move en mass, rather they break into and travel in small bands of a half dozen to maybe thirty animals. Those small groups scatter across the hillsides, sagebrush flats, roads and roadsides, north of Jackson.

When an automobile passes close to a lead cow elk standing

along the highway, instead of running, she might lean back stiff legged, draw her head back, wrinkle her nose and bare her teeth, as if some disagreeable odor had just invaded her space. Getting out of Jackson Hole northbound involved navigating through the elk, which in the early morning hours owned the highway.

Pattie and I would migrate at that season, too, escaping the valley's thawing snow banks and "mud season," driving on Interstate 80 to Pennsylvania to enjoy the blossoming of spring at Pine Creek.

Spring

Spring was a season we were fortunate to relish twice each year. We began spring early, from mid April to the end of May in the deciduous forest at our seasonal home in Pennsylvania; and then a second time, beginning late May or June, in Teton Valley and Jackson Hole. In the West, springtime lingers as it gloriously marches across the valley floors and climbs up into the mountains.

At Pine Creek, spring's renewal was idyllically celebrated by a cacophony of bird and amphibian song, pastel greens and colors emerging in the forest, delicate spring flowers, rushing brooks, fly hatches on trout waters, hiking and solitude in the mountains, and cycling mountain roads. And, invariably, not so idyllic, close encounters with fearsome four-foot timber rattlesnakes!

Returning West was always an emotional homecoming when the dramatic rise of the Tetons loomed into view from the Togwotee Pass highway. There was always a tingling of excitement upon entering Jackson Hole. And Pattie would invariably exclaim, "We're home now!" And we'd happily smile at each other in agreement. The Tetons were our home.

Pattie wrote: "I love spring in Teton Valley. No temperature or weather pattern has secure standing. For the past several days, I have lived as Alice in Wonderland. I fell into a turning kaleidoscope. It is springtime in the Rockies—perfectly ordered chaos!"

In Alta, the fragile unfolding aspen leaves would be a pastel green, while the lilacs would be blossoming around our house. Snow would still cover the upper half of the mountains. In the evenings, the mountains were beset with alpenglow. It was all very lovely, and with it, the feeling of our truly being home—feelings that arose from the deep joy of being happily together in a place we both cherished.

Sometimes on sunny June days we would shoulder our skis and hike on the radiant snowpack toward a peak called Mary's Nipple. Making the most of the sunshine and mountain scenery, wearing shorts, T-shirts, and sunglasses, we looked like sunscreen lotion advertisements. We would spend hours hiking up the mountain on the spring corn snow, which resembled white sand and intensely reflected sunlight like a bake oven, tanning us a deep healthy nut-like brown. Then, when we tired of the exertion of climbing up, and after a lunch on the mountainside, we'd point our skis downhill. What had taken hours to hike up took only exhilarating minutes to ski back down.

We both enjoyed gardening and we worked outside in the yard together each year. I would spade and rake the plot and together we would plant a vegetable garden. Pattie planted flowers in containers and colorful hanging baskets on the decks around the house. I would prune the shrubbery and raspberries. Pattie would patiently weed our established flower beds, raspberry bushes, and strawberry patch.

Our place resembled the look of the houses one sees in the mountain villages in the European Alps with all the flowers and outdoor window box plantings. I feel a deep tightness in my chest at the memory now every time I view Pattie's gardening gloves and empty containers sitting unused in the garage.

A small area, maybe half an acre, of original prairie remained across the street from our house. How it escaped the plow, who knows? The dense stand of arrowleaf, balsamroot, prairie star, and other flowers and herbs would put on a glorious spring display, amid native grasses and snowberry bushes, every spring. It required no tending and was dependably consistent and splendid every year.

Springtime in the valley encouraged cycling, which we did almost daily, riding to the Teton River and over to Horseshoe Canyon and back; or to Victor from Driggs, through Bates and the farmland along the west side of the valley, through all the rarified barnyard odors; and, for a more serious workout, up the steady steep grade of Ski Hill Road to Targhee Resort.

If all our physical activities were not enough, through all seasons, we regularly worked out at fitness centers in Driggs and at the Aspen Resort in Jackson. Pattie also participated in and excelled at Anusaua Yoga. We exalted in our healthy lives. Physical fitness was a prerequisite for our active lifestyle.

"I cannot imagine life without work as really comfortable," Sigmund Freud wrote, nor could we. Being productive or useful, I believe, is a necessary part of a life well spent. We scheduled our work hours into the above seasonal activities as it demanded, but what constituted "work" is a relative concept. For some, what we considered play would have been impossibly hard work; and what we thought of as work, was undoubtedly beyond imagination for many—definitely esoteric, mostly abstract, sometimes far removed. We were, as poets may in some cases appear to be, distantly and happily detached from the labors of mainstream society.

Our work was mostly an extension of the activities we enjoyed. Field work for my consulting projects generally involved being outdoors in pristine settings, for example, doing baseline studies for the Rocky Mountain Elk Foundation, mapping the vegetation on Montana's Flathead Indian Reservation, or federal and local government environment and biological assessments. It often encompassed travel to remote places, long solitary hours in the field, hiking varied and difficult terrain, making and applying specialized and obscure biological observations, science, and principles, and independently researching, preparing, and submitting reports.

Pattie was always researching and working on writing a new piece. Together, we wrote, photographed, and published articles based on our outdoor activities, observations, and travel experiences. This eventually evolved into traveling to challenging off-the-map locations and writing about those places—East Africa, Madagascar, the Galapagos Islands, Ecuadorian Amazon, and the Alaskan wilderness. It was endeavor filled with adventure and novelty. It had its own challenges, and it was definitely not for everyone, but it was never "work" for us in the conventional sense.

Deeply and perennially rooted, our love for each other remained as beautifully dependable as the wildflowers annually gracing the Tetons' mountain meadows. As we built indelible and wonderfully delightful memories together on the west slope of the Tetons and in our travels, we were also creating an enjoyable, rich and enviable life. Together, we consciously and purposefully sought out and created authentic experiences, so called "experiences of a lifetime." What we remember becomes who we are.

> Memories are the keepers of the spirit
> and the holders of the hearts,
> where the flowers of the dreams allow a life
> to linger forever in our souls.
> —Author unknown

CHAPTER 14

FREELANCE WRITING

People who lead 'routine lives' have a bad reputation in our culture. But life is paradoxical. In situation after situation, this pattern recurs: order and discipline are the prerequisites for creativity and daring.

— David Brooks

Pattie and I shared in learning the business and frustrations of freelance writing together. We often did research as a team, helping one another. We were each other's muses. Pattie had a talent with words and vocabulary, a strong education in literature and creative writing, and an active and imaginative mind. Her game of choice was Scrabble. She had been the editor for her college newspaper and had strong opinions about grammar, which I frequently ran afoul of with my loose country-boy interpretations of the English language. My strength and contribution was my natural sciences and technical background, combined with a strong sense of pragmatism.

Our writing styles contrasted. A skilled word crafter, Pattie was sometimes criticized for being too exuberant or flowery. In contrast, with my background in biological sciences and natural history, I tended toward being technical and descriptively terse; or as I was once accused, pedantic. But in researching and writing stories, Pattie and I made a nice team—yin and yang, the power of us.

Together, we photographed and wrote pieces on a broad range of subjects for a wide variety of magazines and anthologies. The fun was in the research, travel, reading, and interviewing people. I have a foot-thick binder containing the stories we published. I entitled and labeled the binder and its contents *Pattie and Earle's Story Book.* It rests ponderously on our living room coffee table, a reminder and compendium of places and times we delighted in together.

Some of the magazines we wrote for had national circulation; a few were regional, such as: *Montana, Jackson Hole, Teton Valley, Yellowstone-Teton Country,* and *Teton Home* magazines. Other periodicals we frequently contributed to included the **Washington Post**'s *The World and I* the Cowboy Hall of Fame's *Persimmon Hill*, the Rocky Mountain Elk Foundation's *Bugle,* the **Denver Post**'s *Travel Section*, and *Southwestern Art.*

Pattie was particularly gifted at interviewing people, descriptively profiling the interiors of trophy homes, businesses, notable local families, celebrities, gifted artists, and distinguished professionals. She was a "people person," capable of presenting everyone and everything in an appropriate, auspicious, and knowledgeable manner. Pattie's subjects generally felt good about themselves and their work after being profiled in one of her well-written pieces.

Describing Western watercolor artist Jean Halverson, for example, Pattie penned:

> Some paintings detail perfectly scenes in Nature. Jean Halverson's paintings render their essence . . . Hers are watercolors that reanimate viewer's souls. Her paintings allow them sunlight at midnight, flowers in winter. They preserve such traces of community as a dusty path to a barnyard or Belgians harnessed to haul hay, their labored breathing trapped by cold air.

Writing the foreword to mountaineer and plein air artist Joe Arnold's book, *Mountaineer's Dawn*, Pattie penned:

> His work is recognized instantly—high-altitude panoramas painted in situ. An annual participant in Cody, Wyoming's

Buffalo Bill Art Show and Sale, show organizers nicknamed him "the plein air artist of thin air." One past brochure describes a painting of his as "done at the end of a rope, the artist's feet hanging over a yawning precipice." On summits where most mountaineers won't linger, Joe sits sketching with pastels, sometimes tied into an anchor in the rock.

Considering *Teton Valley Magazine*'s regional nature, it carried an exceptionally diverse range of subjects in those years, including international travel, which was ushered in with one of our travel stories in the Winter 1999/2000 issue. Pattie and I were regular contributors, publishing articles in every issue of the magazine up through and including its notable tenth anniversary.

The ten-year anniversary of *Teton Valley Magazine* was celebrated in their Winter 2007–08 publication. In her retrospective piece for that issue, Pattie wrote:

> I was already a freelancer when my writing premiered in *Teton Valley Top To Bottom*. The story concerned my experience cycling on Grand Teton National Park's snow-cleared road in April 1997 and registering the park's first wolf sighting in over fifty years. Like those wild canines, I was new to the Tetons, and becoming a regular contributor to this magazine was a great introduction to living here. I wrote the life stories of natives and newcomers. . . . Whatever their chosen career, nearly everyone wants me to do the best job possible, and I'm no exception. When strangers began greeting me in the grocery store, recognizing me from my contributor photos and professing to check each issue's table of contents in hopes of finding my name there, I knew I was home.
>
> For the first time ever, I had ready access to and time to explore wilderness areas. Call me presumptuous, but I had a great time writing about my new loves—wildlife,

wildflowers, skiing, biking, hiking, canoeing, and "peaking" after setting foot on the summit of the Grand Teton. . . Where I end up after I start writing surprises even me. Every odyssey has hardships, and certainly my decade-long journey with this magazine has had its spiritual side, too . . but it's also been a helluva lot of fun!

In 2014, the director for the Murie Center, a conservation organization located at Moose in Jackson Hole, wrote:

> When I [recently] happened upon an article [by Pattie Layser], it made my eyes well up because it captured the spirit of wilderness. In *A Chance Encounter*, she describes [an] incomparable interaction with a pair of wolves in Grand Teton National Park, while riding her bicycle, at a time when wolves had yet to be seen [there]: "the frontrunner turned his head to gaze at me in passing . . . he stopped my heart with his direct stare. . . ." Pattie closed the article with, "Never again will I be in the Park without scanning the land, hoping to see my pair of wolves." What a beautiful way of suggesting the hope that is present in wilderness . . . elation and hope.

My first article for *Teton Valley Magazine,* like Pattie's, appeared in the magazine's premiere issue. It was entitled "Confessions of a Backcountry Drinker." The tongue-in-cheek essay was born from our experience of running out of water on a long hike across the Teton Range from Jackson Hole to Teton Valley on a warm summer day and resorting to a practice common in my earlier years, drinking unfiltered water directly from the mountain streams and springs:

> Our craving for water had become acute. Lingering snowfield reflected sunlight, basking us in radiant heat. Our thirst was simultaneously honed and mocked by a

sparkling millrace of headwaters emanating everywhere as
we made our way through the be-flowered alpine splendor
in the late summer sunshine . . . I filled my water bottle
at the base of a crashing cascade chute while inhaling the
refreshing cool vapors and splatter. She [Pattie] looked
dubious. With a maniacal grin, I joked, if there is any
giardia in that maelstrom, they'd have to be white water
certified.

The magazine owner and editor-in-chief of *Teton Valley*'s winter
2007–08 anniversary issue identified "Confessions" as one of her "all-
time favorites," rating it high on her "reading enjoyment scale."

Two of our writing endeavors were particularly notable in
engaging us in the communities and history of Jackson Hole and
Teton Valley. First, through the Murie Center in Grand Teton National
Park, Pattie developed a friendship with the renowned conservationist
Margaret "Mardy" Murie, and subsequently wrote several pieces about
Mardy, "A Candle in the Wind" and "Mardy Murie: At Home in
Wyoming's Wapiti Wilderness," *Teton Home* and *Bugle Magazines*
respectively. Second, the proprietors of the historic Flat Creek Guest
Ranch invited us to visit the ranch and write about it and its legendary
original owners, socialite Eleanor "Cissy" Patterson and Teton Valley
homesteader Enoch "Cal" Carrington — the "countess and the cowboy."
Pattie published stories about the ranch and Cissy, "The Flat Creek
Ranch, Always the Real West" and "Tracking the Wilderness Wapiti
in 1916," *Persimmon Hill* and *Bugle Magazines*. While I researched
and published a book on Cal Carrington's enigmatic life story, *I Always
Did Like Horses and Women*. One reviewer called it "…the most highly
documented and researched biography of any notable Jackson Hole
character." The biography received an award from the Wyoming State
Historical Society. Pattie and I enjoyed a lot of entertaining interactions
and discussions in our sharing of research findings and interpretations
with each other for those works.

Little could we imagine or know then how much the Internet and social media would change writing for magazines like the ones that published our articles. It was the last hooray for writers of that genre. We were witness to magazine after magazine winking out like candles in the wind.

For Pattie and me, though, looking back at our voluminous published materials; our writing was more than just stories and photographs; it reflected our lives and lifestyle in those years. Rereading our stories and seeing our accompanying photographs poignantly brings to mind not only the subject matter but also the associated feelings and recollections of our life together in those years.

CHAPTER 15

INTERNATIONAL TRAVEL

Not all those that wander are lost.
— J.R.R. Tolkien

What I am able to share within these pages represents little more than excerpts and vignettes from our travels. I am forced to limit myself and to skip over much of the depth and detail of those experiences. While travel expanded our knowledge, awareness, and understanding, the experience of seeing a look of wonder and delight in each other's eyes further connected us.

While some might find it tedious and laborious, our habit of journaling and record-keeping resulted in our travels truly being learning experiences. We documented what we did and saw for purposes of later writing about our experiences. Things were not just superficially viewed and then forgotten; they were sought out, photographed, researched, mulled over, discussed, laughed and joked about, recorded in journals, and later published, at least in part. For us, it was rewarding and fun.

In our materialistic society with its short attention spans and sound bytes, where gadgets and electronic items rule the economy, the lifestyle we cultivated was almost un-American. We gravitated toward accumulating authentic life experiences, rather than dollar-store materialism, prearranged Disneyland fantasy, or virtual reality. The memories and experiences we stockpiled were priceless, and it all contributed to deepening the intimacy we shared.

Our first travel outside the country, beyond Alaska, Canada, Mexico, and French Polynesia, was to Central America—Belize and Guatemala—in winter around the late 1990s. We discovered a perk foreign travel offered: we could write and publish stories and photographs about our experiences. Better yet, in those years many places were willing to provide discounts and even free accommodations to journalists for the advertising published stories provided for them. Our writing stories led us into more travel.

Belize and Guatemala's World Heritage Site at Tikal National Park provided important learning experiences for us, too. It was hardly what one would consider work; we were having too much fun. The ideal vocation is when what one does for livelihood cannot be distinguished from what they also enjoy as play and recreation. We arranged for several days' accommodations at the Banana Bank Ranch in Belmopan, Belize, to acclimate ourselves before adventurously heading out with just our backpacks without any prearrangements, relying on our *Lonely Planet* guidebook.

The Banana Bank Ranch was our introduction to tropical forests and jungle: large breadfruit and rain trees; epiphytes, including bromeliads and orchids; clear starlighted nights suddenly transformed into torrential tropical storms; nighttime screams of a jaguar encaged behind our cabana; continual background of bird sounds—toucans and parrots; a possum in the dining room rafters; geckos, roaches, and other uninvited fauna rustling around within our cabana; habituated spider monkeys and iguanas scampering above us through the trees. We were captivated! A working ranch and plantation, Banana Bank advertised "jungle horseback adventures." After the resort's guide observed Pattie's and my riding skills and saw we could both stay on a horse, we ended up cantering around the plantation—more adrenaline! We were also given access to a dugout canoe. Putting our canoeing know-how to work, Pattie and I explored the Belize River. Our reconnaissance of the misty and swift flowing jungle river went way beyond what our hosts were used to their guests undertaking.

Departing the Banana Bank, we were schlepped to a local market place, where we boarded a bus to San Ignacio, located in the uplands.

The bus ride turned into the stereotypic overcrowded Third World public transportation, complete with chicken crates and mothers with crying babies jammed in on top of us. Pattie could not contain her giggles at the whole scene, especially when a baby burped up on me as if scripted.

From the dusty highland settlement of San Ignacio, we made a side trip to the astounding Maya ruins at Tikal. A photograph of Pattie and me standing together at the top of a Tikal temple is among the montage of images hanging in our Alta kitchen.

A Tikal Park guide pointed to a giant ceiba tree and exclaimed, "That is *Yaxche*; it is sacred to the Maya people." That observation opened up a new awareness for us: the spiritual role trees have played in indigenous and ancient cultures worldwide. It led us to the literature on sacred trees, such as that by author Nathaniel Attman *(Sacred Trees: Spirituality, Wisdom & Well-Being)* and historian Simon Schama *(Landscape and Memory)*, and the singular importance and role of trees in mankind's cultural history and cosmologies.

A repeated theme in many indigenous cultures, the ancient Maya believed a giant ceiba tree grows from the center of the Earth and is rooted in the spirit world. In Africa, we would find the baobab is similarly revered; in Scandinavia, it is *Yggdrasil*, the ash; for Germanic tribes, it was the oak; in Siberia, *Tuuru*, the larch; and for the North America Iroquois, the Eastern white pine, the Tree of Peace. At the dawn of time, forests and trees were highly esteemed and spiritually revered. Compare this reverence for trees to modern society's monomania for commoditization of forests into wood products.

From San Ignacio, we hired a taxi for $125 US dollars for a nearly an all-day drive on a then unpaved jungle road called the "Hummingbird Highway" to Placencia. The out-of-the-way costal hamlet of Placencia offered the best beaches in Belize, which were then mostly undiscovered. Luckily, the greasy red clay soil road surface was dry the day we traveled. Otherwise the swath of unpaved road through the jungle would likely have been impassable.

Along the way, deep in the tropical rainforest, we passed the access leading into to the 150-square-mile Cockscomb Jaguar Preserve. Designated in 1986, the entrance road at the time appeared to be little more than a trace in the jungle.

At Placencia we were able to rent for $50 per night what was, relatively speaking, an upscale palm thatched cabana on stilts located next to the beach. Pattie journaled: "Fan! Window screens! Guatemalan curtains, an Oriental rug; no electricity, dinner by candle light— peering down the tub and sink drains, I see the sand below!" Pattie called it "the poor man's Caribbean."

The few tourists present were a cosmopolitan assortment. The local beer, Belikin, rhymed with the abundant and ubiquitous pelican. Huge six- to eight-foot long habituated leopard rays glided past, patrolling the shallows along the beach. They seemed to be as curious about us as we were about them.

On a fishing excursion, Pattie caught a barracuda that was as long as she was tall. We boated to a small island called a *caye*, presumably to barbeque tuna. I say "presumably" since we did not take any fish with us, but instead fished for and caught our lunch—several crevalle jack, a powerful fighting fish, on light tackle—while en route to the caye.

Pattie asked our Creole boatman and fishing guide if he had ever been married and recorded his reply in her journal: "I was married five or ten years to the best woman in the world, but then we just got mad at each other." Why, we wondered? But he volunteered no further explanation.

Martha, a hairdresser of African descent, who set up her shop in a local pub, built out over the water, had lived twenty years in Chicago. She told us, when Americans would ask her where she was from, she would reply, "Central America." Then they'd say, "Oh, yes—Ohio." Martha told us she would like to style Pattie's bush of hair into Afro braids. I encouraged it, thinking that would be pretty wild! Pattie seriously thought about it, but finally declined the offer.

Pattie was fascinated with the village's Creole children who rode boats to school wearing crisp uniforms and at times would swim alongside our boat "like a school fish." She described "a little, adorable, curly headed girl who brought her plate of rice and beans to sit wordlessly beside Earle on his beach towel, content to sit close and eat."

Upon our return to Alta, Pattie wrote and published a lovely piece about the Banana Bank Ranch, illustrating it with our photographs, and entitling it: "Basking in the Beauty of Belize." Carolyn Carr, wife of the ranch owner, was an artist and she and Pattie had connected immediately. They would later meet up when Carolyn made trips to the United States for art shows in Jackson Hole. Pattie began her Belize story with an enticing quote from Carolyn: "We are far from the real world and near the things you only dream of." How true that proved to be for us.

When her story was published in 1999, Pattie forwarded the Carrs a copy, and they sent her the following e-mail: "Dear Pattie. . . . We were simply delighted with the article . . . the expressive, imaginative text and beautiful photos. . . . The article is a treasure for us. May the Lord's blessing be upon you this Christmas season.—Love John and Carolyn Carr."

Our travel in Belize provided us with an encouragement and fascination for exotic locations that marked the beginning of a decade of globetrotting for us. We found agreement with Mark Twain's observation in *Innocents Abroad:* "Travel is fatal to prejudice, bigotry, and narrow-mindedness."

Regardless where we went in our travels over the years, everyone was invariably drawn to and loved Pattie. "How lucky we are that the smell of coconut soap, photos, this journal, or sharing a memory can bring back such special times," Pattie penned in her journal.

We discovered not all travel was soul satisfying, however. Longing to reconnect with our Tahiti experience, we opted to make a quick reconnaissance of Maui. We diligently searched the islands of Maui and Molokai for the kind of authentic experiences we had found in

French Polynesia. Other than the South Sea tropical climate, for us it was simply nowhere to be found. Maui was manically over the top with commercialism and development. That appeared to be what most American tourists were comfortable with and expected. When we were on Bora Bora, Pattie had made a journal entry of conversation she overheard on the bus:

> A couple asked another if they should bother going to Moorea? (Asked the same question, Earle and I would have practically broken our necks nodding emphatically, enthusiastically, unequivocally Yes!!) The couple asked responded by shrugging uncaringly. "It's different," they replied, "not as nice, not as developed."

They would have liked Maui. It was tawdry and heavily *developed*.

On Maui, major highways, bumper-to-bumper traffic, hawkers and promoters, and everywhere a crush of people, inescapably greeted us. Fresh fruit in the tropics? Forget it; it was shipped in from the mainland at twice the price. I recall the price for one small avocado was five dollars.

The locals openly displayed sneering contempt for tourists, not that I blame them. Try to find a hidden canyon to explore away from the mob scene, the access would be fenced and gated off with No Trespassing warnings posted. Tourists were kept to a revolving circuit of promoted places designed to extract dollars from their pockets.

For sedentary people who liked short walks along the beach, shoulder-to-shoulder with others, and sitting on the seaside benches to watch the sunsets (gotta get there early to get a bench), it was fine, I suppose. It reminded me of a friend who once told me he was going to vacation at Palm Beach. I asked, "What do you do there?" He replied, "Nothing, that's the point."

Doing nothing was not our style. Giving it our best shot, we snorkeled at the Ahihi Kinau Marine Preserve, dined at Peaches and

Crumbles Café, envied the skill of wind surfers at Ho'okipa Beach Park in Paia; and paid homage to the large banyan tree in what was once the old whaling town of Lahaina. Somewhere near Lahaina, we observed green sea turtles that impressed us.

We also hiked Waihee Canyon, visited the Seven Sacred Pools at Ohe'o Gulch, hiked to Waimoku Falls, walked Sliding Sands trail in Haleakala National Park, and rode the Maui Princess to Molokai and back, observing humpback whales along the way. Beautiful places, but all maddeningly overrun with other tourists and reduced to giving off a carnival or Disneyland vibe.

There were the highlights I identified in my journal notes: the sea turtles, distant humpback whales, our boat ride to Molokai, the tropical sun, and Pattie's suntan! A photo in the framed montage that hangs in our upstairs bathroom shows Pattie and me, tanned and smiling, standing close to each other on the stern of the Maui Princess, with Pattie holding onto her hat to keep it from blowing away.

Next, we traveled to La Paz, Mexico. Arriving there, Pattie wrote in her journal:

I love our hotel Club El Moro—arches, atriums, fountains, bougainvillea, hummingbirds, canaries, and thatched roof bar accessible by the swimming pool with the Mother of all Margaritas! Cost: $1.00 US. Inside—bright, cheerful, colorful tile abounds. Cool on the feet, happy to the eye; an arched stained glass window in the shower, ceiling fans—we slept on or in a giant clam shell and breakfasted on the balcony overlooking the sea.

Renting a weathered Volkswagen Beetle, we drove north through cedron forests to the off-the-beaten path village of Todos Santos, a small coastal settlement with ancient mango and palm orchards. There we discovered a small hidden bay, with a clean sandy beach and crashing surf—a place where local fisherman launched their *pangas*.

The concentration of assorted gulls and pelicans on the beach was astounding. Pattie wrote, "Startling a huge colony of birds, they take flight and we are eyeball to eyeball with hovering reddish-billed pelicans."

The photo-montage in our kitchen has an image of Pattie running barefoot on the Todos Santos beach, arms ecstatically raised, amidst a wild storm of sea birds getting airborne. While we were exploring the beach, a whale poked its head out of deep water close to shore. In a role reversal, it appeared to be watching us.

From Todos Santos, we drove to the village of Puerto San Carlos. Located about 200 km from La Paz, the town had bougainvillea-lined dusty streets and a splendid seaside setting. We rented a "suite" at the Los Conchos Resort for $45 a night.

Actually, the so-called suite was the only room the Mom and Pop accommodations boasted. It was spacious, with a lot of empty space. The shower consisted of a cold water pipe coming straight out of the wall, without a shower head; our bed spread was a U-Haul blanket pad. But the place was reasonably clean and came with the usual complement of Mexican dogs—sleeping hidden by day, barking all night.

The people in Puerto San Carlos were happy and friendly. A lobster dinner for two cost us only thirteen dollars. But what we were excited to discover was that we had stumbled onto a premiere whale-watching site—Magdalena Bay. The bay had an estimated two hundred whales present at the time and hundreds of sea lions.

We went out in a small motor boat with two biologists who were studying whales, and we were introduced to gray whales and whale behavior up close. We did not get to kiss or pet one of the giants, but it was still the best day of whale watching we ever experienced.

A sure test of a couple's compatibility is how well they travel together, especially off the beaten paths in challenging situations. A friend once told us that her "test of a relationship and compatibility is a five-day backpack trip in the backcountry with daily drenching rain storms."

Qualities that help couples get along include joint problem-solving abilities, preparation and planning, pitching in and doing one's share, minimal complaining, and having realistic expectations in common. Obviously, if one wants shopping malls and prefers four-star accommodations, and the other would rather experience outdoor surroundings tenting and subsisting on trail mix, you've got problems.

If unavoidable or uncomfortable circumstances arise, both partners need to bear the discomforts without projecting blame on the other. Being able to see the humor in situations is prerequisite. We experienced challenging travel conditions together at times, but about as much as I ever recall Pattie complaining was when she quoted Laurel and Hardy: "A fine mess you got us into this time, Ollie." On this subject, in one of her stories, Pattie wrote:

> Alas, travel is not all drama: it can also involve a great deal of drudgery—days of planning, inoculations and malaria medications; hours and days spent in airports and en-route destinations; dealing with travel agents, custom officials, border guards and guides. Fortunately, those memories are generally short-lived. Still, the apogee of travel is not necessarily when all goes as planned . . . more often, it is when the unexpected, fortuitous, or serendipitous occurs.

In February 1997, Pattie presented me with a Valentine showing a Monte Dolack menagerie of animals dancing at dusk in celebration of life. On the inside she had written:

A True Valentine

By Pattie Layser, 1997

Ever quaintly charming, and, at most, modestly coy,
Valentines are received shyly, with decorum so sweet.
With eyes averted, and heart all a twitter,

Accolades are accepted, but they generate no heat.
This card's illustrations thrust that thought out the window;
It's a natural aphrodisiac that this painting delivers.
Reminiscent of times when senses are keenest;
Full of starlight and moonbeams and iridescent rivers.
Memories around campfires, privy to night sounds,
Sensing that the animals cavort, when we are not about;
Our fantasies sparking in the flickering firelight,
And embers greeting shooting stars on a heavenward route.
This card celebrates animals; a menagerie wild and free,
Mated in kind and neighbor to mammals, fowl, and fish.
'Tis a benevolent rhythm absorbed through soles as we
hike;
'Tis the harmony and peace for which a world of people
wish.
Love intensifies, knowing ourselves a part of this scheme;
Lovemaking loses guile; it becomes natural and artless.
As the night's air cools sweat of the day,
The night's shadows conceal the heat of the darkness.
A Valentine should acclaim the power of paired adventure,
It should honor rhythms shared with our animal brothers.
It should celebrate the passions born observing the wild,
. . . And this would all happen outdoors, if I had my
druthers!
So, having established the requisite scene,
In mood, tone, and temper, this is a True Valentine.
The natural question arising from this wilderness setting,
Is, Valentine, So Dear, will you always be mine?
I Love You, Earle.—Pattie

Sometime around then, the city of Dubois, Wyoming was doing renovation work to the town's main street. The wooden plank walkways were being repaired and restored. To help pay for the project, individuals and businesses could buy a boardwalk plank with their name carved into it. We had a fondness for Dubois, so Pattie invested in a plank with our name on it. It was installed in front of the Dubois Mercantile, and it read: "E & P Layser."

Afterward, every time when we were in Dubois, we had to find and admire "our plank." It was there, and so were we, symbolically durable as ever. Nearly, two decades later, I checked and the plank was still there though very worn down. Our name was becoming barely decipherable. There was a strange feeling of time's passage. In December 2014, large structural fires razed that side of Dubois' main street. But our worn plank, I'm told, survived the blaze.

CHAPTER 16

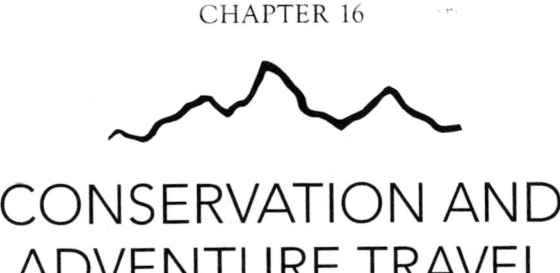

CONSERVATION AND ADVENTURE TRAVEL

The wild creatures I had come to Africa to see are exhilarating in their multitudes and colors, and I imagined that this glimpse of the earth's morning might account for the anticipation that I felt, the sense of origins, of innocence and mystery.

— Peter Matthiessen, *The Tree Where Man Was Born*

Travel to remote and exotic destinations needs to be put into the context of the era. Nowadays, we can hardly imagine the experiences of nineteenth-century explorers, such as Richard Burton, Henry Stanley and David Livingston in Africa. When Livingston departed Zanzibar for continental Africa, he wrote: "This is the first place I have known in Africa to rest before starting on my final journey. It is an illusionary place where nothing is as it seems." It literally became his "final journey." Zanzibar, we would discover, was still an "illusionary place."

When Peter Matthiessen explored the "primordial spirit of man" four decades before us, traveling was vastly different from luxury safaris in East Africa today. And safaris even a decade ago were different from today's ever increasing provisions for comfort. Early journeys were all before the export and adoption of Western culture, rapid air transport, modern conveniences, and over-the-top commercial tourism and ecotourism, plus the availability of modern technology everywhere you go. It all combines to homogenize today's travel. Homogenization is continuing and ongoing, but awesome wildernesses, off the beaten customary tourist routes, still remain in East Africa for those seeking to find them.

An Alta neighbor who had an interest in a London travel agency and friends in East Africa was keen on having us visit Africa. He particularly wanted Pattie to write about his friend, Lizzy Theobald, a young woman who had been promoting black rhino conservation in the Selous Game Reserve in Tanzania, when she suffered an untimely death from malaria.

In June 2000, Pattie and I flew to Arusha, Tanzania, to begin a three-week safari. Afterward, in "Africa: 12-Ply-Tire Road to a Four-Star Adventure," Pattie wrote: "I traveled to Lizzy Theobald's favorite part of East Africa to document her legacy of rhino preservation. There in the Selous Game Reserve, I met rhino specialists from conservation agencies around the world."

This first trip to Africa proved to be among our most unforgettable adventures. It was transformational. We had hired our own guide, driver, and Land Rover for just the two of us. The local beer was appropriately named Safari. We learned the standard tourist Swahili vocabulary: *Jambo!* (Hello!) *Habari gani? (How are you?) Nzuri (beautiful), Asante (thanks).* We thrilled with the abundance of extraordinary wildlife, the friendly and fun loving people, and reveled in true wilderness. Our experiences and photographs were to knock your socks off. Pattie wrote:

> The Land Rover's open roof uncorks blue sky, red dust. I ride standing up on its back seat, my head out the top, stampede straps anchoring against the backlash of my hat's brim. A roll bar and my wide stance brace me against the roughest road I've ever traveled, but I could ride like this forever. Africa is out there!

Years later, I discovered an unpublished whimsical notation in Pattie's journal: "I shouldn't be surprised that I could long for a place after being there just a short time . . . I miss wild Africa."

Our first visit to Africa always remained special in our minds. It had introduced us to a new level of adventure, excitement, novelty, and further possibilities. It was an uncommon learning experience; and, for us, too, it was Karen Blixen's (Isak Dinesen's) *Out of Africa*, dreamingly and exotically romantic.

Tanzania marked the point where we began consciously focusing and designing trips to observe and write about rare, threatened, and endangered wildlife. Our articles were generally written in popular format, but conservation issues and messages were also embedded in them.

We published one or sometimes several articles about each of our different trips. Pattie had given me a 35mm Nikon camera as a gift. It was before digital cameras. Outfitted with a 28–300mm zoom lens and fine-grain film, we did our own photography in support of our stories.

From Tanzania, we visited Zanzibar Island, located in the Indian Ocean off the East African coast, where we intended to photograph the rare and threatened red colobus monkeys in Jozani Forest Reserve and explore medieval Stone Town.

This was before some of the reserve's monkeys had been habituated in order to allow tourists opportunity to observe and photograph them up close. Unguided, Pattie and I searched deep into the Jozani's tangled second-growth red mahogany forest and swamp. The unmarked and unmaintained loop trail dwindled to barely an overgrown trace. We saw and heard monkeys in the dimly lighted forest canopy, but they never allowed us to approach close enough to photograph them.

Somehow we managed to encounter no venomous snakes, only a few leeches, and we avoided getting lost in the jungle maze. When we emerged from the swampy forest several hours later we were covered with black ooze muck. Even our laid-back driver, Vinnie, whose most common pronouncement was "Not to worry," had become alarmed waiting for us. Smeared with mud and bedraggled, we joined Vinnie in laughing at ourselves.

I recently uncovered Pattie's notes where she had recorded a conversation with Vinnie:

> Vinnie was a tall African with a ready smile. Stretching out to cover ground, his lank limbs caught up with his body a full thirty seconds later. He pulled from his pocket dirty bills that wouldn't feed him and his tour van both. Vinnie grinned. He fed the bus, and he dreamed aloud.

> "I want to go around the world," declared Vinnie. "I started out once," he said matter-of-factly. "Went to Istanbul. Have you seen it? It's a nice place."

> "They wouldn't let a black man go on through Greece, so I stayed five years, until I ran out of money. "But," grinned Vinnie, "someday . . ."

Pattie had added an after note: "That's the way I feel about returning to Africa ... *Someday!*"

In 2001, we traveled to Ecuador, where we visited the Galapagos Islands on a small yacht, observing the different island's incredible diverse and rare endemic species, and the stringent protection programs for the unique island habitats.

Pattie began her article with: "'Charles Darwin—he is a very good friend of mine,' Harry says. Dark glasses hide his eyes, but a sly grin takes hold. 'And,' he says . . . We listen intently as Harry, our naturalist and tour guide, tells us ancient truths about his birthplace, Galapagos."

After the islands, we proceeded inland and onto the rivers for another Ecuadorian adventure: the headwaters of the Amazon, "Earth's Richest Biological Habitat," as I entitled my article. Accessed only by motorized dugout canoes through miles and miles of jungle waterways, we spent a week at the remote Tiputini Biodiversity Research Station. It was located within the 2.5-million-acre Yasuni National Park, a designated Biosphere Reserve. I wrote:

The boatman expertly maneuvers our dugout en route. The wilderness waterway meanders between walls of tangled vegetation. Blind turns give the illusion that the river ends suddenly, leaving us engulfed in the steaming jungle. Flocks of iridescent tropical birds burst out in front of us, manically disrupting the moodiness of the rainforest. Mist patches mystically appear and disappear as if the forest itself is a single living, breathing organism.

Oil and gas development was beginning to encroach upon the Park. Tiputini was not a place you went to "vacation." A "challenging immersion into wilderness and rainforest ecology" would more accurately describe it. It was only for those who were serious about spending time deep within unspoiled Amazonian jungle. The daily downpour and pounding of tropical thunder storms, constant near 100 percent humidity, and a need for headlamps even in the middle of the day, gave a clue why it was appropriately called rainforest. One never dried out. Cameras had to be kept in special "dry boxes" when not in use.

Our next adventure was galvanized by the country's election of the George Bush–Dick Cheney presidency. We feared the so-called "1002 lands," the coastal plains, within the nineteen-million-acre Arctic National Wildlife Refuge, would be opened to oil and gas development. The Bush–Cheney administration had declared development of those lands a high priority.

We wanted to witness and experience this awesome Arctic wilderness firsthand before development threatened to change it forever. Among the things, we planned to observe was the spectacle of the Porcupine caribou herd's post-calving aggregation. The caribou represent the life blood of the Arctic, and since time immemorial, the coastal plain has provided their essential calving habitat.

In 2002, we joined a small group to float the Kongakut River from its headwaters in the Brooks Range to the Beaufort Sea in the

Arctic Ocean, and then paddle along the Siku (Icy) Lagoon shoreline of the coastal plain to Demarcation Point within Arctic Refuge. There we had arranged to be picked up by a bush plane on a seaside gravel bar and flown to the Inuit settlement of Kaktovik, and from there back to Fairbanks. In the opening of my published story, I wrote:

> Somewhere a whistle shrilled—the agreed upon signal for bear in camp. I unzipped the tent and peered into the glowing 2 a.m. Arctic sunlight. A startled red and black cross fox stared back from across the river gravel bar, and then abruptly disappeared into the willows. I had dreamt the whistle, but the wild setting outside the tent was very real.

Pattie's published Arctic Refuge story began:

> If it's true that people love what they know, then I would like my writing to channel the wonders of Alaska's Arctic National Wildlife Refuge for others. But how? The refuge is so different from anywhere I've been before, I'm left with metaphors that only suggest the Arctic; words that approximate a place many people will never see, a wild place I'm asking them to love. If I tell others what it's not—car-choked roads, relentless whining air traffic, cell phones, gangs, condos, latte shops—can I save the Far North from becoming a place of legends, literature's second "Paradise Lost."

In the two weeks we were in the Arctic, we were not disappointed. The Arctic Refuge with its huge landscape, serene beauty, and wildlife represents some of the last true wilderness on Earth. We crafted and published four articles, with supporting photographs, about our Arctic experience. Pattie wrote three of the four. And we did witness the Porcupine caribou herd's spectacular post-calving aggregation and migration.

In 2003, we occupied ourselves within the contiguous United States, traveling to Havasu Canyon and Canyon de Chelly National Monument in Arizona, and writing about our experiences there. We also published on regional topics, such as berry picking in Teton Valley, Yellowstone Park's magical waterfalls, backpacking in the Bechler River area, Lake Yellowstone Hotel history, and wolf watching.

In her writings, Pattie explained: "Admittedly, with Grand Teton and Yellowstone National Parks and thousands of acres of wilderness in our backyard, we don't need to necessarily roam the globe to experience adventure."

We continued our traditional seasonal patterns of summer and winter outdoor activities in Wyoming and portions of spring and autumn spent in the Eastern deciduous forest. Our travel to exotic locations and our singular experiences together served to draw Pattie and I even closer, increasing intimacy and further solidifying our bond—a deepening of our passionate connection; so deeply were we drawn to each other, I think we felt it in our bones.

On February 14, 2004, I presented Pattie with a valentine with the following message: "Dearest Pattie—Whatever the day whatever the season, my heart belongs to you always. The years go by, but you will always be my sweetheart. Love You, Earle." Included with the valentine were two tickets to "The Great Love Songs of Broadway" performance at Teton Village's Walk Festival Hall in Jackson Hole, Wyoming.

In 2004, we trekked to Alaska's McNeil River Bear Sanctuary. Acquiring a permit to visit the bear reserve requires application and drawing through an international lottery system (we applied for two years before we were drawn). We tent camped literally among the bears with the small group of successful applicants and were guided by Alaskan Game and Fish personnel within the reserve.

McNeil River is appropriately called the "River of Bears." As soon as we arrived in the bay by float plane and clambered onto the shore, we began seeing giant brown bears everywhere, surrounding us and our campsite.

Pattie exclaimed, "Oh, my God!"

I was speechless. We had been delivered into a primal dreamscape punctuated with colossal bears. The Alaska brown bears are the largest terrestrial omnivore in North America. Photography opportunities were hair-raisingly close up and everywhere all around us. Drop your camera and it would have registered an image of a bear.

A grinning State of Alaska wildlife technician warmly welcomed us. A likeable bear reincarnation of a man, Tom waded into the icy bay waters by the floatplane without benefit of hip waders. Curious, I asked why? "My legs are too big to fit into hip boots," he rumbled.

The high-rise outdoor privy, built to access by a ladder so the door would open in deep snow, was papered inside with Gary Larson bear cartoons from the *Far Side Gallery*. A sign warned: "If the toilet begins shaking while you are in it, do <u>not</u> open the door. A bear is rubbing itself." It was not a joke.

The close-up viewing of Alaskan brown bears concentrated at the McNeil River Falls during salmon season is a wildlife spectacle equal to any in the world. A conservation issue has been the sport hunting of the semi-habituated giant bears, ambushing them as they cross the ground between the McNeil Preserve and Katmai National Park.

Between us, Pattie and I wrote and published four articles and numerous photographs on the McNeil River Bear Sanctuary. In her story opening published in *The Denver Post*, Pattie wrote: "In the lower 48, the dreamscape at this game sanctuary would be a nightmare. Cresting a low-rise, we suddenly were standing within 40 yards of twelve 700–1,400-pound Alaskan brown bears."

Nowadays, one can also view the McNeil River bears on the Internet via electronic surveillance by a webcam installed at the falls. To my way of thinking, observation by remote camera is a hollow substitute for the live and sensory experience of actually being there immersed in the land and natural setting—the cold and wet, the odors and noises. Added to that is the uncertainty involved with the close proximity and interaction with one of the largest land omnivores on the planet.

Later that summer of 2004, in timely celebration of the Lewis and Clark bicentennial, Pattie and I canoed and camped along a 120-mile stretch of Montana's Wild and Scenic Missouri River, beginning from Coal Bank Landing below Fort Benton to the takeout at the Charlie Russell Wildlife Refuge. Biting deer flies, rattlesnakes, afternoon upstream winds, and powerful prairie thunderstorms accompanied us.

With guidebook maps and the Lewis and Clark journals, we were able to find the Corps of Discovery's actual campsite locations and land features referred to in their diary entries, places that are still in existence—such as the renowned White Cliffs, where Lewis recorded there were: "endless seens [sic] of visionary enchantment."

Our adventure nicely translated into a number of articles related to the Lewis and Clark bicentennial and the Corps of Discovery's route along Montana's Wild and Scenic segment of the Missouri River. A story I wrote for *Paddler* magazine was entitled "Paddling through Time."

> Like the Corps of Discovery, on this stretch of river, we encountered swarms of mosquitoes, biting deer flies, and at one point we were caught in a violent prairie thunderstorm. I wrote: "Forebodingly dark prairie sky accompanied by thunderous rumblings and lightning flashes bore down on our riverbank encampment, bringing to life one of Lewis's journal entries describing 'a cloud [that] arose to the SW and shortly after came on attended with violent Thunder Lightning and Hail."

In June 2005, Pattie parlayed her Alaskan bear experience into a journalist assignment with a BBC crew filming *The Bear Diaries*, a documentary on black, polar and brown bears. Pattie accompanied the film crew shooting the brown bear segment, which included BBC luminaries Jonathan Scott, Adam Chapman, Gavin Thurston and Simon Cole. The production was filmed in a wilderness location at Hallo Bay, adjoining Katmai National Park.

In traveling to Hallo Bay, Pattie, had to make five airline

connections: Idaho Falls to Boise, to Seattle, Anchorage, Homer, and finally a bush flight to Hallo Bay. En route Pattie mailed a post card addressed to Earle and Benji Layser: "In Anchorage waiting for the next leg. Long Day! ... missing you guys already. Gorgeous, clear, bright, warm day. Great views flying over Prince William Sound, et al. Beginning to get excited about playing bear paparazzi! Love you, P"

If there was ever any question about Pattie's independent abilities and keen sense of adventure, an excerpt from her unpublished notes and draft of the BBC manuscript should dispel any doubts:

> Early on my first day, a sow and three cubs approached. It was exciting. My point-and-shoot camera framed the four in award winning style, but quickly Mom's body alone filled my boxed image. I lowered my camera. She came closer. Always with an eye on us, she was cresting a small rise, directly in front of the running camera, five feet away from Gavin's lowered head while looking into the camera.
>
> The sow and her wayward three passed by, heading down toward the meadow behind us. There two other sows sat down, signaling they would be no threat to the family. But another bear appeared and gave chase. And this time the bears' trajectory was coming back over the rise directly at me . . . Kevin came alongside my left, his flare in hand. Larry moved up on my right, his flare ready. We three stood steady. The bears veered. I breathed.

Later, that same summer in Wyoming, using pack llamas we made a large circuit in the Bridger Wilderness in the Wind River Mountains. It was an experience encompassing ice storms, scenic high-elevation lakes, spectacular mountain peaks and spires, and stunning alpine flora. An excerpt from Pattie's writings touches on the challenges: "Admittedly, our AARP cards are dog-eared, but no alpine enthusiast wants to think *swan song*. We decided to push our limits: traverse Wyoming's Wind River Range, letting llamas lug our luggage."

There was little problem publishing our photographs and story about our wilderness llama packing in the Wind Rivers. It was another incredible outdoor experience. At one point, in trying to cross a mountain pass, we were caught in an ice storm above 11,000-feet elevation and forced to quickly set up our tent and wait it out. A shivering Benji thought he had arrived in nirvana when he got to be like a person and get inside a sleeping bag. Meanwhile, the llamas, unperturbed, lay down and calmly chewed their cuds, while wind blasting cold and hail and snow drifted around them.

When I think of Pattie and that trip, I recall her relaxed and happy, striding across gloriously beautiful alpine meadows, slack lead rope in hand with the llamas trailing close behind.

Next, in a long-planned junket, we traveled to Madagascar. Ask any American, which is closer, Madagascar or the moon, and they just might pick the moon. An extraordinary country, it was for us another once in a lifetime trip.

The literature is filled with superlatives describing the island and its unique natural features, particularly its endemic wildlife. Extolled as "paradisiacal" by early explorers, today overpopulation, poverty, slash-and-burn agriculture, clearing of primary forest, unsafe urban conditions and corruption all threaten any remaining remnants of paradise.

Madagascar was probably among the most challenging and demanding, but also most rewarding, of our trips. While intensely unforgettable, it was not always glamorous, as when we were required to pick leeches off each other's faces, or when we had to avoid or get through urban areas that were unsafe. With neurons firing on all our brain circuits, the shared experiences, problem solving, and a few stressful events, again only served to further contribute to the tightness of our bond as a couple. The challenges only served to draw us even closer, cementing us more tightly together as a couple.

We had planned a twenty-day trip, originally intended to allow us to observe and write about the island's unique, rare, and endemic wildlife. As our trip progressed, the diversity and unusual aspects of Madagascar's human culture grabbed our interest, too. Of the twenty-some ethnic groups dispersed across the island, some were notably primitive, existing barely beyond the Stone Age. And each possessed its own unique and unusual customs.

Madagascar reportedly has about fifty species of lemurs. Through much travel to remote National Parks, and elsewhere throughout the country, we were able to find, view, and photograph fifteen of them in the wild, including the rare indri.

The three-foot-tall indri, with its green-glow eyes, is the largest living lemur. It is known by the Malagasy as *Babakota,* father of the forest. Only sixty indris were thought to be extant at the time. Its eerie wailing cries could be heard from a mile away. The animal appeared to me to have steel springs embedded in its legs, propelling itself through the forest canopy with astonishing long leaps and speed.

While the trip was definitely not what most would consider a vacation, we did manage to stay in some attractive lodges along the way. Much of our challenging travel was self-imposed for research and exploration. Purposefully seeking out unique places made the travel not only demanding but also rewarding fun. One of our guides liked to boast that he had guided National Geographic explorers. Our little entourage of two was definitely not on the level of a National Geographic expedition, however.

We doggedly hiked long distances in soggy and humid rainforest to find and observe natural and cultural features. And we searched for rare nocturnal creatures with our Maglites late at night. In some cases, we stayed in exceedingly primitive and uncomfortable accommodations. We pulled bugs and leaches off each other, encountered immense snakes in the jungles, and spent long days afield, traveling on primitive roads and flying to destinations with local air transportation. We put up with these conditions to observe, learn, and photograph as much as was possible in the time we had.

One challenging situation developed for us at Ankarana National

Park in southern Madagascar. Known for its primary forest, colossal limestone bat caves, and tsingy (sharp-edged limestone karst), we had arranged our itinerary to camp within the park.

You are required to have a local guide to enter any of the reserves. Our guide at Ankarana was a young and arrogant Malagasy. We only found out after we arrived that he was not really prepared or equipped to provide camping. Our only accommodation option was a little eight-by-eight-foot dilapidated palapas at the edge of a small village about a mile from the park boundary. Our guide could not understand our distress, assuring us he was doing us a service. In his mind, staying in the thatched hut with no windows and a cobbled together door was a luxury compared to tent camping out in the jungle.

The hut's small built-in bunk occupied more than half the flimsy structure's space. Fortunately, it did not rain and the hard bed did have mosquito netting. The netting was not so much for mosquitoes, but rather other biting critters and creepy crawlies, like poisonous spiders, stinging centipedes and scorpions. They all had ready access through the walls and rickety bamboo floor.

Instead of the sounds of the jungle, we heard the village's sounds: crying babies, barking dogs, crowing chickens at 4:00 a.m., and a constant daytime thumping sound of grain being pounded into meal by primitive means. I have a framed photograph of Pattie sitting on the stoop of our little thatched shack looking dubious. Neither of us knew for sure what we had gotten ourselves into.

Behind a nearby small thatched screen was a pit toilet that always seemed to have a waiting line. You could locate the ghastly site from a long distance if you were downwind by the unspeakable odors it emanated. Pattie spoke some French. While they were standing in the toilet line, a Frenchman remarked to her *"Faut du courage,"* It takes courage.

The first morning, we began early to hike to the park's boundary. From there, we trekked for twenty kilometers on foot within the park's primary rainforest. There were primitive trails, but no roads within the park. Wildlife appeared scarce; I suspect the villagers were eating it—bush meat.

The lemurs kept their distance, remaining high in distant tree canopies. It was ungodly hot, humid, and exhausting. If we had not been in good physical condition, the hiking distances would have proven impossible. For lunch, the first day, our guide had brought us each a banana, which he proudly presented to us at noon. Lucky for us, I had stowed some emergency Clif Bars in my daypack.

We hiked to a huge cavernous cave in the park. It was filled with loudly squawking bats and the cave floor literally crawled underfoot with Madagascar cockroaches. When we had gotten about as deep into dark cave as I was comfortable with, wouldn't you know, the Maglite batteries suddenly gave out. Relying on the glow coming from the cave's entrance to guide us, we groped our way back out of the darkness, shrieking bats cheering our departure.

In the Madagascar article we published, I included some introductory discussion on *famadihana* practices: burial, exhumation five years later, and then a reburial in other than the ground. The Melagasy believe it is *fady* or taboo to bury the dead in the ground permanently. They practice ancestor worship. Death for the Malagasy people is the most important part of life because that is when one becomes an ancestor.

Another one of our guides, a local Malagasy woman who claimed to speak five languages, explained the custom to us: "For five years after my father was gone it did not seem like he is dead. But [after the exhumation] viewing the corpse, I know he is really dead; he has become an ancestor . . . we celebrate, we drink rum, we dance and sing, we do not cry." The bones are then taken and re-interred in a remote above ground location that the deceased had somehow had a connection to in life.

Pattie and I arranged to be boated out to Nosy Mangabe (meaning "the dark green island") in the Bay of Antongil within Masoala National Park, where we camped in the primary rainforest. It did not rain; it deluged. Rainfall averages ten feet of precipitation annually there with unrelenting soaking humidity. Set on a platform under a permanent fiberglass roof, out tent was dry and comfortable enough. At night frogs croaked and trilled from every corner of the forest around us. With head lamps and our Maglites, we searched unsuccessfully for the rare aye-aye lemur in the pitch black of the jungle nights.

Geckos were plentiful on Nosy Mangabe, including the unusual leaf-tailed geckos, which are camouflage artists extraordinaire. Much to the amusement of our guide, it was almost impossible for us to discern them, even though we were just a few feet away.

The guide led us along a narrow island trail to a *fasana* (a Melagasy reburial site) hidden under a cavernous rock overhang deep in the jungle. The site was set among hung boulders covered with shaggy mosses and tangled lianas, and surrounded by immense buttress-rooted trees. Small concrete and wooden caskets had been lugged up the mountain on the jungle trail and placed under the ledge. A six-foot boa snake lay draped across one of the caskets. In the gloom of the rainforest, it was a dreamlike scene right out of Hollywood's *Raiders of the Lost Ark*.

We learned that flat-tailed geckos were not the only experts at camouflage on the island. Returning towards camp on the narrow jungle trail, the guide suddenly turned and frantically tried to squeeze back past me.

"Snake, Snnnaake," he shrieked.

I expected to see an average sized ground boa, maybe five or six feet long. Instead, when we were able to focus closely on the dimly lit forest floor, an enormous fourteen-foot-long snake was disclosed. Lying tight alongside and paralleling the trail, the cryptic coloration of the camouflaged reptile had not become visible until we nearly stumbled over the snake.

It reminded me of a reptilian creature out of Hollywood's *Jurassic Park*. We would encounter boas or pythons as long or longer length on other African trips, but nothing that matched the intimidating heavy culvert-like girth of this snake. There was no way around the snake, the undergrowth was too thick to get off the trail and go around it. We hesitated there for a while catching our breath before gently tip-toeing past the creature, passing within two feet of it on the trail.

Once back home, I found an exotic-looking birthday card for Pattie with ring-tailed lemurs pictured on the front of it. Inside I had written:

> A ring-tailed lemur message: Dearest Love, It has been another wonderful year with you. Happy Birthday! The years pass all too quickly, but I'm grateful for our love and time together. I'm looking forward to many more birthdays with you and many more exciting adventures. Have a birthday more wonderfully rare and exotic than a Madagascar creature! I love you, Earle.

On our twelfth wedding anniversary (September 18, 2005), Pattie gave me a large card with a beautiful mountain scene and a bear in the foreground. Inside, she had clipped and pasted photos of us and written: "To Earle—My wildly wonderful, bigger-than-life lover! Our marriage began on a mountain 12 years ago, and we've been bagging peak experiences ever since! I love you and I love our life together. Happy Anniversary—My Love—Always, Pattie."

In addition, Pattie also presented me with a large coffee table book by James Balog entitled: *Tree: A New Vision of The American Forest.* Inside she had inscribed: "For my true love, Earle—Love is like a great tree: It is elegant. It's grounded. It transcends time. It's humbling. It's authentic. Happy 12th Anniversary, Pattie ["

Author W. Somerset Maugham wrote, "We are not the same persons this year as last; nor are those we love. It is a happy chance if we, changing, continue to love a changed person." Very true. My first wife and I had matured from who we were when we first met, irreconcilably growing apart; likewise, Pattie and her husband, too. But Pattie and I experienced a continual growing together—our love continued growing progressively stronger and deeper over time.

Contrary to Maugham, I do not attribute this to "happy chance" alone, but rather, in addition to our high-octane shared experiences, to recognizing and knowing who we were and respecting each other as equals. Our relationship was consciously valued, respected, and deeply cherished by both of us. It gave immense joy to us and to our lives together.

PART III

AUTUMN'S CHANGING SCENE

CHAPTER 17

LIFE ALTERING EVENTS

Sometimes something catastrophic can occur in a split second that changes a person's life forever; other times one incident can lead to another and then another and another, eventually setting off just as big a change in a person's life.

— Jeanette Walls, *Half Broke Horses*

My mind searches for reasons for the catastrophically life-altering and unpredictable events that would come uninvited into our lives. Was it because we were too happy, our lives too rich, our love too grand, so that we owed the universe a tragedy?

Did we somehow offend a deity? Did we overreach? Was it all predestined? Genetically preprogrammed? Were we exposed to hazardous substances? Or was it simply random—a cruel crapshoot? It becomes an entanglement of unanswerable *whys*.

Guilt tries to elbow its way into my thoughts. There are, however, simply no good reasons or answers for what happened to us. If our meeting on that long ago April day had been providential, was the suffering that we were to experience also preordained; a type of pitiless fate? The *Stanford Encyclopedia of Philosophy* states, "Fate seems unordered and cruel because we cannot understand providence." Unordered and cruel, indeed.

We were common people; never ungrateful, arrogant, or big headed. Both of us only had to recall our roots to be humbled and feel gratitude. Unassuming and grateful for the richness of our lives, we carefully cultivated all we enjoyed. Pattie was also one of those rare women who seemed totally unconscious of her exceptional beauty.

Our assets were not heavily invested in technology, so when the euphoric dot-com bubble burst, we dodged that bullet. Our finances survived and investments continued to prosper. That part of our lives stayed intact. But despite an unpretentious, deliberately conservative, health- and fitness-conscious lifestyle, both of us would experience the tragic destruction of our wellbeing. As I have described, we shared everything in life. Now we would come to share something horribly devastating and beyond our control—cancer.

In May 2006, Pattie and I were happily enjoying our customary springtime sojourn at Pine Creek. We were excited to be returning to Africa in a few days—Uganda this time. Then in the dark of the night, we received a horrendous and life-altering phone call.

Pattie's oldest sister had shockingly been found dead in her Memphis residence, an apparent suicide. Pattie's sister had never communicated feelings of hopelessness to us. There were unsubstantiated rumors—debt, guilt for failure to live up to her own self-imposed expectations, depression, isolation—but no one seemed to know or understood what really had happened or why.

Hugely distraught, Pattie flew to Memphis to be with her two other siblings for the funeral service. She wrote a friend: "My sister shot herself, leaving behind a trail to a person none of us even remotely recognized. I understood none of it." Heartbreak was contained in those words.

As I think about it, even now, I can feel Pattie's anguish. I am much more aware now, too, of how the sudden death of a loved one can engulf one in incredible pain-filled grief. The unexpected loss of her sister and her subsequent quiet but deep mourning became a part of Pattie's being. She generally bore it silently, keeping most of her feelings of grief private. Though, forever afterward, the question "Why?" would continue to surface and Pattie would weep quietly, tears coursing down her cheeks.

We had planned our trip to Uganda in June. Our departure unintentionally turned out to be only a few days after Pattie's sister's funeral service. Pattie came home from Memphis, and a day or so later we left for Africa. I do not remember if we discussed postponing the trip, but I believe we must have. If Pattie felt conflicted about doing the trip, I cannot recall her saying it. Under the circumstances, she chose to defer mourning. Perhaps it was not a good thing to do, but Pattie made it a point never to inconvenience others or me with her private feelings. She personified grace under pressure.

Once in Africa, though, Pattie seemed to immerse herself into the colorful travel and appeared to have set her emotional distress aside. In a story she later published, she characterized the trip as: "Boundary busting travel . . . we saw Uganda in the season of butterflies!"

Uganda was at one time touted as "the most beautiful of African countries—the Pearl of Africa." That was before civil strife and the dark despotic days of Idi Amin, when his army ravaged the country. We planned to follow in the footsteps of famous nineteenth-century Nile River explorers, Livingstone, Burton, and Stanley. Our itinerary included equatorial rainforests, mountain gorillas at the Bwindi Impenetrable Forest, chimpanzees at Kibale National Park, rainforest at Budongo Forest Reserve, game viewing in Queen Elizabeth National Park, the Nile headwaters at Murchison Falls National Park, the marshes of Lake Victoria, and vast savannahs. We would be covering 1,600 miles by land rover across the "land of red dust."

We were apprehensive about part of our itinerary into the northeastern part of Uganda after learning that only days before two National Geographic explorers had been killed by the Lord's Resistance Army, a rebel force, which had crossed into Uganda from the South Sudan along the same route we were taking. The insurgents had achieved notoriety for killing park rangers and their massive destruction of elephants. They illegally traded the ivory tusks for supplies and ammunition. It is an understatement to say, fortunately, we did not encounter this rebel group.

In our explorations, we sought out a menagerie of rare wildlife amid Uganda's remaining natural habitats—mountain gorillas, chimpanzees, leopards and lions at close range, the huge goliath heron, and the rarest of rare birds, the five-foot-tall prehistoric looking shoebill stork.

We found and photographed the shoebill from a tipsy dugout canoe in the extensive marshes surrounding Lake Victoria. Our guide could not understand our persistence in wanting to find and photograph the bird. After days of searching and finally finding the rare shoebill, our guide impatiently checked it off: "Okay, we saw it—good. That is done."

A local guide led us to an unusual bat-roosting cave deep in the forest, where we focused on photographing the thousands of large, squawking, flapping, smelly bats. A large ten-foot python had taken up residence there, too. The snake lay unmoving, casually draped across the cave floor below the unlimited food source. Suddenly the guide hissed: "Don't move."

Following his gaze toward the back of the cave, we startlingly discovered that we shared the confined darkened space not only with bats and snakes, but also with a leopard at breath-taking close range—probably less than twenty-five feet! We were inside a leopard's lair! Beside seeking the cool confines, he was undoubtedly there to pick off occasional easy meals from the cave walls.

Gasping with surprise, a rush of excitement and adrenaline flared though me; fear for some reason never occurred to me. Instead, I jerked the camera up to photograph the large cat. Although the leopard had lain there stealthily watching us, as soon as it knew we were aware of its presence, it quickly turned and darted out the back of the cave.

It had been a dangerous situation. Luckily, there was an escape out the back of the cave for the cat; otherwise, it could have been disastrous. The leopard trapped in those close quarters would no doubt have come out over the top of us.

At Bwindi Forest, we observed, photographed, and made close and personal acquaintance with rare mountain gorillas. On two different days tracking, we observed and photographed bands of gorillas at very close range. Along with her "Gorilla Tracking Certificate" issued by the Uganda Wildlife Authority, Pattie proudly displayed in our living room a photograph of a huge silverback she took with a point-and-shoot camera. She had encountered the male gorilla by herself, alone and unguided, almost at arm's length, along a jungle path near our hotel. It was an amazing experience and one that Pattie recounted to friends and others many times. In her published story, Pattie wrote:

> Something's up, and it's not the wind. I grab binoculars to investigate, and camera, in case of whatever. Crossing the road, I start slowly down a faint foot path to glass the trembling leaves. I'm glassing . . . glassing . . . Wow! A gorilla baby! Practically inside the village . . . in the treetops. It's all about being in the right place at the right time! "WAURUMPH!" The guttural warning explodes from the dense foliage, and a silverback catapults into view, a seeming arm's length away. He gallumps across directly in front of me, turning his head to lock eyes.

A sea of poor people and banana plantations and cultivation surround the densely forested uplands of the Bwindi Mountain Gorilla Reserve, portending a shrinking habitat space and an indefinite future for the rare primates. But for now, substantial ecotourism income derived from gorilla viewing ensures a respite from core habitat destruction and illegal hunting.

In Uganda, Pattie and I once again celebrated South Africa's Dr. Friedrich Von Breitenbach's eloquent characterization of Earth's remaining rainforests as "living nature's mightiest manifestations." Writer Willie Oliver said, "Forests can awaken the child in us . . . reawaken memories." The more we explored, the more we believed those characterizations to be true—ancient forests are magical places!

We were fortunate to revel in breathtaking primeval forests in our travels in many parts of the world. They were enchanting with their colorful mushrooms, lichens, mosses, flowers, ferns, lianas, colossal giant towering trees, shadowy daytime darkness on forest floors, and secreted animal denizens—God's creations. Imbued with mystery and wonder, these were places that had remained hidden and apart from modern humanity, economic markets, technology, and gadgets.

But how to convince others of the forest's intrinsic values in view of modern society's unending demands for tropical wood, ever expanding urban areas and forest clearing, and the world's poor people dependent on farming cleared forest areas?

Over the years we discovered guides universally had a never-ending litany of funny excuses. Because of our insistent searching for rare animals, we heard them all. I compiled a list of excuses on the topic of why or why not an animal could or could not be found, or could only be found sometimes:

Feigning disbelief and exclamation: "You see? No, you no see?" followed with: "It is listed in book for tourists—but no can find."

A need for more monetary encouragement: "Maybe find—you pay me first."

Humoring the client: "We saw one here . . . once."

Claiming interfering dangers: "Cannot stop here, elephants crush vehicle," or "Don't like snakes there."

Arguing it was not a scheduled item: "It is not on itinerary."

Being indifferent; giving brush-off: "They are elsewhere now," "Sometimes we see but not now," or "We go look later, maybe."

Avoiding blame: "It is not my fault," "Not want to guarantee we see it," or "Road too dusty to see."

At Bwindi Forest, near the end of the Uganda trip, a frightening event of a different kind occurred: Pattie suddenly unexpectantly experienced a worrisome major swelling of her thyroid. There were no prior symptoms. By chance a medical doctor from California was visiting there, too. He examined Pattie's swollen neck and did not express particular alarm. The swelling thankfully resolved somewhat over the days that followed. Outwardly, Pattie appeared to ignore it. It turned out to be a harbinger of things to come.

Returning to the United States through New Jersey, we both agreed the city of Newark seemed more foreign, dangerous, and alien than any place we had been in Africa. After several days at our Pennsylvania residence to recuperate and regain our energy, we drove back across I-80 to Wyoming. Scenes of Africa played through our minds and in our discussions. It was June 25 when we finally arrived back home in Alta.

CHAPTER 18

THE HELLISH DISEASE REVEALS ITSELF

If you would behold the spirit of death, open your heart wide unto the body of life. For life and death are one, even as the river and the sun are one.

— Kahlil Gibran, *The Prophet*

Within a short time after our return, at the advice of physicians, we anxiously arranged for a biopsy of Pattie's thyroid. The redirection of our lives down a rabbit hole had nightmarishly begun. As poet John Keats expressed, through suffering "the world is the vale of soul-making."

The thyroid biopsy was a difficult and painful procedure. Test result anxiety and apprehension weighed heavily. Huge relief followed when it produced a benign result. Our lives returned to normal. The wildflowers in the Tetons' alpine meadows sang to us once again.

The reprieve was brief, however. A short time later, Pattie discovered a lump in her right breast. Pattie was devoted to having an annual mammogram. But as is often the case, it is not imagery that discovers a small nodule. Pattie had found it herself. A physician we consulted tried to minimize our worry, telling us: "It is probably only a cyst."

A biopsy chillingly diagnosed the small lump not as a cyst, but as a "poorly differentiated, infiltrating, ductal carcinoma, aggressive and invasive, without estrogen receptors." At that point, it was classified as "Stage 1" localized cancer. As it turned out, the absence of estrogen receptors would later limit the options and potential for effective chemotherapy. Typical of the insidiousness of cancer, Pattie exhibited no outward symptoms.

The initial job of informing us of the biopsy results had been assigned to a doctor we did not know. His frightening message, which he delivered by phone in a distant monotone, caused numbing shock. Later, another physician also called us and was more compassionate and concerned. The emotional horsemen of cancer galloped full tilt into our lives: fear, anxiety, guilt, depression, distress.

Statistical reports say half of all men and a third of all women will get cancer in their lifetimes. For breast cancer, 70 percent of those afflicted are women over age 50.

Pattie e-mailed friends: "I returned home from Memphis after my sister's service the night before our flight to Uganda. While we were gone, I started having some problems I attribute to stress and grieving. By the time we returned my body was sprouting tumors."

Confronted with one of the most dreaded of diagnoses, the poetry in our lives was abruptly upended. Cancer and the life-altering consequences it portended—its sinister cruelty and the potentially draconian methods for its treatment—became our focus. Stressing the positive, Pattie wrote to friends that "the good news is they found it early and it's small."

While we did not know it then, we would come to learn that early detection in itself does not necessarily assure a positive treatment outcome, in spite of popular media's message. In the meantime we did our best to be proactive in researching our next steps.

We consulted with doctors and talked with friends and other people who had gone through similar experiences. We became glued to the World Wide Web, researching the topic and the treatment choices. Pattie also had friends in the medical profession, who offered us advice. Filled with sick worry and anxiety, we sensed the gathering of a black storm cloud. It becomes simultaneously wholly unreal and all too real when cancer happens to you or a loved one.

No matter what positive spin the medical and pharmacological community tries to put on it, being pulled into the world of cancer treatment and procedures is a frightening, traumatic and life-changing event. In spite of modern medicine and dedicated physicians and medical professionals, *uncertainty of the outcome rules*. "Transitioning through the course of care," as it is euphemistically called, can be a physically challenging and an emotionally tumultuous experience.

Our storybook life appeared to be over. I confess, I responded with a bout of disagreeable behavior, as if that could have made all the distress go away. Both of us were off the stress charts; we reacted irritably. I angrily and resentfully railed, not against Pattie, but against where I could foresee it was all leading—our once intimate and active lives and lifestyle would be consumed by the constant in-and-out of hospitals, doctor visits, medical procedures and treatments, and the energy- and health-sapping disease itself.

Pattie had the stress from the cancer diagnosis piled on top of mourning her sister's death. I grieved the foreseeable loss of our happy, carefree lifestyle. It was depressing. In my lifetime, up to that point, I never had reason to be in a hospital or even to see a doctor, aside from infrequent routine physicals or checkups, and I recognized that was all about to change.

We went forward into the unavoidable fray like soldiers ordered into battle. There was no other choice. We determinedly trusted and prayed we would prevail. The odds in Pattie's favor were good, thanks to the early detection, our informed treatment decisions, and the fact that Pattie was fit and otherwise healthy, as well as being strong mentally and spiritually. We did everything we knew to do to assure the best outcome. Every step of the way, Pattie researched procedures and drug therapies and continued to consult with various doctors and knowledgeable friends. We approached each decision point believing we were well-informed. I could not conceive of anything other than that Pattie would prevail over the disease.

Pattie wrote: "I am in good hands. Earle's shook but is great to me. I'm determined to beat this." Cards and letters quickly stacked up, along with a flurry of supportive e-mails.

My mother, who was then approaching one hundred years, wrote in a letter: "I just can't believe it . . . I don't often pray for anything, but will now."

Conversely, one of Pattie's relatives was oblivious, and could not understand our worried concern, commenting, "It is a common ailment . . . just a bump in the road." And still another, Pattie's stepmother, told us: "You do not have to worry about it if you have faith in the Lord."

We first consulted with a respectable surgeon in Jackson. He recommended a lumpectomy, but would not consider doing a sentinel node procedure—removal and testing individual nodes closest to the tumor until they test clear. Instead, he proposed to remove all the lymph nodes on the side where the tumor occurred—a separate incision referred to as an axillary lymph node dissection.

We had researched the potential side effects from total lymph node dissection, which alarmingly could include susceptibility to infections, fluid buildup after use or exercise or from atmospheric pressure changes, with possible major permanent swelling. The removal of all lymph nodes would most likely have consigned Pattie to a sedentary lifestyle and possibly unable to do air travel. It was difficult to accept that possibility.

At the Huntsman Cancer Institute in Salt Lake City, we found a young physician who Pattie termed "the best surgeon" for the procedures. The woman was out of town on summer vacation, but we made an appointment for September 5. Huntsman's literature promoting a "team approach" had grabbed Pattie's attention. While I have since read about that actually happening for some at Huntsman, throughout her treatments Pattie would sarcastically joke about her "team of one." We invariably ended up meeting with the physicians on a separate one-on-one basis.

At our first meeting, the surgeon appeared confident and self-assured. She talked about the "barbaric practices" women suffered under male surgeons in the past; and how her hands were small, so she could work with a small incision. Her positive attitude was infectious.

The surgeon recommended a minimally invasive lumpectomy and the sentinel node biopsy procedure, which was what our research had also led us conclude was the state-of-the-art treatment. Our concerns were minimized; it was all positive and upbeat, giving us hope. I think I naively believed, certainly wanted to believe, that surgically removing the tumor meant that the cancer would be gone and Pattie cured. But cancer, I would come to later learn, does not necessarily work that way. It is not so direct and forthright.

We researched statistics and found the overall survival rates for a lumpectomy with chemotherapy and radiation were similar to those of a bilateral mastectomy. We were not aware of a history of cancer in Pattie's family. All this was before testing for the "breast cancer gene," the BRCA 1 and BRCA 2 gene mutations, and before oncogene-designed therapy were generally available. If genetic and additional molecular testing had been available, would it have led us to a different choice of treatment? There is no way to know at this point.

The Huntsman surgeon was also was involved in conducting trial studies on sentinel node procedures. She informed us she had successfully performed a large number of these surgeries. More confidence was inspired. The whole procedure would be an out-patient operation or at most overnight.

I rented a plush studio room for us at the University Medical Center Suites near the hospital on the day Pattie underwent the surgery. When Pattie awoke in the recovery room, the first thing she did was to smile reassuringly at me.

It should be obvious. Pattie was an unusually selfless person, who generally put love, generosity, and the welfare of others, ahead of herself. She made it a point not to burden others. It carried over even when she was undergoing medical treatments and even on her deathbed. Pattie's uncommon altruism deeply impressed people who experienced her gentle selflessness.

After Pattie was recovered from the anesthesia, the surgeon made a grand entrance. Cocky and full of herself, she dramatically announced: "Well, you will have to find some other way to kill yourself because now you are not going die from cancer." I've often since thought of that moment and the surgeon's self-indulgent pronouncement; thinking back now, I feel betrayed.

On August 14, 2006, we celebrated Pattie's birthday at home in Alta with a decorated German chocolate cake and champagne, as always. In a card I had written, "My Dear Love, from sunrise to sunset, may your day be a journey of the imagination and spirit. I love you very much, Pattie. Every year with you has been precious. Here's too many more good years. Happy Birthday!—Earle."

Within days after being back from the hospital, Pattie finished up her Uganda gorilla story. When she submitted the story she included a note to her editor friend:

> I "feel" like she [the surgeon] got the cancer and that my prospects are good, but after reading about chemo-brain, etc., I finished this rough draft Thursday night. Even if I never feel like sending it out, I have my thoughts down for Earle and me to help remember the remarkableness about this trip . . . So say a prayer for me in the coming weeks.

In Uganda, I had kept the most detailed travel journal ever. As Pattie noted above and wrote in her magazine article, the trip had been a remarkable adventure far off any common tourist route. I still have vivid mental images of our time in Uganda. But other than contributing a sidebar about endangered primates to Pattie's story, I have never attempted to publish anything about that trip. With my ongoing worries for Pattie, I was unable to motivate myself to go through the trying process of submitting queries and mustering the concentration necessary for writing.

Shortly after returning from the surgery at Salt Lake City, a friend e-mailed: "Dear Pattie, We have been thinking of you and hope that your surgery went well . . . we caught sight of you biking near town. We were glad to see you out and about." Most people would have come home from the surgery and stress and collapsed in bed for a week. No doubt seeking a calming return to normalcy, Pattie, had gone cycling.

In a one-to-one consultation, the leading breast cancer oncologist at Huntsman told Pattie and me that her chances for a five-year survival without chemotherapy or radiation were 67 percent. But with the addition of both chemo and radiation, it could be improved to 82 percent. Statistically, these were pretty good odds based on the study population. To me the consultation seemed detached and unreal, maybe because I wanted to believe it applied to someone else, perhaps, but please, not my Pattie.

The oncologist urged: "If it was my wife, I'd want her to do the chemo." Pattie determinedly elected to do both chemo and radiation. Termed "adjuvant therapy," the objective was to kill any remaining cancer cells to achieve the best survival odds possible.

Looking back, perhaps we were both wishfully trusting. If only we could have depended on the statistical probability of it actually working. What the oncologist did not tell us, though, was that for an individual there were in reality only two possible outcomes: zero or 100 percent. I never guessed the outcome for Pattie could be anything but 100 percent positive.

At that time, we really did not fully understand that the aggressive nature and pathological threat of different forms of breast cancer can vary greatly. In fact, it was never really explained. We would later learn that "breast cancers" are not all the same. Various forms can differ in their molecular characteristics, treatability, and in the disease's life-threatening nature.

I believe we both incorrectly assumed, too, that if a person survived for five years after treatment, it meant that person had beaten the cancer and were cured. I now know that is not necessarily true either. The cancer can return after five or more years. And there may not be mortality data beyond that common statistical reference point. A person can die from cancer after five years and two days, but still be reported among the sample population's statistical survivors.

Pattie went to a beautician friend and through many tears had the hair-dresser shave off her lifetime shock of beautiful long curly hair. It was a pragmatic approach to not having to contend with clogged drains. Her extraordinarily attractive hair would never again have a chance to achieve its former glory. Pattie began shopping for a wardrobe of stylish and nice looking wigs.

The disease was a deadly intrusion into our lives, but it did not diminish our love and loyalty for one another. To the contrary, it drew us even tighter together. We stood staunchly together hand-in-hand in a type of shared desperation. The psychological and emotional effects were inescapable—fear, apprehension, horrendous stress, irritability, and depression. Life-threatening, the disease and its treatments were a menace to all we enjoyed and loved.

On September 18, 2006, I wrote in a card showing a mysterious scene of the moon rising among clouds: "Once in a Blue Moon, Dearest Pattie, a love comes along like my romance with you. Thank you for thirteen lovely years. Happy Anniversary to My One True Love—Earle"

Pattie's sentimental card showed a boy and girl in vintage clothing sitting together lakeside hugging one another. In it she had written: "To the Fire in My Life, Earle—For all the wonderful memories of yesterday . . . the promise of today . . . and the dreams we share for tomorrow . . . I love you. Happy Anniversary #13. The alchemy of our love will turn 13 into a lucky number! Forever yours, Pattie."

Pattie had added a handwritten Teilhard de Chardin quotation: "Someday, after we have mastered the winds, the waves, the tides and gravity, we shall harness for God the energies of love. Then for the second time in the history of the world, man will have discovered fire."

The chemotherapy the oncologist prescribed was dose-dense

therapy with doxorubicin, which was also known as "red death." "Dose dense" meant a stepped up frequency of drug administration. As dose-dense therapy could result in increased problems with side effects, it was not for everyone. Highly toxic, this was not a new or miracle drug; it had been around for a long time. Alarmingly, the drug's side-effects could include heart damage, liver dysfunction, and bladder damage; other side effects included hair-loss, nausea, and vomiting. And the drug itself was known to *cause* cancer. . . potentially generating metastases.

While in our experience the oncologist's bedside manner and empathy rated near the bottom of the scale, he came highly recommended and was said to be well-respected among his peers. Others we consulted did not contradict his proposed treatment or methods. It worried us though when he could never seem to recall in which breast the cancer had occurred. I've since become more wary, having seen that most physicians try to avoid contradicting one another, regardless.

Once the decision is made to proceed, patients literally place their lives and future well-being in the hands of the medical system and physicians. I absolutely supported Pattie's decision. I kept my ambivalence and any doubts regarding the prescribed chemotherapy to myself. It was a classic "damned if you do and damned if you don't" situation for both of us.

Pattie trustingly entered into the frightening and nightmarish realm of cancer chemotherapy: a world of needles, blood draws, IV drips, scans and imaging, medical procedures, medications with unpronounceable names, distress, stress and fatigue, and unavoidable side-effects. "Therapy" was a benign misnomer for potentially serious and nightmarishly debilitating effects to one's life and to what before cancer and its treatments had been normal being.

When the time came for the drug to be administered, two nurses, like something out of a sci-fi horror show, shockingly entered the room wearing hazmat suits, masks, and goggles.

Doxorubicin was so toxic that they could not risk getting any on themselves. I was told I had to leave. It was heartrending. I did not want Pattie to see how upset I was; I left with tears streaming down my cheeks.

Alone, Pattie suffered the potent drug being intravenously introduced into her system over the course of a three-hour period. I do not believe I would have had the courage myself to have submitted to it. If one endured this kind of punishing treatment, they deserved to be cured.

Not until we showed up, did the drugstore think to check for the anti-nausea medication supposedly ordered five days earlier. But then it turned out, it had actually not been ordered by oncology. Someone had failed to place the order. And no local pharmacies had the drug. When we got home, Pattie was violently ill. The nausea, retching and vomiting occurred not just for a few hours; it was for days. When the anti-nausea medication was finally obtained, it interfered with sleep.

Pattie wrote to a friend: "I really didn't expect to be this sick the first go-around, but I'll know better how to prepare for the next dose. The nurse said the nausea and sickness should pass in a day or two . . . I have to say, it's all surreal and scary."

Pattie was a brave soldier. We were led to believe that the chemo treatments, benignly called "therapy," were the gateway through which one must pass to improve the odds for long-term survival. Determinedly vowing to beat the cancer, Pattie courageously did her part, undergoing the enervating treatments and suffering the ugly side effects. Considering the distress one is put through, a person is forced to trust in the system and that the chemotherapy is actually accomplishing its intended purpose of improving survival time and bettering the odds. Yet one does not know at the time if it is working or not. There really is no way to tell.

One frequently hears the expression "fighting the cancer," but in my opinion, the military metaphors are misnomers. They are rationalizations that distract attention from the destructive treatments. If it were actually possible to "fight," it would all be more understandable. At the time it may seem like a war, but in truth, rather than fighting, one surrenders, giving up control. Cancer patients must endure the loss of control of their lives; submit to the ghastly procedures and treatments; and tolerate the pain, side effects, uncertainty and crushing psychological impacts.

Cancer patients do not "fight." They withstand, they endure, and they try to figure out what to do next. There are things one can do to be proactive, such as appropriate diet, exercise, meditation, research and involvement in decisions, a positive mindset, and prayer. Pattie diligently practiced them all. Ironically, all those strategies are generally considered to be outside of the standard protocol procedures and medical care. Many physicians get uncomfortable or cynical in discussing them.

The metaphor of combat and fighting a battle may be more galvanizing and heroic sounding, but maintaining faith and the will to endure discomfort and pain, fueled with a strong determination or reason to survive become foremost. It is a myth that cancer is a win-lose proposition where the outcome is determined by the patient's attitude and grit. Terminal illness is *not* an opponent you can physically fight and conquer. An implication that a sick person "lost" because they did not "fight" hard enough can be inappropriately associated with that metaphor. Even winners can get sick and die.

Besides Pattie's intense passion for life, I know our love for each other helped power Pattie's spirit and will to endure the therapies and survive the disease. She bravely did whatever was required, or was told was necessary, to beat the cancer. She did her part, and we trusted the medical professionals and system to do theirs. Regardless of the outcomes, Pattie was a winner.

Our lives had taken an abrupt turn from ski slopes, trout streams, and mountain meadows to cancer hospital waiting rooms. There I would observe the unfortunate people who were life-threateningly sick, depressed, physically ravaged, and some barely functional. It was incongruent that Pattie, appearing outwardly healthy, well-dressed, attractive and fit, should have been there. Many times, I disbelievingly blurted out to her, "You don't belong here."

Where other patients would show up at the oncology ward in a depressed and distressed array, Pattie would attractively and stylishly dress for her hospital and doctor visits. It was something she would continue to do throughout all her appointments. I believe, and often said, it worked against her. Because she looked too good, too healthy, doctors and nurses did not take her condition as seriously as they might have otherwise.

For the most part, the oncology nurses were compassionate, capable and professional, and Pattie responded in kind. Smiling and personable, she would keep up a cheerful chit-chat with them and other patients around her. It was as though she took it upon herself to lift everyone's spirit. Pattie for the most part suffered stoically, uncomplainingly through it all. The intravenous injections of the potent chemical continued, once every two weeks for the prescribed five infusions.

The side-effects of violent nausea and vomiting, in spite of medications to counteract it, followed for days after each infusion. I am oversimplifying by not mentioning the other medications and detailed advice given to minimize still other side effects, such as: stress, insomnia, neutropenia, mouth sores, fatigue, hair loss, reddish-colored urine and constipation. The last few days between infusions allowed some near recovery. Pattie would rally, regaining some of her strength, only to repeat the debilitating treatment.

It all weighed heavily on us psychologically. Pattie was determined to get through it, as though climbing to the summit of a challenging mountain or racing to a finish line. Depressed and grieving, I would escape into projects. Pattie, feeling lousy, on edge and irritable, got upset with my withdrawal and what she perceived as my inattention to household chores.

I recall her being uncharacteristically angry, chastising me for "wearing a robe all day that stank and needed washing," or for not "using enough soap to get the grease off of pans" after I had done the cooking. It all sounds trivial now. Contrite, we would both apologize and make efforts to do better. I cannot imagine the fretful difficulties less close couples must go through under similar circumstances.

There was not much respite between completing chemotherapy and reporting to Salt Lake City, where Pattie was to undergo radiation treatments. We moved into a Chase Suites' studio in the city for the duration. Pattie underwent radiation therapy five or six days a week, beginning the last week of November and into mid-January. It was as regular as going to work each day; only Christmas day and Sundays were missed. The radiologist team was competent and conscientious. Unlike chemotherapy, Pattie's radiation treatments, while sometimes fatiguing, proved not to be debilitating. Although there is a chance the radiation treatment itself can cause cancer.

We tried to make the most of our free time in the city—a routine of walking the dog, restaurants, theater, shopping, and working out every day at the University's fitness center. Pattie enjoyed the opportunity to shop and explore the city's different stores.

On top of it all, however, some family members unconsciously or uncaringly seemed to go out of their way to add to the stress and difficulties. We spent Christmas, just the two of us, alone in Salt Lake City. The whole time, we heard nothing from my son and daughter-in-law, who were less than an hour away. Perhaps it was best. They were in the ugly midst of threatening each other with divorce *again*; brandishing threats of divorce, alimony, and child custody outcomes like clubs to punish each other. Meanwhile, they were burning through their finances with attorney fees. They could see no further than their own problems.

The impression our daughter-in-law created for herself at the time was that of a coarse and close-minded drama queen. Suspicious and distrustful of outsiders, she had grown up in a small Mormon community sequestered in an isolated side canyon above Salt Lake Valley. Her uncontained air of religious-based superiority contrasted with her common expressive phrases: "Hell's Belles" and "Bullshit," and remarks that her husband "had been raised without morals." On the occasions when she visited our home, she never left without managing to break something, perhaps purposefully. Pattie's thoughtful, pleasant, and outgoing smiling demeanor triggered the daughter-in-law's base insecurities. She seemed to be hugely threatened by Pattie's attractiveness and intelligence. We did our best, but after our illnesses, we generally tried to avoid her performances when we were required to visit Salt Lake City. There was enough tension in our lives without adding her uncalled for inane and inconsiderate behaviors.

Our stay in Salt Lake City was the first Christmas together that we did not go into the forest and cut a tree to decorate. Pattie's sister, Donna, postal mailed us a small potted rosemary bush shaped into the form of a tree. It became our Christmas tree; we even decorated it. The elaborate decorations at Temple Square were also cheerful reminders of the holiday. But the season's most cherished gift for boosting our spirits was that Pattie gained back her strength day by day. Nearly six months after having fallen into the dark hole, light showed at the end of the tunnel. We were able to breathe freely again.

During this time, we worked on improving our physical conditioning through daily visits to the Utah State University's fitness center. Nearly two months into our daily workouts at the university fitness center, we were both in as good or better physical shape than before the cancer. I had worked up to doing sets of dozens of chin-ups and reps of bench presses with over my body weight. Pattie seemed able to work out on aerobic conditioning machines indefinitely.

Pattie had made friends with her radiation team, taking a potentially negative situation and turning it into something positive, as she always did. They held a party just for her, celebrating the completion of her treatments. I remember this Salt Lake City stay as being a positive one, as we regained hope and put our lives back together again. Pattie had said she was going to beat the cancer, and it appeared she had.

When we arrived back home in Alta in mid-January at night in the dark, the deep snow was not cleared from the driveway, and it was twenty below zero. The local Mormon boy renting our studio apartment above the garage—entrusted with keeping an eye on things—had left the area two days earlier without giving any notice. He had shut the heat completely off in the apartment over the garage. I could hear water running. Pipes had frozen and burst, water was gushing into the ice encrusted garage and pouring through the wall into our house.

CHAPTER 19

THE INDIAN SUMMER OF OUR LIVES

*Each golden day was cherished to the full, for one had the feeling
that each must be the last. Tomorrow it would be winter.*
— Elizabeth Enright, *The Four-Story Mistake*

In the Tetons, autumn generally arrives early. The change of
season is dramatically announced by killing frosts and snow dusting the
mountain summits. Clouds and mists encircle and for days hang over
the mountains. There is a sweet sadness, a melancholy feeling; summer
is over, and winter will soon encase the land in whiteness.

The initial cold snap is generally followed by a dry period with
clear cool nights and sunny days—a time of cobalt-blue skies, cool
but comfortable temperatures, and low-angle and -intensity sunshine
which illuminates the colorful fall foliage making it literally glow. This
beautiful and magical interlude before the final onset of winter is called
Indian summer.

One cannot go through what we had without being changed
forever. More than ever, we recognized and valued the wonderful life
we shared. Knowing it was precious and fragile, we cherished it. We
had a bias for living life as we had known it, a desire for normalcy.
What we returned to was a period in our lives akin to the transient but
sweet glow of Indian summer.

On Valentine's Day, Pattie presented me with a framed picture
showing two shadow figures on a walkway holding hands, over which

she had drawn and colored a heart. Within the heart, she had sketched our names on an arrow and the year, 2009. In the bottom right corner she included a quotation from Wendell Berry's *The Blue Robe*:

> How joyful to be together alone as when we were first joined in our little house by the river long ago, except that now we know each other, as we did not then; and now, instead of two stories fumbling to meet, we belong to one story that the two, joining made. And now we touch each other with the tenderness of mortals, who know themselves.

We settled back into our traditional winter activities: skiing, frequent trips to the fitness center, writing, and for Pattie, yoga. In late winter, we made our accustomed trip to the Lamar Valley in Yellowstone National Park for wolf-watching and visiting friends in Bozeman. In mid-April, we undertook our annual trip across the country to Pennsylvania to enjoy springtime in the deciduous forests and see friends and family back there. Life was good. And it seemed back to normal again.

We dropped down to Memphis, as we regularly did to visit Pattie's family and do all the usual activities there of going to Beal Street for barbeque, seeing the Peabody Hotel ducks, and dining and dancing at the exclusive downtown Summit Club, where Pattie's father was a member.

In crossing the state of Tennessee, we would always stop off at Pattie's Aunt Evelyn's. A feisty, smiling, fun-loving elderly woman, she was a retired school teacher living in Knoxville. The first time we visited Aunt Evelyn, while others were in the living room, she beckoned to me follow her into the kitchen where she produced a bottle of Wild Turkey bourbon. She poured us each a conspiratorial drink, straight up. Soon she motioned me into the kitchen again. This time we each had an ice cream bar.

When we returned to Alta in the first week in June, I arranged for us to take a quick trip to Alaska's Kenai Peninsula to fish for salmon and halibut. This time we rented a small RV in Anchorage, and it worked great for us. We could pull up riverside where salmon were running, and have our accommodations immediately at hand. No hassle with setting up tents, finding camping sites, or motel reservations. And, by good fortune, we had arrived just when the Kenai River sockeye salmon run was at its peak—fish were surging up river in large numbers.

We battled a lot of sockeye salmon. Pattie thrilled to it. When you hooked up with the powerful fish in the Kenai River currents, it became a major struggle. There is photograph in our upstairs wall montage showing Pattie standing on a boulder in hip boots, determinedly braced, her rod heavily bent into an arc from the weight of a struggling wild salmon.

We went out on a Cook Inlet halibut charter near Homer, Alaska. Halibut fishing can be hard work. The depths the fish are at may be up to two-hundred feet or more; the sinker used may weigh five pounds; currents are strong. Just reeling in the line and sinker without a fish is physically demanding. Add a thirty-pound halibut or larger to the end of the line, and it can require an enormous amount of effort and upper body strength.

There are tricks, however, to reduce the amount of heavy lifting. But most fishermen are inclined to be macho. They stand up lifting the full weight with their arms and upper body, cranking away. After a few times of just reeling the line in to rebait, release rock cod, or bring in a heavy, resisting halibut, they generally have had it. Exhausted and aching, they are done and want no more.

Pattie was the smallest person onboard the charter. But she figured out her own method. Laying the heavy rod across the gunnels, and then straddling it, she would crank the reel. Enthusiastically, she caught and brought in more than half of the entire charter's limit of halibut, which included some fairly large fish—thirty pounders. The worn-out contingent of would-be halibut fishermen could only watch. The boat captain dubbed Pattie "Halibut Woman." She proudly relished it. The title made her grin.

CHAPTER 20

EUROPEAN ALPS

The quality of life is determined by its activities.
— Aristotle

I had promised Pattie earlier that I would arrange a special trip to celebrate her being cancer-free and our fourteenth wedding anniversary. Known as the Great Alpine Traverse, it involved sixteen days of hiking across the European Alps through five countries: France, Switzerland, Italy, Austria, and Germany.

Some nights on the Traverse, we would be staying in renowned four-star luxury resort hotels—rooms provided with plush robes and comforters, eating well-prepared cuisine, drinking fine wines—and other times, we would stay in rustic mountain chalets and huts, which for us were pretty comfortable, too. Unlike our previous Spartan-travel when we combined it with work, there would be guides speaking several languages leading the way and schlepping our luggage. We would be hiking every day, sometimes long distances with strenuous mountain crossings, but carrying only light day packs. There was no steamy jungle or off-the-map arctic tundra, just glorious alpine surroundings and historic mountain villages, and all very civilized.

Pine Creek served as an East Coast jumping off point for many of our trips. Driving there earlier in autumn than usual, we arranged a one-way car rental. Dropping the car off at Newark's International Airport, we then flew to Chamonix, France, on September 4, 2007. Charles Dickens once responded to Chamonix by noting that "he could not imagine anything more stupendous or sublime."

Our trip was straight out of the Swiss tale, *Heidi: Girl of the Alps*. Like Pattie did in her first encounters years earlier with the high-elevation grandeur in the Teton Mountains, she elatedly twirled around, arms raised in the glorious alpine settings, while singing the lyrics from the theme song of *Sound of Music*: "The hills are alive with the sound of music . . ." We both felt elated and on an emotional high with having our lives back. We witnessed spectacular Monte Blanc, the Matterhorn, the Engadine Valley, the luxury of the Glacier Express train, impossibly grand and elegant four-and five star hotels, and much more, too.

Over the course of the two-week trip, several happenings were stand outs. We discovered a local harvest festival in Austria's Hinterthal near Maria Alm, which Pattie referred to in a published story as her "favorite trip experience." She wrote: "I saw Heidi's fair beauty; I saw Heidi's grandfather handcrafting wooden shingles. I ate pretzels and plum tarts." And me, I drank Bavarian beer served in large schooners served by blonde Heidi look-a-likes, after all of which, we had to stagger several miles back across the mountains on foot, and ride the tram down to the village where we were staying.

On another adventure, we hiked from one side of two glacier-filled mountain valleys in the Bernina Range to the intimidatingly faraway other side. We crossed the two glaciers, the Morteratsch and Pers, with a local mountain guide in the lead. Our destination, the Berghaus Diavolezza lodge, was perched on a far rock summit, barely visible in the distance. Binoculars were required to see it.

Half of our party opted out. Pattie nervously elected to do the hike. I followed her lead. For hardcore mountaineers, this traverse would have represented a walk in the park. But for Pattie under the circumstances, this hike represented a validation of her cancer free recovery. If she could accomplish this challenge, certainly it would confirm she was strong and healthy.

Our guide circumvented crevasses, led us across swiftly flowing streams on the glacier's surface, and at places cut steps for us with his ice ax. Crossing the loose moraine rock rubble when getting on and off the glaciers was even more hazardous, as was the final ascent up very steep terrain and the face of the unconsolidated lateral moraine to Berghaus Diavolezza. Pattie's determined completion of the glacier crossing was a deeply emotional experience for her and everyone. Her arrival at Diavolezza was celebrated with hugs and joyful tears from other members of the group.

On September 18, our anniversary and the final day of the trip, we were in Salzburg, Austria. In the evening, we attended the awesome and ancient Baroque Hall of St. Peter's, an 800 A.D. medieval monastery transformed into a dining hall and entertaining venue. Between dinner courses, the Amadeus Consort, Salzburg's acclaimed musicians and singers, performed the timeless music of Mozart, dressed in period costumes in the romantically elegant and historic setting.

Unknown to us, our guide had informed the musicians that it was our anniversary. Thereafter, for the rest of the evening as Pattie and I sat close to each other—smiling, holding hands beneath the table, glancing over to meet each other's eyes—every performer proceeded to announce they were dedicating their song to us in honor of our anniversary.

Along with toasts of fine wine, a special chocolate dessert was decorated and dedicated to us, too. It all went beyond starry-eyed; it was a once in a lifetime experience by any standard. It was an extraordinary tribute and celebration to us, contributing more sealant to our already deep and tight bonding. The memory of that evening would resonate in our minds forever.

I provided the photography and Pattie the narrative for a beautiful piece about the Alps and our experiences. Published in *Teton Valley Magazine,* Pattie entitled it "The Great Alpine Traverse":

> Weave together these vignettes: sundown's flamingo-winged alpenglow in Maria Alm; dawn's chilled golds at sunrise in Diavolezza; forests of larch and spruce and mountains of auguilles, their needles of granite piercing the

underbelly of heaven. Imagine fantastic fromage at every meal, cheeses synonymous with 'smile.' Every home, every store has flower boxes . . . perfection in each petal of every flower.

When we had returned to Alta, Old Blue had a birthday: twenty-one years old with three-hundred thousand miles. We remorsefully traded Blue for a new 2009 Tacoma pickup through President Obama's "Cash for Clunkers" program, supposedly designed to help stimulate the economy. Old Blue was consigned to the crusher. Although the truck's body was rusted through at places, it was still running strong. I still feel a great deal of remorse over Old Blue going to the crusher. There were so many wonderful memories associated with the old truck.

In Pattie's 60th birthday card, I had written:

To Pattie My Love—Wishing you a walk in the forest and a whiff of wild flowers . . . something for your soul. Our love abides now and forever. This is a special birthday, an age you enter with grace and beauty, which is so much who you are. Thank you for being you. Happy Birthday! I Love You.

Pattie had frequent scheduled checkups by her surgeon and the oncologist. They performed visual observations and manual physical tests for tumor recurrence. We were relieved each time, believing everything was always okay. What did not occur to us, and inconceivably apparently did not to the physicians or the head oncology nurse either, but certainly should have, was to conduct scans.

We found out after the fact several years later that scanning had actually been recommended in Pattie's charts, but was never followed up in our doctor visits. Apparently the oncologist or head nurse never read the chart notes. Either that or they simply failed to follow procedure. Pattie always said, she "fell through the cracks." Whether earlier detection of metastases would have changed the eventual outcome there is no way to know.

In addition to Pattie's regular cancer treatment follow ups, she had become insistent that we both have annual medical checkups—health fair blood profiles, the family doctor physical, and checkups for her with the gynecologist—all standard stuff, recommended practice, certainly nothing unreasonable or new.

For a number of years, I had been reporting annually to a local family practitioner. When asked the routine questions about whether I had any health issues, we went through a cursory checklist discussion. Perennially, I voiced concern over a frequent and sometimes urgent need to urinate. The physician every year immediately attributed it to prostatitis. But then, a follow-up prostate exam and PSA test would invariably contradict that diagnosis with "normal" results. The doctor would smile, and sidestepping the puzzling issue, invariably say: "It is age related; you're just getting older."

And, of course, I was relieved to be blissfully sent on my way with the usual feel-good complimentary remarks about my excellent health. It never occurred to me at the time to be tested for an infection or other possible reasons for my symptoms, nor apparently did it occur to the doctor either. It was another case of inadequate attention by a physician because the patient appeared healthy, as compared to if I had looked unwell or had a history of serious illness.

I continued to cope with having to go frequently by regulating my intake of liquids, especially diuretics like coffee and beer, and by making preemptive trips to bathrooms. I rarely let a chance at a urinal go by unused—no more than a small inconvenience.

For Pattie's 2010 birthday, in a card depicting a back-lighted bull moose on a frosty autumn morning, I had written: "To my love and lover—May you blaze a trail into a grand and glorious year! Happy Birthday—May it be among the best of years! With all my love. — Earle."

CHAPTER 21

GRAND CANYON

We are now ready to start on our way down the Great Unknown . . . We have an unknown distance yet to run; an unknown river to explore.
— John Wesley Powell, 1869

In September 2010, I arranged for us to participate in a commercial raft trip through the Grand Canyon of the Colorado River from Lee's Ferry to Lake Mead—279 miles, 162 major rapids!

The guides and people in our group were great—enthusiastic without any complainers. We hiked spectacular side canyons, observed the incredible geological formations, spotted wildlife, photographed each other and the ageless canyon scenery, and played at the various river stops. After daily checking of our bedding for the ubiquitous scorpions, we slept comfortably on cots in tents or under the stars on the sandy beaches.

Pattie and I appeared healthy, among the strongest and fittest in the group. Everyone enjoyed Pattie's adventurous and pleasant sociable nature. In going through the tremendous rolling whitewater, such as renowned Lava Falls and Crystal Rapids, Pattie would crawl out onto the pontoon outrigger and lie there clutching it, exposed to the sensations of whitewater spray and adrenaline washing over her. *Carpe diem*!

When we returned home, Pattie published a story accompanied by my photographs about the experience, entitling it: Shining Waters,

Ancient Stone: Downriver in the Grand Canyon —

> North America has other canyons. Gouged by the Snake River's whitewater, Hell's Canyon is deeper. Mexico's Copper Canyon is longer. Still. Canyon country scribe Edward Abbey found those who love the Grand Canyon address it as "the canyon"—as if there were no other comparable feature on the face of the earth. . . .

It would turn out to be our last travel story. What we did not know, nor could anyone at the time have guessed, since we both seemed vigorous and healthy, was that cancer was silently and insidiously growing inside both of us. For our lives, the "golden days" of Indian summer were drawing to a close. Soon winter's onslaught and darkness would arrive.

CHAPTER 22

DEATH IN THE FAMILY AND ANOTHER CANCER DIAGNOSIS

Being deeply loved by someone gives you strength, while loving someone deeply gives you courage.
— Lao Tzu

In late October 2010, shortly after our Grand Canyon trip, and after my autumn ritual of elk hunting and firewood gathering, we repeated our customary drive across country to touch base with the autumn hues of Pennsylvania forests, and to visit our Eastern friends and my elderly mother.

The farmstead in Pennsylvania was a great place to entertain. We encouraged family and friends to visit us there. Pattie had taken over my mother's tradition of baking apple pies and had developed her own special recipe for the wild cranberries we picked. Honoring a family tradition, Pattie always roasted a turkey in autumn while we were there, too.

In the warm autumn, we sat on the open porch and indulged ourselves with Grandma Utz's old-fashioned hard pretzels, Pennsylvania Dutch extra-sharp wheel cheese, and Yuengling Lager, from the oldest brewery in the United States. The brewery dated back to 1829. We hiked in the mountains where the trails were deeply covered by fallen leaves, cycled the scenic sixty-five-mile Rail Trail, and connected with family. It was an opportunity for Pattie and me to spend enjoyable quiet time with each other. Our lives happily seemed to have returned to usual, something we all seek after life-threatening events.

Over the years, when we felt like it, we had also made road trips to nearby Eastern attractions: designated Natural Areas; James Fennimore Cooper's workplace at Cooperstown, New York, on Otsego Lake; the Bond House in historic Philadelphia; Cape May, New Jersey's beachfront and historic district; the wineries in New York State's Finger Lake region; and the cherry blossoms at the National Monument in Washington, DC.

On one such excursion, we hopped a flight to Chicago. I wanted to visit the Field Museum and see their taxidermal rendering of the notorious Tsavo man-eating lion. The man-eating lions gained notoriety during the building of the Uganda-Mombasa railway in 1898. The story was made into a Hollywood movie in 1996, *The Ghost and the Darkness*. Pattie had in mind to visit Macy's flagship store on State Street, a National Historic Landmark. She somehow knew about the store's famous Walnut Room, the longest continuous running restaurant in the country. I think she may have read about it in a novel. Most all she wanted to experience one of their famous chocolate martinis served with an edible orchid. We also attended a musical production at the Ford Oriental Theater. Built in 1926, it boasts a lavish massive domed ceiling ringed with ornate sculpted seahorses and goddesses.

On October 9, we received word that Pattie's father had passed away at age 87. It was not unexpected; he had been ill for some time. But it was a sad blow nevertheless. We arranged to fly to Memphis at once.

Pattie had been close to her mother, Carolyn, who had deceased before Pattie and I met. Separated by distant locations, her father and stepmother had still been a part of our lives for all our years together. Pattie's father had been supportive of our marriage, and although it was foreign to him, our lifestyle, too.

Pattie's family name was Bell, and while she was reluctant to speak of it, her pedigree went back to the earliest settlement of Virginia,

Tennessee, Missouri, and Arkansas. Her linage was peppered with an impressive array of relatives who served as members of those state's territorial governments, as Indian fighters and trail blazers, veterans of the Revolutionary War and the war of 1812, state governors, congressmen and senators. Her father had been a tail-gunner in WWII and a prominent Memphis attorney. Her great-grandfather and grandfather had laid out the streets for sections of the city of Memphis.

I was among the pallbearers at the funeral. Pattie's father, in a traditional graveside service, was buried next to his first wife and children's mother in Memphis's large and historic Memorial Park Cemetery.

That same autumn, a nephew in Pennsylvania, who had become a good friend, was killed in a vehicle rollover on a mountain road. Then the person who had been my best friend in high school lost a long battle to cancer. All three of Pattie's aunts passed within relatively short time. Pattie's older sister was gone already. My father and three of my half-siblings had also departed, and my mother although still living, was 104 years old. Pattie and I both had entered a stage in life that was marked by staggerring loss and mourning. The graves of deceased parents, relatives, and friends lined the waysides of our consciousness.

After our return to Pine Creek from the Memphis services, on a mid-November morning, we were on a strenuous hike beginning from the valley floor and following up a steep ridge toward the mountain top. Approaching the upper part of the mountain, Pattie was trailing close behind me, when a whitetail buck stood up from where it had been lying hidden in dense laurel only thirty feet away.

The regally antlered animal and I looked at each other for what seemed like a long time. The buck did not show fear. It finally stalked away into the evergreen laurel thicket, moving very deliberately and stiff-legged. It was the messenger for what came next.

I had one of my commanding urges to pee. Instead of the expected yellow stream, like a ghastly horror show, there was a startling gush of blood and blood clots. Both Pattie and I were shaken. In pulse-pounding shock, we headed off the mountain.

The images remain vivid in my mind. It was the opening scene for what would become a continuing and horrendous change to our lives; a time and place underscoring the beginning of a total change in the exceptional lifestyle we had enjoyed and treasured. I can still point to the exact spot on the mountain where it happened. It is the place where our world began crumbling down around us.

It was a Friday afternoon. Try to see a medical specialist when you are from out of town and without an appointment on a Friday afternoon. Reluctant to go to a hospital emergency room, we called an old schoolmate and friend, who was retired from the medical community and whose wife was a significant force on the local hospital foundation board. They in turn called a urologist they knew socially; then they called back to inform us that the doctor had agreed to see me if we could be at his office before closing time.

With pulses racing, we were out the door and into the car immediately. It was a fifty-mile drive to the urologist's office, part of it on a narrow winding mountain road. A crowded waiting room greeted us. It was filled with despondent people who, by all appearances, were seeking relief from insufferable maladies. After the usual filling out of insurance forms and other questionnaires, I was surprised to be ushered directly into an operating room.

An overworked urologist with a professional air of no-nonsense about him showed up just as quickly. Without introductions, I was questioned in a rapid-fire manner about my symptoms. A nurse prepared me for a cystoscopy.

Magnified full-color images of the inside of my bladder appeared projected real time onto a large monitor screen. Even to my untrained eye, I could see the inside of my bladder was an abnormal mess. Riddled with tumors, the bladder wall was leaking blood at places.

"Cancer?" I asked, already knowing the answer. "Yes," was the dreaded confirmation, "urothelial cancer." The urologist cauterized some of the bleeding places, randomly clipped off some tumors, and installed a catheter. The nurse assisted with attaching a leg bag. It all seemed dreamlike and unreal.

The urologist's dire diagnosis was that the cancer was not confined to the bladder, but that it had spread into adjacent tissue and organs—a deadly condition. I naively questioned him what my chances for survival were, hoping for some positive assurance. He replied, "Fifty-fifty," a non-committal answer that further underscored the seriousness of my condition. A long pause, then in an offhand manner, he drove the coffin nail: "You've had a good run."

The physician asked me for a name of a hospital for him to make a referral. Some names of renowned East Coast cancer hospitals came to mind, but I hesitated until we could research them. Impatiently, he wrote out a referral to Hershey Regional Medical Center in Pennsylvania.

Pattie had been left alone in the waiting room. She was worried sick. Not wanting to frighten her, I tried calmly to explain what had taken place. She was shook; we both were. I remember the nightmare-like ride down the elevator, both of us in trance-like shock, with me about to throw-up. I hobbled to the car, the catheter and leg bag restricting my ability to walk. Benji was waiting for us, tail-wagging. Pattie had to drive, my leg bag prevented me.

It was Friday evening. We began anxiously and urgently researching bladder cancer and cancer hospitals: M.D. Anderson in Manhattan, Sloan-Kettering in Philadelphia, and the University of Cincinnati's Center for Bladder Cancer. Both of us were exhausted, but sleep was impossible. Bladder cancer it turns out is the fifth most common cancer in the United States.

In the morning, it being the weekend, no one answered the phones at any of the major institutions we called. Our urgency and desperation was maddeningly met with inane and impersonal recorded messages: Press one for . . . press two for . . . to leave a message press . . . . . If you are dying, please leave a message.

We called the Huntsman Cancer Institute in Salt Lake City where Pattie had received her treatments—surprise! A real person actually answered. In the interval, we had had a while to think about the difficulties and time required even to obtain an appointment at one of the big name institutions; also the intimidating logistics of moving into temporary quarters in the strange surroundings of a major city, which most certainly would be required for an indeterminate time during treatments; and, the travel logistics for follow-up visits. And, what would we do with Benji?

It was a seemingly impossible situation, nerve-wracking and frightening. Emergency lights were flashing in our minds; sirens going off to man battle stations. Time was of the essence. But regardless of the panicky urgency and the pumping adrenaline and anxiety we felt, it all seemed stressfully beyond our control.

Calling the Huntsman Institute again the next day, we were amazed when the person answering remembered our name. That cinched it. We were already familiar with Huntsman and Salt Lake City from Pattie's treatments there. It was readily manageable for us, which was an important consideration.

We were given an appointment to see an urologist in two days; or better yet, as soon as we could get there. I called my older son. A pilot for American Airlines, he called the Chief Pilot, who arranged for emergency seating for us on a flight from Rochester, New York, through Chicago, and arriving in Salt Lake City. It was stress relieving not to have to make those arrangements ourselves on short notice under the circumstances.

We left Benji with a neighbor friend; drove four hours to Rochester, New York; left our vehicle in airport parking; and boarded the flight with my catheter and leg bag flopping uncomfortably at every step. On the plane, I discovered that in the rush and confusion, I had put my pants on backwards. Within hours we were in Salt Lake City, where we checked into the now all too familiar Chase Suites.

Cancer is the plague of the twenty-first century. And, in spite of a supposedly enlightened society, it still has underlying social stigma. I felt like we were the equivalent of modern day untouchables. Where had our cancers come from? Both of us sickened in spite of healthy lifestyles and model diets. Was it luck of the draw, genetics, radiation leakage from the nearby Idaho National Energy Laboratory, pesticides applied in Teton Valley farming? Secondhand smoke? No way to know. The Pennsylvania urologist had said I must have been "exposed to something." But what and where?

A day later, after an initial consultation with the Huntsman urologist, I was scheduled for a pre-operative assessment. Put under anesthesia, I remember neither awaking from the procedure at the hospital, nor the trip back to the hotel. I only recall afterward lying on the couch in the hotel room and that my son and Pattie were there. Another catheter had been installed. The pain from whatever procedures had been done was intense; a deep raw visceral hurt, the kind of pain one never forgets. Without pain medication, I flopped around uncomfortably on the couch gasping for each breath, trying not to groan aloud.

The next day, we limped back to the hospital to learn the results. A relaxed smiling physician's assistant greeted us, saying: "First, the good news is we do not agree with the Pennsylvania urologist's assessment. Our determination is that the cancer appears to be confined to within the bladder."

Learning the cancer was contained within the bladder, and that it had not spread into surrounding tissues or organs, was hugely significant. It was an immediate relief. It meant I had a fair chance to accrue some more birthdays.

Pattie and my son were present when my two treatment options were offered up:

One: A type of immunotherapy, wherein a solution of *Bacillus Calmette-Guérin* (BCG) would be injected through a catheter into the bladder, starting with once a week for six weeks and progressing with variable schedules continuing over a two-year period.

"Two years?" I questioned.

It is a treatment generally reserved for *early* bladder cancer. Combined with surgically removing the tumors, it is intended to *slow* the cancer's growth and reoccurrence. And it has its list of side-effects, of course. The patient's life necessarily becomes tethered to the hospital and procedure schedules. If it does not work one is back to having no choice but a cystectomy.

<u>Two</u>: Radical cystectomy. My bladder, prostrate, and lymph nodes would be surgically removed. My plumbing would be rearranged by an ileal conduit, a urinary diversion and stoma created from a segment taken from my small intestine. Removal of an organ like the bladder is major. The surgery comes with a host of side effects and serious risks.

Over the course of several discussions with the surgeon, who ducked and dodged questions and minimized my concerns, it was obvious he favored the cystectomy. Further conversations revealed that his last patient had died after electing the BCG treatment. The patient's cancer had metastasized and spread aggressively in spite of the immunotherapy treatment.

A physician assistant told us, the radical cystectomy would allow me to "get out in front of the cancer." Bladder cancer has high reoccurrence rates. Life is full of choices, but it appeared that if I wanted the best chance for any longer-term survival, I had only one disagreeable alternative. I was advised that because I was in good health and physically fit the odds were in my favor to withstand and recover from the operation.

In retrospect, I recognize that my resolution and strong desire to survive came from my love for Pattie. I did not want to leave her alone, nor cause her more grief. I loved her and our life together; I was not ready to give it up. She, along with all we enjoyed together, made my life meaningful and gave me courage and strength. Together we were a force, we could beat this. But it wasn't going to be free of difficulty. As poet John Keats penned, "It surprised me that the human heart is capable of containing and bearing so much misery." Keats was referring to the emotional impact of his terminal condition and his simultaneous deep affection for a young woman.

The day for the surgery began early. I do not recall much after being given a sedative that put me on the edge of going under. I remember a physician's assistant telling me to bend forward to facilitate his doing a nerve block, and feeling a crunch as something was inserted into my back or spine. After that, nothing.

I awoke over ten hours later in a hospital room bed. Pattie was standing over me holding my hand, looking distraught and tired from worry. My son, Brett, grinned at me from the bottom of the bed. Pattie had sat outside the operating room for the entire ten-hour surgery getting updates. She had trailed along behind as they had wheeled me down the hallways and elevators from the recovery room to the hospital room.

I had been split open from belly button to sternum; two different drains were embedded in me. I could hardly move or feel my arms, they had been restrained in a crucifix position, apparently for the entire procedure; the corneas of my eyes were scratched from my rubbing them at some point. I could not feel my legs below my knees or my feet from the resulting neuropathy. This peripheral nerve damage has never fully resolved, leaving me with a tendency to stumble clumsily at times. And later, I would have to deal with a hernia. The athletic body I had cultivated as part of my identity and lifestyle was gone, forever changed and misshaped. But I was conscious; I was still alive.

The surgeon made a grand entrance into the room. The first thing he said was: "You are going to have to find some other way to kill yourself now because it won't be cancer." The exact same pronouncement Pattie's surgeon had made after her surgery? Grinning, he added, "I liked operating on you; you have good tissue." Was that a leer, not a grin?

I am certain the surgeon must have had compassionate things to say, too, but I cannot recall them. I suppose, surgeons must be able to divorce themselves from the idea that the patient they are working on is a person and only pay attention to the exacting procedures. There is a never ending progression of patients to deal with.

Exquisite pain like electrical jolts arrived as the spinal block began wearing off. I was attached to a morphine drip. Having spent ten hours in surgery, I would spend the next ten days in the hospital. If one must be in a hospital, it would be difficult to find a more modern, clean, and up-to-date facility than Huntsman. The back of my large private room was all glass. The expansive window looked out on the Wasatch mountainside, where I could watch deer and trail runners go by. But it was still a hospital, an institution. Hospitals, I learned are not restful places.

Pattie and Benji stayed in the hospital room with me the entire time, except for Benji needing to go out for his routine. Pattie slept on a hard futon. Every two hours during the night, interns, nurses, and attendants made the rounds to check on me, measure vital signs, take data, and administer medications.

Benji would not get up, but would growl at the constant intrusions. Pattie was also awakened every time. It was hugely exhausting and stressful for her. Stubbornly adamant about her role as my advocate and guardian, she would not consider leaving me there alone.

When I was able to get out of bed, we were told I must walk laps around the circular hallway perimeter, at least a half-dozen rounds or more every day. There was a chalkboard hanging on the wall at the doorway for me to keep score of the number of times.

We went on pretend hikes doing twenty laps or so—very slowly of course—going up and down the elevator, using both floors, pretending to vary elevation and terrain. Benji stayed tight at heel, with me pushing the wheeled stand, on which all my bags, pouches, IVs, and tubing were hung. A smiling Pattie socialized and conversed with me, the nurses, and other patients. When the nurse checked our walking tally, she was disbelieving and annoyed. It amused us that the nurse thought we were fudging the numbers.

A strange side effect of the surgery was that my bowels "went to sleep." Oddly, they had shut down. Who ever heard of that? That meant for about a week I did not have a bowel movement, even though my appetite returned somewhat and I ate nearly full meals. Where did it all go?

I was informed I would not be released from the hospital until I had a bowel movement. As if I could control it. Around day eight, things started to wake up. It began as a disgusting foul green ooze over which I had no control. In addition, my body was producing large amounts of strong-smelling gooey mucus through my stoma.

I was a repulsive, filthy mess—untouchable. Trying to bathe with all the connective tubing and not get my incisions wet was a problem. Pattie had already gone the extra mile. I did not want her to suffer from this indignity, too. I was enough to nauseate almost anyone, and I didn't want her to associate that with me.

A young black nurse offered to help. I do not think she was American. Enrolled in a type of nurse study program, her name was Angel. She really was an angel; she caringly helped to clean me up. Over the years since, I have frequently recalled her kindness. I thanked her profusely, although, it was hardly enough.

Midway through the hospital stay, Pattie began complaining about her back hurting. We attributed it to stress and her sleeping on the hard futon, or at least I did. Pattie would tell the doctors and interns about her excruciating back pain. They would listen politely, expressionless, then recommend she make an appointment to see a specialist. None offered to help; she was not, after all, a registered patient.

We did not know it then, but would learn all too soon, back pain can be a symptom of cancer metastases. Three different people we knew, who later died from cancer, had their symptoms begin initially with pain in their lower back, metastases on the spine.

Finally, I was released from the hospital, but we did not go far.

We returned to a studio at Chase Suites. I was neither confident nor strong enough in my condition to travel. We were afraid not to stay close to the hospital and doctors. A nurse came to our hotel room each day to check on my condition; administer necessary tests, medications, and bandaging; and assist in managing my urostomy. The stoma was a foreign and scary new part of my anatomy, which without warning, periodically spat out a stream of yellow mucus-filled fluid.

We stayed at Chase Suites for a few weeks after my hospital release, tethered to the hospital and nearby medical assistance. We made plans to check out on Christmas Day—a holiday gift to ourselves, we said.

There was a feeling of relief and anticipation to be going home, to return to our lives and all we cherished. I resembled the grievously wounded soldier returning home from the war. The weeks of stress had taken a toll on Pattie, and she was exhausted. Less than midway into the five or six-hour drive with winter road conditions, Pattie struggled to stay awake and finally had to pull over to nap.

When we reached Sugar City, Idaho, only forty miles from Alta, Pattie had to stop to rest again. We pulled into the empty grocery store parking lot. No one was around on Christmas Day. We were sitting in the car in the empty lot dozing, when a police car rolled up. The officer came over and asked what we were doing? Benji greeted the policeman, wagging his tail. Pattie explained. The officer looked dismayed. We were in a pathetic state of affairs for Christmas Day.

Shortly afterward, we were underway again on the snow-packed highway. And, soon we were walking across our Alta threshold, the same one that I had happily carried Pattie across on our wedding day years earlier. Not only were we thrilled to be home again, we felt relieved and grateful to be back in a familiar and safe place—a place we associated with happy and loving times. We had been gone nearly three months.

Our house remained just the way we had left it in October. Friends had looked out for it, shoveling snow, watering plants, and regulating the heat. Pattie and I were recognizable as the same persons who had lived there before; but, in reality, we were no longer the same. Apprehension, nervous anxiety, depression, tension and uncertainty were unwanted house guests that had inescapably followed us home.

Before my cancer diagnosis, we had made plans and arrangements to travel to Chile and Argentina that January—Patagonia and the Straits of Tierra del Fuego. I had paid a trip deposit. The trip along with our former lifestyle had come to a crashing end with my cancer. Our international travel plans were canceled, never to be revived. Journal pages left forever blank.

Changes had come rapidly and unexpected, altering our lives forever. The health and attendant psychological impacts would be continuing challenges. The medical challenges both of us had been through had taken a toll, both physically and psychologically. I felt as if I had been taken to the edge of death's doorway. Our spirits were battered, but despite it all, we clung steadily to our love for each another. Shared stress and problem solving can work to draw some couples closer—a type of "spirit creation." More than anything, love gave us strength. What made me want to go on living was Pattie.

CHAPTER 23

RECOVERY

But in a war, sometimes just by staying alive, you win a victory. You come home bleeding; your arms and legs are broken, your head wounded. But you are still alive. You reach your home, and you have a chance to recover.

— Paul Coelho, *The Pilgrimage*

Pattie had somehow found the above quote from *Pilgrimage* and without saying anything, had taped it to my computer monitor, a reminder to persevere. Perhaps someone had given her that same quote after finally returning home from her near-death experience from a ruptured cerebral aneurism and surgery when she was twenty-five years old. I don't know.

In Alta, a home-care nurse came by each day to check my vital signs and blood-thinner levels, and to assist attending to my strange new anatomy, the stoma. I was unable to do much. Pattie had a full-time job taking care of me and pretty much everything else.

Thinking back, I remember her anxious and worried looks, but also her loving attention, smiles, and encouragement, too. Friends would stop by to visit, reminisce, shovel snow and generally help us out. I would either lie down or sit up on the couch while we talked.

As the physical healing of my wounds progressed, we again incorporated a routine of going to the fitness center—simple physical therapy for me, anaerobic stress-relieving workouts for Pattie.

Looking out our window at the Grand Teton and snow-covered

landscape, I grieved for our past lives and lifestyle. Our wintertime activity of downhill skiing was impossibly beyond my capability. Walking on snow, I shuffled along using ice-creepers attached to my boots. For the first time in my life, I tasted the disagreeable condition of physical incapacity and nagging depression.

My confidence in my body was destroyed. I felt vulnerable, weak and fragile. I had to hire high school boys to do regular winter chores. I was unable to perform simple physical tasks, such as shoveling the snow off our driveway and the back porch, or splitting firewood.

At the hospital in Salt Lake City, I had tried to learn what might realistically be physically possible or advisable for me post-surgery. I had read a brochure that proposed that people who had undergone my surgery be legally classified as handicapped. It did not help my confidence.

Wide-eyed hospital staff told us about people they knew who had undergone my surgical procedure and were able to walk a mile or even swim. They repeatedly told us of a person who amazed them by scuba diving. These were sedentary activities compared to what we were used to doing. Of course, many of the hospital staff and nurses had no idea; they were sedentary themselves, unable to imagine the active lifestyle Pattie and I had enjoyed.

What the doctors and hospital staff failed to consider or avoided dealing with is that healing from such horrendous surgery involved more than just the physical wounds; there was a huge psychological component, too. Post-surgery psychological issues included the patient's need to reconcile with a new physical self— something I struggled to do without the benefit of counseling. What should I realistically expect my post-surgical physical capabilities to be?

We attended a fund raiser for columnist and wildlife enthusiast Bert Raynes' Pika Foundation in Jackson, where a couple of my pika photographs were on display and *Green Fire: Stories from the Wild*, my book containing a pika story, was being sold. We bumped into a concerned acquaintance there who told us her father had undergone the same surgery as me. She told us that "he came home and sat down in his chair and pretty much never got up again." It was not an uplifting story.

My valentine to Pattie on February 14, 2010, showed an Argentine couple embraced in a sultry tango. Inside I had written: "To Pattie—My Valentine—I love you with all my heart . . . Happy Valentine's Day!"—Earle." It was a close as we ever got to our planned South America trip to Patagonia.

Pattie bolstered my spirit with her elaborate valentine: a unique folded flower, with flowers and verses on one side and my picture framed in a heart-shaped wreath of roses. On the reverse side she had written: "Welcome Home 2 Loving & Being Loved! With you, my love blossoms every day. All my love 4-Ever! Happy Valentine's Day, Earle! xoxo Always, Pattie."

In March, over three months post-surgery, two of Pattie's women friends invited us on a cross-country ski tour. I often wondered if Pattie had cleverly suggested it to them to get me outside. Whether it was necessary or not, I took the precaution of wearing a four-inch wide ostomy belt to hold my new anatomy together. Amid familiar surroundings of crisp winter air and deep unbroken powder snow, we skied for miles up South Leigh Canyon, then followed what had once been a logging spur road to a far ridge in the forest.

Thankfully, our friends did not hold back, go slow, or think to show sympathy. The exhilaration of being outdoors again, coupled with my ability to keep up, was restorative. Being outside and actually able to ski was a physical and emotional turning point in my recovery.

In mid-April, we made our annual cross-country drive on I-80 to Pine Creek. A true test of compatibility, three days on the highway, coming and going, may seem interminable to some, but Pattie and I made it a fun time together. We talked, picnicked, and took walks at rest stops. Forested with old-growth burr oak, some of the rest stops in the Midwest are lovely. We had our preferred places where we had regularly stopped to overnight. Each time we did this long trip over the years, we turned it into an adventure.

I do not recall any disagreements ever arising during our close confinement on the road. We discussed whatever came to mind; we joked and laughed. Sometimes we played books on tape and dissected them. Other times, we made short stops at attractions or historic sites to break up the driving, including Buffalo Bill Cody's birthplace in Le Claire, Iowa; the Cody ranch in North Platte, Nebraska; the National Homestead Monument in Beatrice, Nebraska; and, Cozad, Nebraska, where the famous American artist, Robert Henri, was born. Previously, over the years, we had written and published stories about those places, after Pattie first got the idea to write about the town of Cozad and Robert Henri. I often joked that we could have written a guidebook for I-80.

This time when we arrived at our Pine Creek home, the water system was not functioning. The intake at the spring house was plugged. The spring was nearly a hundred yards from the house, up a significant hill through thick and brushy vegetation. I hired a neighbor friend who did handyman work to crawl into the springhouse. Wearing hip boots, he replaced the intake. It was accomplished at night in the dark with me holding flashlights to illuminate the job.

I had to go up and down the hill to the house a half-dozen times to get one tool or another and to test the water flow. It may not sound like much, but it was another post-surgery test of physical capability. Being able to accomplish it further helped to restore some confidence.

We returned to our accustomed Pennsylvania springtime routine: wading the Pine Creek currents fly fishing while marveling at the backlit storm of mayflies; walking mountain trails lined with wildflowers—trailing arbutus, colt's foot, toothwort, violets, bluets, trilliums, Dutchman's breeches, trout lily, twisted stalk, flowering dogwood, and many more. We were excited sometimes to even find the rare and showy pink lady's slipper orchid. All the while we avoided trailside rattlesnakes and, afterward, picked ticks off Benji. Sitting on the farmhouse porch, we were serenaded by cooing doves, hammering pileated woodpeckers, spring warblers—a dozen colorful kinds—and the constant background courtship singing of toads, bullfrogs, and chorus frogs. It felt like a welcoming. It was recuperative: a post-surgery return to normality, or at least something approaching normality.

We both recognized the loveliness of the place and time. We were undeniably sentimental. After all we had been through, there was awareness that all the beauty we were being privileged to enjoy was truly fleeting. We existed but in a moment in time. The fact that we were "just passing through" was no longer an abstraction.

CHAPTER 24

THE INSIDIOUS CRUELTY OF CANCER

The world breaks everyone and afterward some are strong at the broken places. But those that will not break it kills. It kills the very good and the very gentle and the very brave impartially.

— Ernest Hemingway

Pattie continued to complain frequently of low back pain, especially during and after physical activities. Reaching around behind her, she would put her hand on her back as if guarding it. On the long automobile ride across country on I-80, sitting at times became uncomfortable for her. Back in Alta she became reluctant to participate in the yoga she had so enjoyed because of the painful discomfort it caused.

Still, when I proposed one of our day hikes that would get us up into the Tetons' summer display of wildflowers, she looked at me with a quizzical grin as if to say: "Yes! If you can do it, so can I." We drove to the 8,431-feet elevation summit of Teton Pass. From there we climbed north, directly up the steep ridge and mountain face, to the 10,086-foot summit of Mount Glory—a 1,600-foot gain in elevation. As far as hikes in the Tetons go, it was a steep climb, but relatively simple. In years past, we generally hiked non-stop without pause to the top of Mount Glory from the pass. Our less active lives had taken a toll on our conditioning; we were more challenged this time.

Once on the summit, we followed the ridgeline north toward

Phillips Pass. In the rockslides we spotted pika ("rock rabbits"), nature's "little haymaker," with their signature stacks of dried plant material and squeaking calls. Above 10,000-feet elevation the sky becomes an arch of cerulean blue, the lighting more intense. Ancient gnarly whitebark pine trees cling to rocky ridges, while the meadows, swales and upper slopes are adorned with the riotous colors of wildflowers—dazzling displays of bluebells, columbine, parrot's beak, crimson monkey flower, Indian paintbrush, mountain lovage—a patriotic mountain garden of red, white, and blue.

In *The Light of the World*, author Elizabeth Alexander portrayed the transitory beauty of all life in her eloquent description of flowers: "Flowers live; they are perfect and they affect us; they are God's glory, they make us know why we are alive and human. . . . They are beautiful, and they die and rot and go back into the earth that gave birth to them."

No commercial or man-made cultivation can match the glory of God's wildflower gardens in the Teton Mountains. It is hard to imagine the glorious alpine splendor not making almost anyone's spirit soar, from that of dullards to those of poets. For us, it was restorative. As columnist Gary Ferguson aptly penned, "Nature can scour the debris from a broken life."

I took a photograph of Pattie standing thigh-deep in wildflowers with her arms thrust skyward, celebrating and embracing the beauty. The Teton Range peaks thrust up in the distance behind her, like the back of a Stegosaurus. It would turn out to be our last hike together into the high elevation of our beloved Teton Mountains.

In June 2012, a documentary film, *The Stagecoach Bar: An American Crossroads,* premiered to a sold out audience at the Jackson Center for the Arts. After the showing, the Stagecoach Band set up on the stage floor and dancing began. Recalling our courtship years, we watched from our theater seats. But not satisfied with being mere spectators, we soon joined the twirling crowd.

Pattie winced, complaining about her back hurting on some

moves, but the curtain of dark despair temporarily lifted for us. We danced and laughed again, for a short while that evening, the weight of our lives lightened. We returned to being our old selves again, not cancer victims. Our mood change was palpable, an actual conscious shift in feeling, even though it was only for brief time.

On our eighteenth wedding anniversary, the card I gave Pattie wishfully stated, "May you live a thousand years, and I a thousand less one day, that I might never be without you." It seemed very appropriate. Inside I had written: "To Pattie, whom I dearly love, Happy Anniversary on the 18th of September our 18th anniversary— Forever, my love—Earle"

Once a person has experienced the prospect of death from serious illness, there is tendency for hypochondriac watchfulness. The mind remembers and conjures the unspeakable. In Pattie's case, her mother had died from a cerebral aneurism. Pattie had experienced near death from a similar condition at age twenty-five. For the rest of her life, every migraine Pattie suffered raised the specter that it was not just a headache, but the aneurism and death's return to claim her.

Likewise, a person who has had a potentially fatal cancer becomes psychologically scarred. It becomes a monkey on your shoulder. The mind goes to that dark place, a perennial worry of recurrence, waiting for the other shoe to drop. A cough that would normally be attributed to either allergies or a cold, or a shortness of breath, both now raise the worry of lung metastases. Feeling somewhat dizzy or off balance from a poor night's sleep can make a cancer victim suspect brain metastasis. Even a spot of blood on clothing could signify cancer's return. In bleak contrast to when a person is young and strong, the reality of one's mortality is now a constant companion. A friend told me, "We are all what we survive."

We made an appointment for a CAT (Computed Axial Tomography) scan in order to determine what might be causing Pattie's backache. Because of a metal clip used in her aneurism repair, Pattie was unable to undergo an MRI. I do not recall what the scan showed for her lower back at that time, but the image overlapped the lower portion of her liver and lungs, allowing the radiologist to identify some questionable small spots or nodules.

We tried to rationalize it was the benign small cysts in her liver that had been reported there for years. In consultation with the oncologist, our fears were minimized. He smilingly told that Pattie being from the South, non-cancerous spots on the lungs—histoplasmosis—were commonplace. Not to worry. Of course, one badly wants to believe it is nothing, an artifact of the imagery.

Another scan was recommended, this time centered on the lungs and liver. The results from this scan instead confirmed our worse fears—small growths in the liver, and pulmonary specks and nodules.

Given Pattie's earlier intensive treatments for breast cancer and supposed remission or cure, the radiologist speculated if what they were seeing on the scans were cancer metastases, the source or primary tumor might actually be from the thyroid. It had been an earlier concern, but had biopsied negative after our return from Uganda.

Pattie submitted to another biopsy procedure, this time aimed at a liver growth. If it was malignant, microscopic analysis of the cells could determine whether it was metastasized breast or thyroid cancer. Lesions on her spine, also detected by the scan, were now suspected to be cancer metastases, too. Our world began to spin out of control; feelings of helplessness, anxiety and apprehension ratcheted up.

We fearfully awaited the test results. Test result anxiety. One prays and hopes against hope that somehow it is all a terrible mistake. Pattie must be fine; on the surface, she appeared to be and acted like herself. Other than the occasional back pain, she was asymptomatic. It was difficult to accept or believe anything was wrong. Denial? Perhaps. Nervous anxiety ate at us both. We probably did not discuss the "what if?" We did not have to; it was unmentionable. We both knew what was at stake.

St. Johns' head oncology nurse called us a few days later with the results. Pattie answered the phone. I quickly went and picked up the cordless phone in the other room, just in time to hear the nurse say: "It is metastasized breast cancer."

An involuntary and primal cry of despair escaped me: "Noo, nooo, not Pattie."

I sat down on the stairs, sobbing in dismay. With the phone still near my ear, I heard the nurse bark, "Who is that?"

Pattie said, "Earle."

"Well," the head nurse fired back, "it's not a death sentence."

Cancer is a silent killer. Sinisterly lurking in the shadows, it often reveals itself only after it has gathered its deadly forces. I have relived the horror of that phone call countless times. As I write this, tears still well up at the memory. I have since learned the median survival time for metastasized breast cancer is twenty-six months. If that is not "a death sentence," what is? The medical profession should be responsible for giving people the truthful facts, not holding out false hope or playing the seriousness down.

Pattie appeared to receive the chilling diagnosis calmly and very matter-of-factly. I still ponder her reaction. It was as though she already knew and had fatalistically accepted it. Maybe I had been in denial. I had clung to hope for a better outcome right up until the very last. For me, it remained inconceivable. Pattie was so beautiful, so vibrantly healthy looking, so full of life, and so undeserving of this. How could she be pronounced terminally ill? It was heartbreakingly difficult to accept. It was tragic. Grief and sorrow do not wait in the wings, they arrive early—anticipatory grief for what could or would happen to us roared in with a Tsunami-like surge.

Later, Pattie had the composure to chide me. As she put it, I had "screamed and collapsed." I explained, "I didn't 'collapse'; I sat down on the stairs." But, yes, I suppose I screamed, and in a way, I did collapse, too. With the diagnosis of Stage 4 breast cancer our entire world collapsed.

The oncologist recommended Pattie have a PET scan (Positron Emission Tomography) at Salt Lake City. It is an imaging procedure that involves a radioactive substance being injected into the blood stream. The radiotracer measures metabolism. Cancer cells take in the radioactive sugar first. They "eat first," before normal cells and their locations then light up in the imagery as "hotspots."

Worried about all the scan radiation Pattie was being subjected to, I raised a question with the oncologist: "When does radiation-induced leukemia become a concern?" His abrupt response cut off the question: "Cancer trumps those concerns."

Any side effects in his mind were justified and single-mindedly not given any pre-consideration, they were secondary. This was to be a continuing pattern. It had been for my treatment; it was for Pattie's, too. The oncologist autocratically prescribed, with little or no explanation to us—doctor knows best. The nurses and other physicians would carry out his orders and serve as the mop-up crew, treating the symptoms of the side effects.

For the PET scan, we reported to the Huntsman Clinic again, checking into Chase Suites once more. There we had become unfortunately too well-acquainted. People who worked at the hotel facility had begun to know us. Although the food was excellent, my stomach revolted at the idea of taking meals at the hospital cafeteria again. Even though we were treated exceptionally well, I do not have good mental associations with the hospital. A pervasive feeling of dread arises in the pit of my stomach just pulling into the parking lot.

The PET scan was much more involved and required more preparation than other types of scans, including hazmat suits again. I winced at the idea of a radio-active substance being injected intravenously. Again, Pattie bravely endured the procedure. We returned later that afternoon, mentally exhausted, worn out from anxiety and stress. We waited to learn the results.

As though awaiting an executioner's sentence, looking grimly deadpan and expressionless, our guts churning, Pattie and I stood side by side facing a backlit screen. The oncologist displayed the large image on the lighted viewer, and a scattering of small spots lit up and glowed into surreal focus. We stood there transfixed; no one said anything. It was as if the oncologist assumed the image was self-explanatory. Finally, perhaps in an attempt at levity, he said, "Well, at least you didn't light up like a Christmas tree."

I do not recall what was said after that, but only know the scan did not locate a primary tumor from which the cancer had distally spread. Pattie's cancer was diffused in flecks and small tumors or lesions at scattered locations on the liver, lungs, and the lower spine. On this baseline scan, the tumors were notably small, measureable in millimeters.

It was never stated, but in its diffused form, Pattie's cancer was inoperable; nor was a pathway or primary source or origin for the metastases ever speculated. If the doctors had a clue, they never informed us. The thyroid had been ruled out.

The breast cancer, I assume, had somehow distally spread through the lymphatic or blood system. When and how did it get into the bloodstream? Had it already escaped and spread before the first surgery? Had the presence of hidden cancerous cells failed to be detected in the sentinel lymph node procedure or in determining the surgical margins to be clear? Or had the original chemotherapy caused some cancer cells to disperse distally? No possible explanations were ever given.

An unfortunate aspect is that a critique or follow-up review was never conducted to learn where a failure in the treatments may have occurred, and how it might have been avoided for future patients. Potential liabilities in our litigious society prohibit such analysis, I suppose. Yes, there are formally designed and controlled trials for that sort of thing, but hospital files must be filled with untapped case information, too. Meanwhile, the medical model and practicing physicians continue to grind ahead with standard protocol and state-of-the-art treatments and procedures, but without the shared benefit of such information. Privacy rights prevent it. Unless one is part of a trial study, or the physician is personally paying attention, it seems unlikely a person's treatment responses will ever be parlayed into anything benefiting others similarly stricken—especially by overworked physicians, whose style is not to deviate from protocol procedures.

We left from the PET scan stunned into hopeless silence, overwhelmed and sickened by the gravity. An anonymous intern or resident, who had stood behind us quietly observing, boarded the elevator with us. His smooth and hairless countenance spoke of recent or ongoing chemotherapy, and he bore a large raw scar on his head from a recent incision. Smiling, he spoke encouragingly to us: "Do not give up hope. I had testicular cancer that metastasized to my brain." He went on to describe all he had been through in his own treatment. "I am now cancer-free," he announced. His manner and encouragement was inspiring. Our spirits were given a much needed boost. Every time after that when we reported to Huntsman, we would look for that individual. We needed another infusion of the type of hope he had given us. But we never saw him again.

When we again met with the oncologist during his weekly visit to Jackson, he told us: "Don't worry; it is not a death sentence." That should have been a huge galvanizing red flag since we had heard the exact same rote remark from the head nurse. "I have a list of drugs as long as my arm," he said. "If one doesn't work, we will find one that does. I have patients who I have been treating for eight years," he stated. Again, one wants badly to believe it is true.

Chemotherapy is not a cure, but it can prolong life *for some*, depending on the type, aggressiveness, and molecular nature of the cancer. The common qualifier is that metastatic breast cancer is "treatable, but not curable." For us, this was all before the recent advent of so-called "precision medicine" or "targeted therapy" cancer treatments.

The first chemotherapy Pattie received was relatively easy. It was an oral medication, Adriamycin (doxorubicin). She had few or no side effects, not even hair loss. In addition, denosumab, a relatively new drug to maintain bone hardness to protect against fractures related to the bone metastases was administered by injection every two weeks. Maybe it was not hopeless?

Another scan was scheduled in three months to determine the effectiveness of the treatment. I do not believe we fully appreciated it then, but in retrospect, the progression of the disease was advancing, and the clock was ticking. However, we hardly resembled the grasshopper and ant fable; we did not fiddle away our time. Resuming our lives, we both continued doing what we knew to do: researching and checking with other doctors and friends in the medical profession for what they thought and recommended. Becoming enshrouded in a dark veil of depression, worry, and pulse-quickening anxiety was unavoidable. It was our new "normal feeling," which we lugged around everywhere. And it weighed depressingly heavy.

After a two day marathon of medical testing and consultations at Salt Lake City, Pattie emailed friends and family:

Warm greetings. We arrived home a short while ago. We haven't heard Earle's results yet, but we have every reason to expect they will be good. My results were immediate—but disappointing. More tumors had appeared, and some of the existing ones had doubled in size. Based upon a new study indicating that Arimidex works best given in conjunction with Faslodex, I had my first injections of the second drug yesterday. Another scan will be done after a short trial of this combo. If the additional drug doesn't bump up Arimidex's efficacy, we'll look at other treatment options.

Otherwise, our plan going forward is the same as it was before Earle and I went to Salt Lake City: Live each day fully—gather with friends, laugh and love lots, remain active outdoors, learn new things, travel when we can. A Christy Minstrels song keeps playing through my head about living BIG, while we're working with my docs to find the right treatment. I'll sing it for you: "Today is my

Glory, and now is my Moment ... I'll laugh and I'll cry..."
With great thanks for the love and prayers that Earle and
you send my direction Everyday.

All around us, in what was now an otherworldly scene, people
were going about their normal lives, happily laughing, talking, smiling,
and engaging in activities. But like the very old or elderly, our lives had
become weighted down with the realization we would never be a part
of that capable and carefree world again. Our reality existed apart; we
had entered into an entirely different state of being. We now found
ourselves on the outside looking in at life.

Still, for the most part, at this stage, even though anxiety
constantly hummed like a tight wire in the background, you could not
tell that anything was physically wrong with Pattie. She still displayed
good energy levels and her lovely smile. We continued our traditional
activities: going to the fitness center, riding our bikes, fly fishing,
moderate hikes, picking berries, and when snow arrived, participating
in some alpine and cross-country skiing.

However, the overall level of intensity in our activities was
reduced, more to accommodate me at that point, I think, than Pattie.
Feeling vulnerable to accidental injury after my surgically rearranged
plumbing, I had given up downhill powder-snow skiing on steep
terrain. Still it was comforting just being outdoors on the ski hill,
riding the lift together and skiing intermediate groomers in the beauty
of winter, as we had in our life together before cancer.

Weekly trips to oncology in Jackson and my checkups at Salt
Lake City governed our lives. Pattie wrote in her journal:

> I was in jubilant agreement that fifty is the new 30-year-
> old. One day I was an active conservation journalist, then
> suddenly the next, a stricken, puzzled woman, old before my
> preconceived time. Suddenly an anxious insomniac, I railed
> against what might be happening inside my body. If I survived
> cancer, could I accommodate its everlasting companions,
> diminished power and loss of control over my future?

Pattie organized and did local fundraising for Grand Targhee Resort's Mary's Nipple Mountain Challenge to raise money for St. John's Hospital's Oncology Department. She personally solicited donations and prizes from local businesses and individuals. Through her efforts the event brought in a record amount of money. Following the fund raiser, we again made our spring trip cross-country to Pennsylvania, arranging for Pattie's drug therapy to be administered at a Pennsylvania hospital.

First thing after we returned to Wyoming, Pattie was scanned again to determine the effectiveness of the chemotherapy. The mind-chilling determination was that the cancer had continued to grow unabated and rapidly. Some tumors now scaled in centimeters. The same numbness and helpless shock I had experienced standing in front of and viewing the PET scan returned and totally engulfed me. My heart sank. I remember thinking, this could not be happening, it was not real. Pattie, I am certain, must have felt the same way.

Taking a copy of the report home, Pattie, frightened and disbelieving, would read the tumor measurements aloud, as if appealing to some higher power to intervene and make it all go away, like it was a bad dream.

"Not to worry," the oncologist repeated to us "I have a list of drugs as long as my arm." This time, the heavy guns were brought out. Paclitaxol was prescribed in a predetermined schedule and dosage. There was no pill form. The drug was administered weekly by an intravenous infusion at the hospital.

Hooked up to tubing and intravenous drips, Pattie smiled bravely, putting forth a positive attitude, providing good cheer and boosting moral for everyone around her. This time there were medications to deal with the side-effects and other details needing constant attention. My heart cries out when I picture and relive it all again.

The side-effects were significant—peripheral neuropathy, vomiting, mouth sores, constipation, and fatigue. And once again, Pattie lost all her hair. I tried not to show my sick worry and hammering pulse every time we approached the oncology ward, or my barely contained tears at seeing the dearest person in my life suffering the hideously painful treatments. Professional and efficient, the nurses had little tolerance for my distraught and distracting presence.

Our once active lives were now totally reduced to day-to-day dealing with fatigue, the chemo side effects, treatment schedules, hospital procedures, and doctor appointments. We lived under the constant unmentionable dark cloud of where it might all be leading. A heavy black shroud inescapably enveloped us and everything we did or tried to do for momentary respite.

It is different for everyone, but in our case, I do not recall either of us actually discussing where it was all ultimately going to lead. To have verbalized that it was a terminal illness would have been to empower it; admitting the inevitable would have denied hope. Neither of us was inclined to give up hope. Not giving up is a big part of resisting the disease. It was not in Pattie's nature to concede to the disease's progression or to give up. We went about our lives while shadows of uncertainty danced in the backs of our minds.

In Salt Lake City, Pattie shopped for and purchased several high quality wigs. When she chose to be finely dressed and wear her best wigs, it was difficult to believe this was a woman suffering a progressive life-threatening disease. She did not fit the outward image of a cancer victim. Maybe others noticed changes, I did not. She looked gorgeous, slender and fit; and still looked much younger than her chronological age. At least to me, that was the way she appeared. I have since had others tell me they had the same impression.

Pattie continued to show up for every hospital and doctor appointment in dress uniform, like a solider going into battle. Her well-groomed appearance and smiling manner selflessly spared others, including the physicians and nurses, from the emotional trauma and physical pain she was personally suffering.

When the weeks of prescribed intravenous treatment with Paclitaxol were completed, Pattie reported to radiology for another scan. It showed mixed results. The therapy had temporarily shrunk and slowed the growth of tumors in the lungs, but had done little or nothing to curtail the growth of those in the liver.

I can still see and feel Pattie's look of frightened dismay when we were made aware of those results. Then she tried to cover up with a blank expression; something we both did, like expressionless robots. But the hairs on the back of my neck tingled, and my stomach churned nauseously. I wanted to scream. There is no one place a person can point to, grief hurts all over.

The benefit of reducing the lung tumors was short-lived. As was the continuing case, the oncologist did not explain, point out, or discuss much about the results with us, at least that I recall. Any questions were answered perfunctorily—don't ask, don't tell. We mostly learned the progression of the disease from studying copies of the radiologist's report ourselves. Whatever the oncologist thought, whatever the outcomes, the timing, or the particular strategy he was employing, he was disinclined to discuss those details with us. His cards were closely held and played one at a time, with little or no explanation.

Another unpronounceable chemotherapy drug was prescribed. The nightmare routine continued of our reporting to oncology, where Pattie would be hooked up to intravenous drips; subjected to needle sticks, blood draws and repeated testing. She was given shots and prescribed medications to deal with the host of potential side effects.

Pattie incredibly continued to maintain a smiling presence through it all, talking almost cheerfully to the nurses. It was not a façade; it was Pattie, and her selfless way of minimizing the burden on others. It carried over even to the medical professionals who were treating her. And in a way, I suppose, her cheerful demeanor was meant to enlist them—and me—to her cause. Who could resist wanting to do their best for her? Even while writing this, I still feel galvanized. Whatever was done, it was never enough; and from that belief, guilt and remorse arise like potent vapors from a spring creek on a cold morning.

What we did not know, or at least I did not at the time, but would come to alarmingly learn late in the process was this: the more anti-cancer drugs are tried and fail, the more unlikely it becomes any will work. The "list [of drugs] may be as long as your arm," but the cancer sinisterly develops a resistance to drug therapies. In retrospect, it is hard not to feel we were misled by the deadly seriousness of the situation being disarmingly played down.

The nurses were skilled and professional, but they restricted themselves to carrying out only procedures they were assigned. They never stepped across the line. Never questioned, discussed, or commented on the real issue with the patients: Is this drug therapy successfully serving its intended purpose for you? That part was reserved for the oncologist's judgment alone. But the nurses surely must have had an opinion? Maybe not. They appeared not to think about it. As professionals, they were able to compartmentalize their work.

My role was that of the unqualified questioner; a well-meaning husband, a buffoon and layman not to be taken too seriously by impatient medical staff. I played that part, but Pattie and I forged a strong pact to look out for one another in the hospital settings.

We had also connected with other oncologists and friends in the medical profession who dealt with aspects of chemotherapy, and consulted with them on every step and each new drug. They would have had little reason not to point out anything they disagreed with, or any need for any additional treatment, trials, or anything being overlooked—or so we trusted and believed.

Pattie was a smooth-skinned petite person, not a large woman with bulging veins. After nearly two years of needles, frequently as often as once a week or more, it was becoming a challenge to find intact veins and intact places remaining for another "stick." But without orders otherwise, the nurses dutifully continued to press on with the growing challenge.

The oncology nurses continued to hook Pattie up to IVs and do blood draws—more "needle sticks"—whenever she reported. I winced watching. A nurse rising to the challenge remarked, "We can go in through the foot, if necessary."

I could see no end to the need for more IVs and blood draws. It must have been hugely painful, but Pattie never complained. I was the one who finally brought it up. "Pattie needs a Port," I said, referring to a temporary medical device surgically installed under the skin in the upper chest region, through which drugs could be injected and blood samples drawn, reducing or eliminating the need for needle sticks

The head oncology nurse seemed as oblivious to this need as she had with the importance of placing the anti-nausea medication order, or arranging the earlier first recommended scanning. She should have been the one to have recommended the port much sooner. Perhaps she was distracted by her nearing retirement and an illness in her own family. In any case, I recognized the apparent dysfunction: things were falling through the cracks; items noted in charts appeared not be happening.

It was hard for me not to feel like I had betrayed Pattie. I can still see and sadly feel her crestfallen and defeated expression. She could not conceal it—another devastating blow. I believe that for Pattie accepting the port meant conceding that things were not improving. Likely she did not want the reminder of the foreign device's bulge under her skin either. No doubt it was psychologically disturbing, just as the stoma was for me. But after suffering the surgical procedure to implant the port, the continuing relentless march of oncology procedures and tests were made physically easier for her and everyone concerned.

Swept along by currents over which we had no control, Pattie entered into the vortex of late-stage cancer from which few ever return. We unwillingly found ourselves on the tragic path of becoming the kind of lovers that history remembers—heartbreaking drama with an inevitable devastating and tragic outcome. Romance is heightened and comes into play where love is doomed and passion becomes suffering. As poet and scholar Denis de Rougemont has pointed out, "History doesn't bother recording eternally happy lovers."

CHAPTER 25

LAST ELK HUNT

It never dawned on them that life is unpredictable, that one day one of us could suddenly cease to exist. What would be the joy in having left so much unsaid? With what memories would we fill the empty silence?

— Isabel Lopez, *Hand-Me-Down Dreams*

Family is different. Except for our spouse, we have little choice in whom or what we get. But we love them just the same. When I think of the sleepless nights and thoughtless rudeness we dutifully suffered from *family drama*, things you would not put up with otherwise, I can easily become annoyed and upset. Pattie on the other hand was always extra diplomatic, able to turn the other cheek in true Christian-like manner, more than any person I have known.

Yet Pattie, over the years, struggled with family in Memphis, and both of us with my family, too. My mother could be extremely self-centered and manipulative, which she became less adept at concealing after my father died, and as she grew older. My half-siblings were viciously petty. And I had my "damned if I did and didn't" challenges with my children and daughter-in-law. My youngest son, who had showed unlimited potential growing up, went into hiding, off the grid. After a brief work assignment in Russia for a Fortune 500 technology company, he had begun concocting a grandiose and elaborate story that the CIA and Russian KGB were pursuing him.

My older son, who outspokenly repudiated Mormonism, at least to us, strangely chose to live in a Mormon community with his devout Mormon in-laws, Mormon wife, and all her extended family relatives. It is a shielded and communal culture. I do not have a problem with Latter-day Saints, that is, until they behave in a judgmental and provincial holier-than-thou way toward non-Mormons.

I think one reason my mother lived to such an advanced age was her ability in her later years to laugh things off that she recognized she could not change. When she learned her grandson was marrying a Mormon woman, her response was to say, "Now the Laysers have a Mormon line." She found that amusing, laughing aloud as if she had made a funny joke.

Rather than lending support during our illnesses, some of our family members seemed to go out of their way to be difficult, in spite of the stress and challenges Pattie and I were already suffering. Maybe they didn't think. They either did not care or must have thought we would all go on living forever, regardless. It made Pattie and me all the more appreciative of the love and closeness we shared. We would sometimes joke about being thankful for our places of residence being separated by mountain ranges, rivers, and vast prairies.

In the rural West, bagging one's first elk can be a rite of passage. In October, my son and fifteen-year-old grandson arrived to pursue elk in Grand Teton National Park's special hunt. Hunting elk in that area could have been viewed as a tradition and made out to be a special family event. My son and I had hunted together there in the early 1980s when he was a teenager and we lived in Jackson. But it never occurred to him to think of it that way; or maybe he did, and he was somehow threatened by it?

I had recovered from my surgery enough to do some easy hunting, as if any elk hunting was ever easy. It's a large animal and one generally has to cover rough terrain and long distances in search for them, sometimes in deep snow and extreme cold. I am no longer capable of very heavy lifting either. A downed elk is a big animal. Good chance it was my last elk hunt, considering my age and cancer's toll on my body.

Young people sometimes seem to take a lot for granted. Although she was sick, Pattie cooked meals, made lunches, entertained, and enthusiastically led conversations to involve the grandson. Outwardly, she casually presented a gracious smiling persona to everyone.

It never fully registered on my children that Pattie was, in fact, critically ill, that it might be the last time she would ever host a family hunting outing, or that they may never see her again. The narcissism of youth; life focused and revolved around only them. I do not think the *last supper* nature of our gathering ever occurred to them.

Pattie knew the hunting routine. She had prepared lunches and beamingly sent me on my predawn way many mornings, and had listened to my stories afterward. Taking two vehicles, my son, grandson, and I left at 4:00 a.m. to be at the desired location before dawn began snuffing out the glow of stars and satellites from the night sky. Hunting the thick cover in the dramatically scenic Snake River bottom north of Moose, we separated with an agreed upon meeting place and time.

When I arrived at the meeting place sometime later, my son and grandson were not there. However, looking upriver, I saw seven cow elk heading toward me, trotting single file through shoulder high riparian willows and silverberry at a ground-covering pace. Perhaps my son and grandson had unknowingly frightened them in my direction.

They were unaware of my presence. I lay down behind a beaver-felled cottonwood tree, waiting and watching in ambush as they approached. The lead cow suddenly appeared on the river channel embankment within yards of me. With almost reflex action, I killed her instantly with a single well-placed shot. She fell back over the embankment and lay along the water's edge. At one time, I would have been elated; now instead, sadness engulfed me.

In order to kill the cow elk, I had had to detach myself emotionally, deadening a part of my mind. This was not easy to do when I was already on the edge of emotional overload from our living with progressive illnesses. It occurred to me that the torrent of conflicted feelings in killing the elk was similar to what both Pattie and I experienced in reporting to hospitals—nerve-wracking on one hand; and on the other, there was a practical need to keep raw visceral emotion and nerviness under control.

As I have gotten older, I have come to dislike killing anything. Killing a big game animal incites the uncomfortable recognition of one's own mortality. Mostly, I just enjoy being outdoors, especially in the early morning in beautiful natural settings. For me that was always the best part of hunting.

In my daypack, I carried a folding all-purpose saw, a hatchet, two, knives and a sharpening stone for what came next. Struggling alone, I field dressed the large, four-hundred- pound animal. After mentally marking the elk's location, I walked back to my truck and brought it up to where my son had parked. Then, using my cell phone, I called "Johnny Horse Caller," a person I knew who provided elk retrieval services. By lucky chance, he was nearby. We used Johnny's powerfully built Morgan horse to drag the elk carcass to the truck, where we had it lying when son and grandson showed up around lunch time.

A tough, old guy, Johnny was up in years, eighty-something. He charged me twenty dollars in the late 1970s for dragging an elk out. This time, even though it was a relatively short and easy retrieval, as far as those things go, he asked for $125. I didn't argue. He earned it, considering the price of maintaining horses and equipment, the cost of fuel, as well as the amount of time he spent.

But so much for the idea and economics of would-be subsistence hunting these days. People in rural areas used to supplement their diets with game meat because it was readily available low-cost protein. Nowadays elk meat is a luxury relatively few can afford. Don't believe me? Look at the exorbitant price of farm-raised (organic grass-fed) elk on the restaurant menus and in the markets in Jackson!

When my son and grandson arrived, I was purposefully low key about my having bagged an elk. Prudently, so not to appear to rub it in, I said little. My blood-stained clothing and the fat cow elk laying there spoke for itself. Just as I had anticipated, it was obvious my son was put off by my success. No congratulations or "way to go, Dad," which made me even more reticent.

Following his father's cue, my grandson sensed something was wrong and stood there looking down at the ground. I was left to believe my son somehow felt insecure or outmatched. Old demons: "Dad catches all the fish and gets all the game." Possibly he felt I showed him up in front of his boy. Who knows? As I said, family can be different.

Characteristically, I'm certain my son would deny his behaviors. But he was obviously determined to give little acknowledgment to my having bagged an elk. Still, he couldn't totally ignore it; there it lay. I suggested they hang around until late afternoon, and then hunt through the densely forested river bottom again at dusk. Meanwhile, I would take the elk I had killed home.

When the two of them returned late that evening for the dinner Pattie had prepared and kept warm, we learned my grandson had shot a yearling elk at dusk. They had field-dressed it, but it was getting dark and too late in the day to get it out. Grandson's first elk! We had to coax the details out of him at dinner. I am not certain we ever got the full story. Meanwhile, my son looked down at his plate and said little. Pattie and I tried to ignore their unexplained behaviors and toasted the grandson and his first elk. My son popped open another beer, acting abrupt and moody, coolly indifferent or bored.

My perceptions are probably my own, different from those of my son's. I'm certain he would adamantly deny much of what I've said, while offering little explanation. That's the way it usually works. It was, however, the last time they would ever see Pattie.

In the morning, the two of them returned to the grandson's kill site. Luckily, no bear or coyotes had found the carcass during the night. I have the impression they hastily, unceremoniously, chopped the elk into quarters leaving the hide on it. Making several trips, they quickly and efficiently backpacked it out to their vehicle with the arrogant strength of youth.

They stopped off at our house on their way home. When I asked to see Colton's elk, my son showed me the meat bags piled unceremoniously in the back of his Suburban. Unless I would bring it up, we never heard anything more about the grandson's first elk.

I often wondered what was said when they arrived home in Utah. Rather than a celebration, Colton may have encountered his mother's purposeful trivialization of anything associated with Pattie and me. He likely was made to feel disloyal to her family clan if he had enjoyed himself with us. No doubt the elk meat was communally distributed among her extended family and no more was ever mentioned of it.

Two years later, after Pattie had been gone for over a year, my grandson killed a four-point bull elk in Utah's Uinta Mountains with a compound bow and arrow—a major hunting accomplishment. He and his Dad rightly celebrated it at length with his wife's family, friends, and e-mailed us photographs. If Pattie had still been around yet, she would have been thrilled for him; I know I certainly was. I got to talk with him on the phone about it and congratulate him.

But I could not help but remember that Pattie and I had hosted Colton's first successful elk hunt. I could see Pattie again, sitting at the dinner table, smiling, coaxing Colton to talk about his first elk, congratulating him, and a calling him "Little Buddy," as she always had over the years, though he was not so little anymore. Pattie was a kind influence.

When families slip into old behavioral patterns—perpetuating disagreements, knee-jerk insecurities, fueling old angers, chasing demons, punishing, rationalizing, patronizing, even lying—it is destructive at worst, silly at best. It is like a druggie in denial needing just one more fix to be made whole. The satisfactions or rewards one can expect from those behaviors are generally short-lived and never enough; only short-sighted victories. It could not be done to other than caring family members, no one else would put up with it.

Family dynamics can change overtime, and like Pattie, I continued to remain ever hopeful. I suppose we all have our reasons. Some family members' underlying motives and patterns are difficult for them to understand or recognize themselves, or admit to and try to reconcile. Shortsightedly and stubbornly, they cling to long-held resentments and unrewarding behaviors. In contrast, other family members appear disinterested and avoid engaging entirely. Perhaps the latter is a luxury of large extended families. I have observed them side-step, avoid or rationalize disagreeable behaviors altogether with the simple comment, "Bless their hearts."

Pattie always tried building on the positive. Flying in the face of it all, she and I both put up with a lot in the name of "family." Perhaps that is what defines family—a willingness to put up with it all. Even in one's last days.

CHAPTER 26

OUR LAST CHRISTMAS

He felt now that he was not simply close to her, but that he did not know where he ended and she began.

— Anonymous

With Pattie, I did not know which part was the greater: that part of me that was her, or the part of her that was me. Early on we had evolved into one. Love had continued to evolve and grow in the neurons of our brains; we were "two hearts beating as one."

In December 2012, Pattie gave me a large birthday card that advised me to emulate a tree: "Don't think of it as getting older, think of it as new growth." Inside with her artistic longhand, she had written: "Earle, Darling, Happy Birthday! To endless rings of new growth and stimulation, new places and new adventures, new fun outdoors, new people, new cultures. Learning new things. Loving to new depths with you! Always together with my young husband—I Love You, Earle—Pattie."

On the surface, Pattie continued to be herself. It was difficult to accept or believe what was happening. Few would have suspected she was suffering from late-stage cancer. However, bittersweet, this would be the last year we would celebrate birthdays, Christmases, and Valentine Days together.

For lovers, Christmas can be a romantic time. It was Pattie's favorite; for her, the apogee of holidays. The years with Pattie colored and transformed my idea of what Christmases should or could be like.

I admit my vision of Christmas had grown to incorporate a sentimental old-time Norman Rockwell flavor via Pattie. I remember Pattie's bubbling and joyful happiness. Holidays are especially difficult for me now, alone.

That last December, I wanted us to have a Christmas tree and to celebrate Christmas season like we customarily did; once again, reaching for some normalcy in our lives. The disease, chemotherapy, and anxiety and stress were exacting their toll. Pattie's beautiful shock of long dark curly hair was gone, replaced by thin, totally white wisps. Using scarves and wigs, she retained her striking attractiveness. Her beautiful smile, so freely given, remained unchanged.

For the first time since our first Christmas together when we had begun going to the forest to cut a Christmas tree together, Pattie choose not to accompany me. I went off on the seasonal task alone, immersed in silence and my thoughts of past Christmases. We had always gone together on an enthusiastic adventure looking for the perfect tree. I could still take you to the exact spot along the Gallatin River in Montana, where we cut our first tree together, years before while both of us were living in Bozeman.

In today's world, it is safe to say, many never have a real tree or experience the scent of the forest brought into the home. They only know generic plastic ones. Reusable plastic is easier and cheaper. Just pull it out of the basement and plug it in. Less ecological impact? Maybe. With plastic it depends on whether it can be recycled.

We were horrified one Christmas to discover my daughter-in-law, who takes faux pride in claiming to be "country," had purchased and began setting out a really scraggly pre-decorated artificial tree; a cynical plastic version of Charlie Brown's tree. We were left to wonder, what values did she unthinkingly wish to convey to the grandchildren?

Like a kid, Pattie excitedly looked forward to every year's Christmas tree cutting expedition. Cold was ignored as she plowed untiringly through the deep snow. Her laughing enthusiasm was combined with semi-serious discussions in deciding which magical tree was to be honored among the forest's many. It always made for an entertaining and memorable holiday season outing.

Pattie, of course, insisted on cutting only the best-formed and tallest tree. In our area, it had to be an alpine fir, too, which would retain its needles. I was left with reminding her that, although we had a vaulted ceiling, there were practical limits to how big and tall the tree could be; not to mention the work and difficulty for me in dragging it out of the forest. And it had to a size that would fit through the doorway to the house.

Maybe because it turned out to be our last Christmas tree, I remember it so distinctly. Pattie was no doubt not feeling well, or maybe she thought it would make her melancholy. More likely she knew she was not up to the strenuous outing in the deep snow and cold; or maybe it was all the above. For the first time in all our years together, she elected to stay home while I went by myself. It cast a somber shadow over what had always been a fun event. Although she did not openly complain, I am certain she must have felt sad, too. I wonder now what her thoughts were while I was gone. I didn't ask; I was afraid to ask.

As usual, the snow was knee deep and four-wheel drive barely got me close to the location. More on task and single minded than on our past tree-cutting outings, I found a group of densely-branched subalpine fir trees that were close-growing in the understory. In the dim light of a snowy winter day, the trees appeared black-green, their stout evergreen branches flocked with heavy loads of snow. Removing one tree from the clump would be like a thinning release and not adversely affect the overall forest composition.

This particular thicket of subalpine fir had not experienced moose browsing, so the ends of branches were still intact. The tree I selected was evenly formed, and the height Pattie always seemed to desire. A stepladder would be needed to decorate the upper branches. I was strongly aware of Pattie's absence. Without our on-site back-and-forth banter and her blessing, how could it ever qualify as the "perfect tree?"

Back home I tried to bolster Pattie's spirit and enthusiasm by admiring and talking up the tree, and reaching out to hold and hug her. Then I descended into the crawl space underneath the house where we stored our half-dozen large boxes of prized Christmas ornaments. I say *prized* because Pattie dearly treasured the decorations she had collected over the years. They recalled our Christmases past.

Many of the ornaments were unusual, elaborate, or special in some way. Some had been obtained from when she had her gallery; others were personalized with our names or photographs; many of the antique glass bulbs were irreplaceable, gifts from my mother from New York's Corning Glass Works. Every year, afterward, each precious ornament was individually wrapped and carefully stored away. Pattie also set out the same tasteful table decorations each year. It had all grown into a strong tradition for us.

Pattie very seriously, carefully, and artfully decorated the tree this time. Perhaps, rather than seriously, I might more correctly say *solemnly*. I tried to make light-hearted remarks and little jokes recalling better times and Christmases past. And there was the usual: "Pattie, get down off that ladder. Let me do that."

Typically, I was encouraged and allowed to hang some ornaments, but not too many. Pattie had her own vision of just where and how everything should be best hung. For her, it was a work of art calling for her artistic talent.

Over the years, a rivalry developed to see who could put the most attention-grabbing Christmas presents under the tree for each other—big boxes magnificently wrapped, sometimes with only small but costly items teasingly hidden inside. Pattie's gifts always appeared professionally done with elaborate ribbons and bows. Mine? Well, I did my best, but generally could not compete with Pattie's gift-wrapping skills. She had had years of practice gift wrapping in her Bozeman gallery and gift shop business.

Some people shudder at the thought of extreme winters in the Rockies. But snow piled high outside, the wood stove crackling, the decorated tree and lights reflecting, fancy-wrapped gifts stacked around the tree, our closeness and being very much in love in spite of passing years, all combined to generate an old-fashioned warmth and closeness. It was truly a special time of the year for us.

On Christmas morning, while still in our robes and coffee mugs in hand, we unwrapped our gifts, helping Benji with his, too. Then we would get nicely dressed, and drive our four-by-four through the winter wonderland across Teton Pass to the Wort Hotel's or Granary's buffets in Jackson. The Granary looked out on the winter scene of snow-covered Tetons through a surround-glass dining area.

Pattie would be snuggled in one of her beautiful winter coats, set off with high leather boots, and I wearing a new sports coat, items that were often gifts from Santa. One Christmas, we were only able to get as far as Victor, Idaho, before having to return. A blizzard of blowing snow completely closed off the roadway and pass. Like a real family, Brett, my older son, and the grandchildren accompanied us to Christmas dinner on a few of those years.

For this last Christmas I insisted we keep the tree up longer than usual. When we finally took it down, we did so silently and somberly. There was not good cheer, but rather unspoken and underlying melancholy. Pattie carefully wrapped each of her precious ornaments and securely placed them in the boxes as she had always done. She handed the boxes down to me in the crawl space, where I stacked them to await our next Christmas.

Those ornament boxes remain packed away under our house with their precious items. Someday someone will pull them out. I think it would be intolerably painful, too impossibly heartrending, for me to do it though.

The following year in late November after Pattie was gone, I left Alta and spent the holiday season wandering the sandy beaches in Coastal Texas alone with Benji. Far from the Tetons, sparkling snow and evergreen Christmas trees, it held few holiday reminders or memories.

CHAPTER 27

FALSE POSITIVE

She was too gentle to be of this world. When I met her, how could I have known that she was an angel returned to Earth, and, for some unaccountable reason, had chosen to walk for a time hand-in-hand through life with me.

— The Author

Sometime in February, Pattie and I traveled to the Huntsman Institute at Salt Lake City for my prescheduled routine checkup. A urethra wash was conducted and the cells analyzed for abnormalities. A blood test was also done. Bladder cancer commonly metastasizes to the lungs, so a lung x-ray was also a part of the routine. If it shows up on an x-ray, it's all over anyway. We were given to believe that all the test results were okay. No news being good news, we skipped out of there, breathed deeply, and drove home.

Two days later, the phone rang. A Huntsman nurse advised they had found "abnormal cells," meaning cancer cells, in the wash. A detached and dazed feeling of impending doom rose up within me. A feeling no longer new to me, it no doubt resembles the numbness soldiers must experience when commanded to charge directly into deadly enemy fire. I was told to report to the Urological Department so they could do more tests.

Pattie and I resignedly packed up again. It was another sleepless night. In the morning, we got into the car and drove back to Salt Lake City. It was a glum-filled, quiet drive, like traveling to one's execution.

It underscored just how tenuous our lives were.

As I quietly worried, what gnawed at me most was how we were going to manage if both of us were simultaneously afflicted with metastasized cancer. The hair on the back of my neck prickled with apprehension. No doubt another horrendous surgery would be required for me, likely chemo, too. Remembering the difficulties of recovery from my last operation, I knew I would be unable to take care of Pattie. And she was too weakened from her own illness and treatments to expect her to nurse me. I had no idea how we were going to cope.

Reporting directly to the hospital when we arrived, I was ushered into a patient room. Pattie accompanied me sitting to the side of the room trying to remain calm and expressionless. Apprehension must have been flooding over her in sickening waves. The nurses conducted another urethra wash. The urologist did a urethra cystoscopy procedure.

"Looks fine," he exclaimed, his expression reflecting my relief.

A heavy weight lifted. Time had stopped, and then started up again. Tension mercifully eased. I looked over at Pattie, I could see her features relax and a small smile appear. Results of the wash also came back negative. The original wash result was termed a "false positive." We were both too relieved to complain about the unnecessary scare and additional expenses. If cancer had been detected, though, I no doubt would have been scheduled for surgery within days.

We practically ran from the patient room, descended the elevator, got in the car where Benji happily greeted us with his tail-wagging agreeably as usual, and sped from the hospital parking area. Down the street, I parked and we ducked into an upscale Mexican restaurant, where we were seated. We felt the weight lifting. I ordered a margarita with a double shot of tequila. Both of us contemplated what felt like a huge reprieve. Pattie laid her hand on mine. Mercifully, this time we had been spared.

CHAPTER 28

THE PATTIE LAYSER MARY'S NIPPLE CHALLENGE

The things you do for yourself are gone when you are gone, but the things you do for others remain as your legacy.
— Kalu Ndukwe Kalu

Pattie totally understood the importance of doing for others. It guided the way she lived her life—putting others first. With her experience from the previous year in mind, once again Pattie set about arranging Grand Targhee Resort's local fundraising event for St. John's Medical Center's Oncology Department in Jackson. In March, working with the Resort's event coordinator, Pattie gave fully of her time and remaining precious energy, developing advertising materials and news releases, soliciting businesses for donations and prizes, obtaining prayer flags, and helping set up the booths for the event.

On the day of the event, Pattie appeared in costume in support of the Best Costume contest. She had obtained large butterfly wings and an orange-colored wig. With some additional costuming and makeup, she represented herself as a butterfly. We never discussed why she chose to be a butterfly? I wish now that we had.

What amazed me was the stamina she summoned to do it all, including the number of ski runs she made off the top of Fred's Mountain. Not remarkable in itself, perhaps, until you consider it was accomplished in spite of advanced stage-four cancer, ongoing chemotherapy, pain, and medications. It was an unconscious and unpretentious display of an unquenchable spirit.

Besides raffle tickets for prize drawings, such as season ski passes, people could buy a prayer flag, or any number of prayer flags—colorful rectangular cloths—and write the name of a person they knew who was currently (or had been) stricken with cancer on them. The flags were then strung together and flown on the mountain summit like Buddhist prayer flags used in healing ceremonies in Nepal and other high-mountain locations in the Himalayas. I wrote Pattie's name on mine. I am certain many others did, too— prayers spread across the Teton Mountains by the wind for Pattie.

Near the end of the day, it was announced all the participants should report to the top of the mountain again to be photographed with the prayer flags and Mary's Mountain in the background. Although she must have been exhausted, Pattie never hesitated. Like a butterfly, she appeared to flit back up the mountain. I worried about her being tired and skiing back down safely; but before too long, there she was at the bottom of the ski run again. She was a winged butterfly running on her energy reserve, still laughing and appearing to enjoy herself, but staggeringly tired. One had to admire her selfless determination.

For a second time, the local event through Pattie's efforts raised what was a record amount of money. I was told, over twenty thousand dollars. For the oncology fund at St. John's Medical Center, it represented a worthy donation. The fund was set up to provide financial assistance for those undergoing cancer treatments but would otherwise not be able to afford it. Ironically, no one from St. John's Hospital or oncology had shown up to participate in or support the event. I suppose the regular work week in the cancer ward was enough for anyone.

The next year, in Pattie's honor, Grand Targhee Resort would name the event "The Pattie Layser Mary's Nipple Challenge." In memory of her appearance as a butterfly the previous year, the poster advertising the fund raiser pictured clouds of butterflies rising over the prayer flags strung along the mountain top. A women's group that took over running the event were astonished to discover it required five of them to do what Pattie had accomplished single-handed the year before.

CHAPTER 29

LAST TIME AT PINE CREEK

When you go back to your family home, you find it wasn't the old home you missed, rather it was your childhood.
— Sam Ewing

The Pine Creek farm had always been a gathering place for family. When I was growing up, my mother prepared legendary meals there, roasting turkeys with all the accessories and side dishes, including homemade pies made from apples picked fresh from the farm's trees. The meals were served on large antique platters and dishes with colorful patterns celebrating Pennsylvania Dutch farm life.

Over the past two decades, Pattie had taken over that tradition of entertaining and cooking when we visited. My mother, whom we always visited and spent time with when we were back there, had passed away the previous summer on July 3, 2012, at nearly 106 years of age. As she was my last living relative on Pine Creek, her death was another major loss in our lives.

I wrote my mother's eulogy. She had had an incredible life, spanning from the horse-and-buggy days to witnessing space travel and the Internet. In Lebanon, Pennsylvania, before moving to Pine Creek with my father, she had led marches for women's right to vote and had played piano accordion in speakeasies during prohibition. She had owned and operated a business and campaigned for women's rights long before the modern feminist movement came along.

In autumn, we arranged a well-attended memorial service for her at the nearby country church, where she had served as organist for over forty years. She had loved Pine Creek. Poignantly, among her last personal possessions, she had kept a key to the Pine Creek farm house.

Pattie and I scattered her ashes, where my father's had also been spread, on their beloved farm that they had pioneered. Our time at Pine Creek seemed incomplete without her presence.

My mother had always gone out of her way for her grandchildren, and all of them had spent fun times at the Pine Creek farm while growing up. But, oddly, not one of them showed up to pay tribute to her at the memorial service, not even from the Mormon branch of our family who claim "family is everything." I was left to assume, all were "too busy" with their lives.

In April, Pattie and I decided we would attempt our annual springtime cross-country pilgrimage to visit the farm. It was something Pattie wanted to do, even though her disease was growing more worrisome as it continued to advance. We rarely spoke of where it was leading. It wasn't denial; both of us were keenly aware of the progression. It was on our minds constantly and did not need to be underscored.

I arranged our vehicle so that Pattie could lie down on the back seat when she got tired or when her back hurt too much to sit. I insisted on doing all the driving. We brought books on tape along. I had a cousin in Des Moines, Iowa, and we would stop off with them for a respite from the long days of pounding along on the interstate highway.

We arranged for Pattie's chemotherapy and the denosumab injection to be given at a nearby regional hospital in Danville, Pennsylvania. Pattie had phoned ahead to make the necessary arrangements and appointments. Denosumab was expensive. In Jackson it cost $2500 for one injection. We were assured in a phone call that the expenses for the treatments would be similar at the Danville hospital. Pennsylvania is a big welfare state, so we thought, in fact, it might be less costly.

Instead, we were incredulous when the bill arrived for the denosumab. For one shot, it was a lofty $10,000. We called our insurance company, suggesting it was a case of insurance fraud, but they paid the claim without blinking. Incredibly, four times as costly was within their allowable range. The hospital and state's health care system must have used people like us to balance out the difference for residents who did not have insurance and who could not afford to pay.

At Pine Creek we watched the mountainside forests transition from drab bare limbs and brushy grey color to the flush of pastel yellows, reds, and greens punctuated with scattered bursts of flowering shadbush trees. And we witnessed the forest floor erupting into the seasonal carpet of delicate flowering herbs—arbutus, bloodroot, lilies, trillium, violets and more. The daytime songs of dozens of different kinds of warblers and of American toads filled the air. At night owls, chorus and bull frogs resumed the noisy springtime celebration, and sometimes Eastern coyotes joined in. Black bear were frequent guests at the house, much to Benji's howling disapproval. Pattie made a list of a dozen different kinds of birds that came to the feeder at the back kitchen window—cardinals, tufted titmouse, grosbeaks, blue jays, nuthatches, red-winged blackbirds, Baltimore orioles, and more. Her list still lies on a desk in the house. Filled with renewal and bursting with life, spring was a wonderland-like time of the year there. Pattie e-mailed relatives and friends:

> All and all, things are good. 4 ruff days with deep lung pain
> and breathless, but all that subsided and infusion went well.
> Enjoying little walks, all the warblers, visitors and friends,
> a little fishing, and knitting [fashion scarves] on the porch.
> Want to try a short, flat bike ride today. Finally, warmed
> up. Last 3 days gorgeous.

It was delightful to walk in the forest together, ride the bicycle trail, and cast our fishing lines to rising trout once again. This time though, a solemn weight and worry inescapably overhung everything for us—a fragrance of sadness accompanied us everywhere. Simple hikes proved to be benchmark reminders of Pattie's changed condition. She now labored on walks in the mountains she'd had no difficulty with before, and bike rides became problematic. After crashing her bike she confessed to having balance difficulties. Each incremental change was an upsetting reminder of the disease's relentless advancement. Pattie could not hide it anymore. It stabbed at my heart.

Still, we fished below the house at the head of what had come to be called the "Turkey Hole." The name recalled when the Layser place had been a landmark turkey farm. Pattie was still capable of wading thigh-deep in the currents, casting imitator dry flies—March brown, slate drake, gray fox, sulphur Mayfly—with long rolling loops of line toward the far bank to rising trout.

In recent years, it seemed that whenever Pattie fished at a certain location, a great blue heron would show up and stalk the shallows immediately behind her. It was unusual that the heron would allow someone to be so close. If I moved in their direction, the large bird would take wing. I kidded her, "The heron must be your guardian animal, your totem." Pattie would look pleased and smile knowingly.

On one occasion, we walked up an old grassed-in quarry road. Its steep grade had never been a challenge in the past, just exercise. This time Pattie carefully measured her pace. It became apparent it was difficult for her. Near the top, she sat down on a boulder exhausted. I sat on the grassy road bank opposite her. She was unhappily aware of the change in herself. Although obviously disheartened, she did not complain and said nothing.

As I looked about, I noticed a rattlesnake peeking out from beneath a boulder near her.

"There is a rattlesnake under the boulder about ten feet away from you," I remarked casually.

Normally, Pattie would have looked around and made some entertaining comment. Instead, she glared at me, looking annoyed. She thought I was making a poor joke to enliven the moment. The snake remained under the rock, and we left it there undisturbed.

It may seem morbid, but on the last few trips to Pine Creek, we had begun to look at cemetery monuments. We had decided to install a monument in our memory at the Layser family plot in the Cedar Run Cemetery behind what had become the modernized country church.

My father had erected a monument there for himself and my mother in the 1970s, ironically, when he was about my age. He had done it while still in good health, too. Although I thought it odd at the time, I understand now. Time passes swiftly and why entrust your heirs to do it. Go shopping for yourself; get something that in life you liked. Maybe have your photograph taken standing beside it while you are still above ground. That's what my Dad did.

We found a black granite monument and arranged to provide details for its engraving after we returned to Alta. With advanced cancer, one lives day-to-day, moment-to-moment with the constant reminder of one's transience—each hour a small forever we gladly suffer. Arranging for a cemetery monument seemed oddly consistent with the reality we were living. More than anything, it represented a symbolic act—symbolic of our lives and losses. Tombstones honor the dead, even though they may not sit precisely above the respective person's grave.

We did not intend it to, but our black monument, located beneath an immense centuries-old white oak tree, jumps out among the cemetery's staid white granite and marble markers. We had the smooth black granite laser-etched, with the Teton mountain scene viewed from Grand Teton National Park's Snake River observation point. Below the laser-etched panorama, beside our names and dates, we had it engraved with a fitting epitaph we had composed:

> Together we explored the wonders of forest groves,
> glowing canyons, mountain rills, and flowering hills.
> Look for us now in the night sky along the River of Heaven,
> walking together in beauty throughout eternity.

When we reported to Pennsylvania's Danville Regional Medical Center for Pattie's chemotherapy, their oncologist had studied Pattie's medical and treatment records. He wanted to talk with Pattie, perhaps because he was curious. As usual, Pattie looked terrific, dressed nicely with the ravages of chemo hidden beneath a wig. The oncologist, a fatherly figure, dignified and compassionate, spoke softly and kindly. At one point, I made a remark, and he appeared irritated by the interruption. I remained quiet, while he and Pattie conversed. Pattie later told me she had liked him.

"You have had world-class treatment," he told her.

Looking back, I realize he was all too aware of the seriousness of Pattie's condition. He knew all too well the inescapable bitter pill that was coming.

A woman friend, who was a local Orvis fishing guide, got the novel idea she wanted to hold an event, which she called, "Fishing in Skirts." It was intended to celebrate women fly fishing.

Pattie bought some new flies to match the ongoing hatches and a fancy new landing net for the occasion. The women wore their waders under dresses while they fished. It drew some quizzical looks and remarks from the male-dominated populace of sportsmen on the creek, which was the women's intent, I suppose.

There is a photograph of Pattie in her fishing vest, casting, and wading, her white hair peeking out from beneath her Dubois, Wyoming, Cowboy Café baseball cap, the new net slung over her back. No one who did not know would have suspected or believed she was at that time very sick. Photographs of the women were posted on the Orvis website. One showed Pattie laughingly holding up a small fish she had caught. It was the last week of May 2013.

PART IV

WINTER'S DARKNESS AND DESPAIR

CHAPTER 30

THE SENTENCE

I see people who die a few minutes after the doctor tells them there is no hope of a cure. They give up and go. Others get angry and find joy in proving the doctor wrong. Something within them is challenged and hopeful. Hope is the divine motivator.

— Bernie Siegel, *Love, Medicine and Miracles*

The regimes of chemotherapies Pattie underwent appeared to be subjective trial-and-error procedures, heuristic at best. We had been repeatedly assured the list of available drugs "were as long as the oncologist's arm." We were told, "Something would be found that worked." We wanted to believe, but nothing worked. Did the chemotherapy and all the associated suffering actually extend Pattie's survival time? There is no way to know.

We continued to search for trials and made it known to the oncologist and hospital staff that we were interested in participating in trials. Yes, there were a lot of ongoing trials, but none that we could find were appropriate for Pattie's stage-four cancer. Most trials were narrowly and academically designed for some small facet or method of treatment specific to a particular condition, early cancer stage, or single medical procedure. No magic bullets. Doctors and nurses, and our oncologist, whom we repeatedly asked about trials, would look at us blankly. They were unaware of any fitting trials.

I thought I had finally discovered a possible trial startup that sounded promising. It was intended for stage-four breast cancer that had resisted all other treatments. The pilot study involved proteomics, individualized specific treatment using molecular profiling for late-stage breast cancer to determine what therapies might be most appropriate and work best, so called "personalized or precision medicine." It would have served the purpose of this trial to provide Pattie with the best treatment possible.

The trial was to be conducted at a university near Washington, DC. I made several phone calls and spoke with the study's lead professor, expressing our interest and willingness to travel there. Pattie appeared to be an ideal candidate. It all appeared hopeful. Then we heard nothing more. Phone calls were not returned. A secretary informed the doctor had left on a trip to Europe. Apparently, the study had not received anticipated funding.

Within short time after returning to Alta from Pennsylvania, Pattie was scheduled for another CAT scan to determine the effectiveness of her latest and ongoing chemotherapy. We put our trust in hopeful prayer; it was all that we had left. Like a child, one desperately wishes, pleads, and prays to a higher power for it all to somehow turn out favorably; as if wishing had the power to determine the outcome.

Over the course of Pattie's treatments, our waiting to learn the results was accompanied with those silent supplications—and fingernail on chalk board test-result anxiety. And after each type of drug therapy, the scans had alarmingly and devastatingly shown the tumors continuing to multiple and expand in size. Every time it was like being slammed and crushed by the worst outcomes.

Reporting to St. John's Medical Center to learn the latest scan results, we waited nervously in the small patient's room, trying to appear calm, but in reality, wanting to scream, feeling sickening dread and anxiety.

The oncologist entered the room and sat down before us. Generally, he made polite little remarks about how lovely Pattie looked. This time, without any preliminaries, he blurted out: "You have three weeks to three months to live." With hardly a pause, he added, "You'll go to sleep and not wake up."

Pattie's face flushed red, and she began sobbing quietly. I was too shocked to say anything. What could one say?

The oncologist looked uncomfortable and said: "My wife asks me what I do; I tell her, 'I make people cry.' You may want to just use the time you have left without any more chemo treatments," he said haltingly and stood up to leave. Then almost as an afterthought, he added, "There is one more drug that *might* extend your life a month or two."

Wiping her tears away, Pattie nodded she would do it. Tears rolled down my cheek, down both our cheeks. Giving up was not her style, she clung fiercely to hope and life. Defeated in all that she had undergone up until then, she was still willing to try whatever might work to extend her life.

The oncologist grunted, "I thought you'd say that," and left the room.

Contrary to earlier assertions, Pattie's metastasized cancer had been a "death sentence." Putting any other spin on it had been irresponsible, it was holding out false hope. Those who are unfortunate enough to develop metastatic breast cancer are in all likelihood going to die from it, as was mentioned earlier, odds are within twenty-six months or less. At this writing, medical science has yet to change that fact. In the United States, breast cancer is the second leading cause of death in women. And contrary to general impressions some studies have shown the mortality rates going up, not down.

Some physicians are uncomfortable with frankly discussing the prognosis. Perhaps it was thought best for the patient not to be informed about the potential dire outcomes early on. Instead, doctors and staff hold out hope, even if it is false hope. Extending hope is a part of the medical professional's job. That is fine, but it should be done within the context and disclosure of the full reality and seriousness of the situation. Otherwise, it represents misleading information and a lie by omission. I also suspect, some of the failure to inform fully is motivated by our medical system's preoccupation with minimizing any chance for liability.

While it may not be universal, I have since had medical professionals tell me they purposely do not tell patients the full story or they sugarcoat it to maintain a patient's psychological well-being. In the words of one nurse, she did not think "patients would be able handle the truth."

Patronizing patients is a horrible disservice. Especially in the case of life-threatening illness, having all the facts in advance can motivate people to make better, more informed choices, seek new or additional treatments, and do critical planning that they might otherwise feel they can put off. Plan for the best, but also be thoroughly and realistically counseled, about the real likelihood for the worst.

CHAPTER 31

WAITING FOR SPECIFICS FROM GOD

Being a survivor doesn't mean being strong—it's telling people when you need a meal, company, a ride, whatever. It's paying attention to heart wisdom, feelings, not living a role, but having a unique, authentic life, having something to contribute, finding time to love and laugh. All these things are qualities of survivors.

—Bernie Siegel, *Love, Medicine and Miracles*

Pattie was unquestionably a survivor. She continued to live, laugh and love until the very end. My mind goes to dark corners as the question pervasively nags—did we do all we could have done for her? Yes, rationally, I know we did all we knew to do. And all that appeared available and possible. But in the pathos of mourning my brain does not let it rest. Rather it plays the "what if" or "if only" tape over and over again. Guilt and regret invariably try to elbow their way in.

When Pattie's cancer appeared the first time, we thoroughly researched the potential treatments. We followed specialist's understandable recommendations. There was logic to it. At the time, as far as I know, neither genetic testing for the breast cancer gene nor ontogenesis was generally available. Still, statistically, the odds were that Pattie should still be with us. A recent study comparing lumpectomies versus double mastectomy indicated comparable ten-year survival rates of 82 percent. Why did Pattie fall into the population's statistical fringe, the 18 percent wasteland? What happened? Why? My mind looks for answers, but I find none; there are none.

After years of being his patient, the last face-to-face we had with the oncologist was abrupt and final. There was no ongoing follow-up. No doubt there were questions later directed to him by the nurses, but I do not recall that we had any more direct contact. It appeared the oncologist had washed his hands of the unpleasant aftermath. The next phase, so-called "palliative treatment," was pretty much handed off to the nursing staff and other physicians.

After Pattie's cancer metastases were discovered, it had felt like the medical treatments became a free-for-all. There is no standard of care—diagnostic and treatment guidelines—for women with progressive metastatic breast cancer. Suffering brought on from the drug side-effects was difficult to separate from the disease itself. I assume there was a systematic and logical sequence to the prescribed drug therapies; but whatever it was, it was never explained. Whatever benefit may have been gained from the chemotherapy is unclear and unknowable.

Could Pattie and I have done anything differently to change the outcome? Probably not, but why did the medical system leave us mulling this unsettling question, rather than assuring us we had done all we could? The Pennsylvania oncologist knew about closure; without our asking, he had quietly told Pattie that she had "had world-class treatment."

Following the St. John Hospital oncologist's bluntly delivered prognosis, Pattie, who outwardly still appeared very much herself in nearly all respects, wrote friends and family movingly alerting them to her condition: "To all of you who fill my life with joy—it's hard to write about something that seems unreal to me . . . the doctor's prognosis for my survival is weeks . . . maybe months. I read the report but I'm waiting for specifics from God."

Friends and family were disbelieving; none wanted to believe it. Only a few months earlier, Pattie had been strong enough to spend all day downhill skiing at the Grand Targhee Resort's Mary's Nipple event. And I have a photograph showing Pattie wading and fly casting at Pine

Creek, taken only a few weeks before receipt of her death sentence prognosis.

There is an unnamed, unmapped waterfall on the North Fork of Teton Creek near where we live that Pattie and I occasionally visited. From the trailhead, it is a short walk through dense spruce forest on a barely discernible trace that ascends steeply. In June, only days after the chilling prognosis, Pattie and I made our way up the familiar path. We did not pause to rest or gain our breath, but kept going up through huckleberry and honeysuckle bushes and around the downfall. The exertion felt good. It was not a place one might expect to find a person with an advanced terminal illness.

Mists rose and snow-melt waters roared down the narrow defile. At the brink of the gorge and falls, the forest opened up into level moss-carpeted ledge rock punctuated with large glacier deposited boulders—a microcosm of solitude and natural beauty. If the natural world provides spiritual support and inspiration, this enchanting and restorative spot represented a place where that eternal connection might be felt. It was a place for meditation, reconciling deep thoughts, or perhaps for prayer.

Bathed in the heady aura of the mist's dissolved oxygen, or as some term it, "negative ions," we lingered. There was a heavy underlying sadness. A nesting pair of water ouzels claimed the glen as their home, busily darting up and down the chasm. In my mind, I named the waterfall "Pattie's Cascade," in honor of Pattie and her deep love for the Tetons. Maybe a cartographer will one day put the waterfall on a map and decide to use the name: Pattie's Cascade.

At home, visits from friends, family, and cards and e-mail correspondence continued to pour in, a constant coming and going of communication and concern. Pattie's women friends brought food dishes, potted plants, and flowers. The sisterhood emerged, support that women offer one another in times of serious distress. Our refrigerator bulged to overflowing with the offerings. It all underscored my continuing deepening dismay.

Pattie taught herself to knit what I called "fashion scarves." Her many productions were lovely and artfully creative. Pattie had always excelled at crafts—knitting, needlepoint, stained glass, sewing, decoupage, floral arrangements, wreaths, and music boxes. She did it all. Many of her artistic creations decorate our home. She smilingly and selflessly began handing her scarves out as gifts to friends and relatives. She never verbalized it, nor did I or anyone else, but they were obviously intended as remembrances, one of her last acts of kindness. Where did Pattie get that idea; or for her, did it just follow naturally?

Pattie's younger sister Lisa visited. When the sister and her husband were leaving after a four-day stay, Lisa tried to minimize the intensity of the moment by saying encouragingly, "We'll be back again next year to see you." Pattie's self-control became undone; she burst into tears. She knew her condition made that unlikely, and that it was the last time they would ever see each other. Pattie rarely burdened others by expressing self-pity. Through it all, she resolutely acted to minimize concern and not to cause others worry.

Friends from Arizona and Wisconsin that we had met on our Grand Canyon raft trip visited. We went out to breakfast and enjoyed conversation. We walked them into Pattie's Cascade on the North Fork of Teton Creek, where they adored the natural setting. But this time, climbing the steep pathway, Pattie began experiencing shortness of breath and difficulty of balance. I walked behind and helped her. She never complained, but it contributed to my layers of concern.

The last resort drug therapy Pattie had elected to do was eribulin, also known as Halaven, a brand name. It was intended for late-stage patients whose cancer had progressed in spite of prior multiple rounds of chemotherapy. We were told it could possibly increase survival up to two and a half months. Pattie was determined to go on for as long as possible in hope that a new cancer drug or an effective treatment might be discovered. Hope against hope. But two years later, as I write this, there has still been no such advancement.

The side effects of the eribulin were indescribably horrible. It destroyed both red and white blood cells and lowered Pattie's potassium levels to the point of inducing dizziness and causing balance problems. Blood chemistry testing a week after the initial infusion indicated her levels of red and white blood cells to be so low that we were told another dose of the drug would have been fatal. It took more than two weeks before Pattie's blood chemistry recovered sufficiently to allow her to do another eribulin infusion. The resulting side effects were the same as the original dose—debilitating. It took another two weeks again for her blood chemistry to begin to approach normal. That was the last chemo Pattie received. She had no strength to do more. Was her brave suffering worth it? Did the drug do what was intended, and actually prolong her survival? No one can say.

A kind of deep numbness set in for me. I have lost track of the sequence of some details. The disease progressed in a series of irretrievable and interconnected losses in both Pattie's health and function—small defeats and disappointments that continued to cumulatively add up.

At one point, I brought up Pattie's complaint of dizziness and balance issues at an oncology appointment, rather than first ascribing it to the chemo and other drug side effects, it was immediately assumed to be brain metastases—the worst possible case scenario. When a brain scan was proposed, I recoiled in horror, and the brain scan proposal was dropped. I do not believe Pattie ever developed brain metastases, but if she had, what good would it do anyone to know at that point? It would have been untreatable anyway, and the knowledge would have only underscored an already distressing situation, making it appear even more depressingly hopeless.

With an eye to what lay ahead, Pattie requested consultation with a pain specialist. The pain doctor was an easy-going personable young fellow. He prescribed additional pain medications and calmly advised us on their use.

Pattie was saint-like. It makes one wonder how she was able to calmly smile and talk amiably and matter-of-factly, discussing the disease progression and use of pain medication as if casually inquiring about a topic of conversation, or for academic purposes, as though seeking information for someone else. Thinking back, I felt deadened and dazed.

Sometime after that, I made a comment to a nurse about Pattie's shortness of breath when we had hiked up to the North Fork waterfall. The nurse looked alarmed; right away she had Pattie walk up and down the outside hallway. Then she measured Pattie's blood oxygen level with an oximeter. It registered slightly below normal. Pattie was sent to radiology for a lung x-ray. The x-ray revealed the ominous beginnings of a plural effusion, a buildup of fluid between the lung lining and chest wall.

We were sent home with a prescription for an oxygen concentrator and bottled oxygen to be delivered to our home. When the concentrator was delivered and set up, it made a noise resembling the loud rhythmic thump of a heartbeat. The disturbing sound pounded throughout the house, a grim and constant reminder of a life being sustained. The person who delivered the machine indifferently played it down, calling it "just white-noise." Pattie began having to wear a cannula attached by tubing to the concentrator.

To diminish the machine's distressing noise, I moved the concentrator to a far location in the basement and attached thirty feet of tubing. With that length, it allowed Pattie to go anywhere in the house and outside onto the deck, too. Two sizes of tanks for portable use had also been delivered. But for the most part, our day-to-day world had gone from the vastness of mountains and rivers to a radius of thirty-feet indoors.

As we had in past years, Pattie and I attended the annual Alta community picnic, this time with me carrying a portable oxygen bottle in a day pack and Pattie wearing a cannula. Some neighbors were glad to see us, gave us hugs; others, as you might expect, were uncomfortable and kept their distance as if we were contagious. Pattie talked to the former, did not impose on the latter, and tried to bear up through it all. It was not easy.

A year earlier, Pattie had applied for a breast cancer survivor program called, "Casting for Recovery." She was excited to learn she had been selected to attend. It lifted her spirit, only to be disappointingly crushed once more when she was told she was not going to be allowed to attend because she needed to be on oxygen. We were informed that since the event was being held at over 7,000-feet elevation, it was considered too risky to allow someone needing oxygen to participate. I called the person in charge, pleading, offering to drive Pattie back and forth each day and to carry her oxygen bottle for her, all to no avail. The things in life Pattie looked forward to and enjoyed and that would have given her spirit a much needed boost, were one by one slipping away. Pattie did not cry, but her deep disappointment showed. Recalling her reaction is painfully sad for me.

My mother's passing away less than a year earlier added to the distress. Over the years, my mother had, through her own free will, transitioned from the country farm to an in-town apartment, then to assisted living, and near the end involuntarily into a nursing home, which she despised. Confined to the nursing home by age-related infirmities, she had lost her desire to live.

I had received a late night phone call of her critical condition. My flight to Pennsylvania got hung up in Chicago, where I had to overnight. Between Pattie's condition and my mother's passing, I was in a weary mental state. By the time I arrived at the small town where she had been living, my mother was gone. Unlike the independent manner in which she had lived life, she had died dependent and in an institution, alone.

Pattie and I were led to reflect on our own mortality and legacy. There is a name for it: "anticipatory grief"—grieving begun already before the inevitable actual loss. We had already for some time been silently mourning our lost lifestyle. The incremental losses in our lives were cumulative, building staggeringly upon each other, growing like a gathering storm.

I wanted the legacy of Pattie's and my name to live on *together* through lasting contributions to what we had enjoyed most in life: deep commitment to nature, the land, and each other. We had talked about it many times in the prior years and had come to absolute agreement on what we proposed for the Pine Creek property's eventual disposal. My mother, too, had agreed with us. Before her death, she had urged us to sell the property to the Commonwealth of Pennsylvania's Department of Forestry and Conservation.

The family property adjoined state forest lands, a designated state wilderness area, and it had critically valuable stream frontage and bottomland. Pine Creek was a state-designated "Scenic River." As there were few other intact properties remaining in the Pine Creek valley like it, it was uniquely important for its recreation value. I had always envisioned it remaining in the family. But no one in the family had as deep an attachment to it as Pattie and I; and importantly, neither did anyone appear to have the interest in, or the financial capability for, maintaining it.

At different times, years earlier, we had tried to talk to my sons about their interests in the property. The younger son pretended indifference, which was a reply in itself. He had not visited the farm or his grandmother in over fifteen years. My oldest son reacted as though we were trying to stick him with something that was a liability. "It won't pay for itself," he said angrily. At his outburst, Pattie and I looked at one another, but I did not try to argue with him. However, those being the attitudes, we felt justified in our concern that after we were gone, our heirs or other private interests would likely try to maximize the property's substantial cash value by subdividing it.

During our previous time at Pine Creek, we had met with the State Department of Conservation and Natural Resources administrators. Our property was on their priority list for acquisition should the opportunity arise. Pattie and I agreed to and arranged for a sale of the property to the Commonwealth. It would transfer to them upon our deaths to be managed in perpetuity for public outdoor recreation as a part of the adjoining 146,540-acre Tiadaghton State Forest, State

Game Lands, and as Scenic River frontage. The sale of what had been a cherished family property weighed heavily on us as another loss in our lives.

While Pattie, as half-owner, signed the first round of papers, the transaction was not actually finalized until after she had been gone for nearly a year. It had involved much bureaucratic back-and-forth, which was finally circumvented when the District and State Foresters personally stepped in and became involved, based on the property's prior designation as a priority for acquisition.

Next, Pattie and I endowed an *"Earle and Pattie Layser Distinguished Professorship in Conservation Biology and Policy"* at the University of Montana College of Forestry and Conservation in Missoula. It would begin after we were both gone and was designed through education to help insure that the wildlife and wilderness in the Northern Rockies, which had played such an important part in our lives and relationship, would continue to exist into the future. The university gift celebration was described under the chapter on Legacy.

The university installed a rock monument with an attached large brass plaque along the walkway leading to forestry school building. The plaque shows a skyline representation of the Teton Mountains and a reminder or gentle admonishment to passersby and students entering the forestry college: "We have cherished the Northern Rockies. Now it is your life's landscape. Keep these wildlands and all their wildlife forever intact—Earle and Pattie Layser."

It was poignantly significant that the legal forms for the above two matters were the last papers Pattie was physically able to sign. Instead of her artfully flowing longhand, she struggled to pen cramped signatures, but determinedly managed them on both the Pine Creek and University of Montana documents. Then she looked up at me, proudly smiling as if to say: "There, we did it."

Pattie's other sister, Donna, and a niece, Evelyn, who had been the flower girl at our wedding, visited and stayed with us for nearly a week. We would gather on the back deck in the morning for a pleasant breakfast surrounded by sweet-scented lilacs, raspberry bushes, and potted flowering plants. Pattie had planted the latter with my help only weeks earlier. While she had been still able, Pattie had searched for solace among the flowering plants in the local greenhouses. Invariably, she brought something home to plant.

For breakfast, I'd prepare Pattie her favorite fruits—watermelon and huckleberries. When she was still healthy and active, Pattie had always enjoyed breakfast. Now, she appeared disinterested in eating and would toy with her food. She had also begun drinking tea rather than coffee. A friend had recommended tea made from red clover as having anti-cancer properties. When Pattie was still able, on her outdoor walks, she had collected red clover. Little medicine bundles of her dried red clover still hang in our home's plant room, another tender reminder of Pattie that I have been unable to remove.

In a haze of painkillers, Pattie remained her gracious self, amiably chatting with her sister and niece at breakfast. Although the others didn't seem to notice, I was sadly aware that she had begun to mix up her stories. It really did not matter though; it was Pattie agreeably laughing and talking.

During those last days, in the cool and pleasant morning settings, we were impressed by the butterflies that seemed attracted to Pattie, flitting closely around her. Likewise, hummingbirds would hover right in front of her face as if peering into her eyes, or maybe into her soul.

We sat there entranced, while Pattie, smiling knowingly as if she alone possessed the secret power, calmly accepted the unique attention. It would not have been remarkable, I suppose, except for the fact, every morning the butterflies and hummingbirds seemed to focus their magical attentions only on Pattie. They appeared like her spiritual companions.

Pattie had entered the end stage in life, where spirituality for some begins to border on the mystical. The blue heron, mentioned earlier, hummingbirds, and butterflies, all seemed appropriate spiritual companions for Pattie. Amazingly fitting totems for her, they symbolized her gentle but resilient spirit and her relationship with nature. Native Americans believed the spirit of the person never dies, that it can become associated with a particular part of nature—an animal, bird, or land feature. Particularly fitting for Pattie was also her association with Jackson Hole, the landscape where the Teton Mountains rise dramatically from the Snake River plain.

Pattie's sister, Donna, was entranced by the scene with the butterflies and hummingbirds. I'm not sure if Donna knew about "spirit beings," but as she later remarked to me, she will forever associate hummingbirds with Pattie and their last time together. Seeing hummingbirds invokes memories of those last hours together with her sister and brings tears to her eyes.

I was reminded of the poster for the Grand Targhee Resort event, which had associated rising clouds of butterflies with Pattie. I remembered, too, a better and happier time not many years earlier in the rainforest in Uganda, Africa, where we were enchantingly engulfed by blizzards of butterflies. Pattie had referred to it as: "Uganda's Season of the Butterflies." There was also our last season fishing at Pine Creek, where I observed great blue herons and Pattie uncommonly close to each other, both fishing. I had teased her that the heron must be her totemic animal.

Curious, I looked up what those three totemic animals signified: the butterfly represented "going through life in beauty, continuously unfolding with grace and lightness"; the hummingbird an "enjoyment of life and a playful optimistic outlook"; and the blue heron was known for "independently choosing one's own way and being a peace maker." I was amazed at how closely those three animal's totemic descriptions really did match Pattie's life's path and spirit.

Now, friends sometimes tell me they saw a blue heron and are reminded of Pattie; others say the butterflies they saw made them reflect on her; and Pattie's sister, Donna, has told me she will always think of Pattie whenever she sees a hummingbird. And I—I am reminded of Pattie by all those, but feel her presence the strongest when I am in Jackson Hole, north of the town, where the mountains rise spectacularly from the valley floor. It was where she had recaptured her strength and began a recovery from her life-threatening cerebral aneurism years before; beginning a new life. Later, it was the place where we had married; and also, where we had spent a great deal of time outdoors in the shadows of the Teton Mountains, celebrating life and our extraordinary love for one another. It was a place Pattie loved and deeply identified with. She called it her "life's landscape."

CHAPTER 32

THE GREAT MYSTERY

[My friend] Basso has departed this strange world a little ahead of me. That means nothing. People like us . . . know that the distinction between past, present and future is only a stubbornly persistent illusion.

— Albert Einstein

Those who know me recognize that I have always been a practical person, grounded in reality, and probably not a person they would generally expect to reflect on otherworldly matters. But living at the edge of life's greatest mystery with Pattie in those last years and final days changed me forever. Reflections on life-altering occurrences, spirituality, and afterlife, inescapably and pervasively come to mind.

Pattie was an exceptionally spiritual person—more than anyone I have ever known. In those last days the quiet strength of her spirituality resembled the Divine. Her angelic nature was enhanced by the tragic fact, that at her relatively young age, she was able to calmly face and accept her mortality, despite her love of life. While not religious in an orthodox sense, Pattie lived her life committed to selfless principles that all the world's major religions recognize.

I believe Pattie saw the divinity in every moment in every day and in every part of nature, in the sense of Ephesians 4:6: "God is over all and through all and in all." Being with her, one saw the richness of her spirituality, not unlike the luminous glow of flowering mountain meadows in springtime.

In her late-stage progression and alternating mental states, we were bonded together, drifting along the path of life's final and most mystical journeys. In the inescapable end, I knew Pattie would leave me and go on alone passing through that mysterious gateway, but we had not come to the point of separation yet. Somehow she seemed to have transcended fear of death; at some point, she appeared to me to have quietly and with dignity accepted the inevitable, that her earthly time was nearing an end.

On one occasion, she and I were sitting on the deck in the early morning when she gave a little start. Appearing to be intently focusing on something across the other side of the porch, I quietly asked her, "What do you see, honey?"

"People I haven't seen in a long time."

"Who?"

"My mother and grandmother," she replied very matter-of-factly. Both had been deceased for a long time.

I gently asked, "Is that frightening or comforting?"

Without hesitation, she responded, "Comforting."

Fearful of being intrusive or causing alarm, I did not pursue it further. Strangely, I felt like I would have been invading the sanctity of her privacy to have asked more questions. She offered no further explanation either. Her calm unemotional acceptance of the incident gave me pause.

Was it hallucinations or was it, as some would believe, a visit by loved ones from the "other side?" Why her mother and grandmother, whom she had loved, and not others? Pattie used to reminisce about playing in her grandmother's yard with her cousins as a child, chasing butterflies and lightning bugs. If blessedness in a person could bring loved ones to visit from the afterlife, Pattie would have been one to do so.

We normally did not allow Benji on the bed, but Pattie began coaxing him up. He would lie tightly against her, like her guardian. She loved Benji. Feeling him snuggled against her was no doubt reassuring. Little wonder some ancient and Native American cultures sent horses, pets, and sentimental personal possessions into the afterlife with their owners.

At one point, I read her a story that she had written and published years earlier in the anthology, *Spindrift*. Entitled "Twenty Below," it is a lyrical composite of Pattie's observations during our first winters together. More specifically, it was about her fantasy-like discovery and embracement of winter's beauty. Forcing myself not to choke up, I tried to read calmly. Lying there looking up at me, as I sat on the edge of the bed reading, she listened intently with a haunting expression of what I can only describe as childlike wonder.

> I turned my skis on edge to push off quietly. Winter's solitude and beauty merged with my frosty breath . . . heralding a private epiphany . . . I could feel boundless tensions unraveling, trapped emotions being sprung, pure joy released . . . each day...a singular pleasure. During many long years spent walled into cities, I [merely] thumbed through calendars full of pretty days. But today, I blow kisses to my restlessness . . . [otherwise] I might have missed first light piercing crystal-wrapped tree branches . . . hurried past the song of pine grosbeaks, and the sedate gathering of ruffed grouse. I might never have taken time to share life with the wild snowshoe hare that I encountered along the way.

I had purposefully delayed bringing Hospice Services into our home, refusing to concede what hospice's presence foretold. It was not denial; I knew where it was all going. Compassionately, I wanted to shelter Pattie—and perhaps myself—from admitting to the frightening inevitability for as long as possible. I resisted the inescapability. I clung tightly and protectively to our precious last remaining days, hours, and minutes together.

Pattie began to exhibit more signs that the end was near. She began displaying alarming involuntary physical movements. The medical term for it was myoclonic twitches. She seemed to be aware of the uncontrollable movements, but appeared to ignore them. She became increasingly weak. When she was no longer able to do it herself, I administered the regime of medications and helped attend to her personal needs.

Friends frequently stopped by to visit with Pattie, kindly bringing prepared foods and flowers, asking what they could do to help. The refrigerator continued to bloat with all it would hold. Other friends offered to remove and replace the accumulation of older offerings that filled the fridge.

While friends would visit and sit with Pattie, I would use the occasions to take Benji for a walk or to go for a short bicycle ride. I did not have the strength to make those into anaerobic stress relieving jaunts. On one occasion on a walk in the forest near our home, I plucked a small branch from a huckleberry bush that was laden with fruit. At home, I put the branchlet in a small vase with water and set it on the dining table. I foolishly thought it would be a nice surprise and might make Pattie smile. When she saw it, it took her a minute to realize what it was, and then she burst into tears. Instead of bringing cheer, the berry bush had the opposite effect. It recalled our enjoyable times in the mountains picking berries, and she sadly recognized she would never do it again. The branchlet of berries was a sad and unintended reminder of mortality and loss.

I lived day to day enveloped in a deepening fog of depression, grief and sorrow. While I remember impressions from that time and certain happenings, I am sure my mind has merged, blocked, or forgotten the details of many things. Feelings of numbness, sadness, and pain dominate my memories. As National Book Award Winner, Joan Didion, expressed in *The Year of Magical Thinking,* "I wake and feel the fell of dark, not day." At one point holding Pattie, I began to cry. Barely able to speak, she gently chastised me for weeping. After that, I tried to conceal my tears and weeping from her.

A woman who was an acquaintance of Pattie's and who had at one time served as a professional hospice nurse took it upon herself to begin coming to the house. At first I was grateful, and it was very helpful. The person was experienced in administering medications and all aspects of palliative care. But then it became strange, and the person's motivation uncertain. She would show up unannounced and authoritatively walk through our unlocked front door into the house, as if in charge. At one point, she helped me change Pattie's pajamas; pausing, looking at Pattie she sighed, "Even after all she has been through, what an amazingly beautiful woman she still is." It was true, Pattie was slender, her skin smooth, and she still appeared fit; hardly what you would expect with a person dying from cancer.

Truthfully assuring the woman that we appreciated her help, I politely asked her to please first call ahead. She took offense and said: "What's going to happen when you wake up and she is unconscious, but still breathing . . . what will you do then?"

I was in vulnerable state of mind. I did not know how to take the question—rhetorically or whether she actually expected me to respond? Did she view all lay people, or maybe just men, or only me, as incapable and incompetent?

I finally conceded to invite hospice into our home. The nurse came and sat at one end of the couch, Pattie appearing stoic and quiet, and perhaps a bit annoyed, at the other end. Occasional uncontrollable twitches grabbed at Pattie, which she was no longer able to conceal, although she tried. Mostly, the nurse told us a litany of her own personal health problems, but then she began reading from a brochure entitled "End of Life Issues."

Amazingly, Pattie rallied, becoming present in the moment. Drawing herself together, she interrupted the hospice nurse. Speaking calmly and very clearly Pattie said, "I'm *not* ready for that yet."

The nurse looked startled; confused, she stopped reading. I wanted to cheer. I had to admire Pattie's defiance. She had not given up to the approaching inevitability. It was pure Pattie. I felt like she deserved a medal of honor for bravery and failure to surrender before insurmountable odds.

I have often told that story to people. Mostly it draws blank looks. I do not know if they do not get it, or maybe how to take it, but to me it was an unpretentious display of indomitable spirit. While the disease was conquering her physically, it never defeated her spirit, or the strength of her character. Before leaving, the hospice nurse assured me: "She's not ready; she's got a long time yet."

The disease did not appear to progress as benignly as the oncologist had informed us it would: "You will go to sleep and not wake up." No longer eating, barely able to whisper any words, wracked with painful coughing, difficulty in breathing, shortage of breath, involuntary movements, elevated blood ammonia levels, and falling blood oxygen levels, her lucidity slipping away, Pattie suffered uncomplainingly; but sometimes she was unable to stifle quiet moans.

I felt overwhelming helplessness and despair as the disease continued gathering momentum. Pattie was the person I loved most in this world, but I could do pitifully little other than attend to her most basic needs—helping her to the bathroom, propping pillows, giving pain medications and cough suppressants, checking her blood oxygen levels, and administering lactulose to help reduce growing nitrogen levels in the blood. Desperate, I called the St. John's Oncology Department and asked a nurse what I could do to alleviate or ease the gathering storm of symptoms. I was told "there was nothing that could be done." I called hospice and was informed that all the regular nurses were busy, but that they would send someone out from the nursing pool.

Pattie was transitioning into a realm that bordered between two worlds—the present and the eternal. She labored for every difficult breath. I was engulfed in anxiety and mind-numbing apprehension. When I held her she began trying to kiss my face and neck with lightly fluttering "butterfly kisses," as she used to call them. Though barely conscious, she fought to speak. In little more than a gasp, she whispered, "I'm sorry . . . I'm sorry."

There was nothing for me to forgive. She was not sorry for herself because she was dying, but lovingly and selflessly empathetic to the end, Pattie apologized because she was leaving me alone. I wept a torrent of tears for her and for us, and the promises and sweetness that our life together had held, which would forever remain cut short, unfinished.

A nurse from hospice knocked at our door, a Guatemalan woman who spoke good English. She was professional and compassionate, and I was tearfully grateful for her competent and timely help. Together we changed the bedding, gave Pattie a sponge bath, and changed her pajamas. Thoughtfully, the Guatemalan lady gently combed Pattie's remaining wisps of white hair. I was thankful for that kindness, a final nod to Pattie's pride in her hair and appearance. As the hospice nurse was leaving, she reassured me: "She is not ready . . . she has a long time to go yet."

But Pattie was having increasing and alarming difficulty in breathing. I increased the oxygen amount the concentrator was delivering; still, Pattie was unable to get enough air. She was panicky and kept brushing the cannula from her face as if she thought it obstructed her breathing. She was suffocating. I kept trying to calm her, talking to her, rushing to put the device back in place repeatedly.

A few days earlier, I had installed a sound monitor next to Pattie's bed. It broadcast the sounds of her labored breathing, punctuated with moans, throughout the house. It was unsettlingly and horribly difficult to bear, hearing the amplified sounds of her suffering. But it was a way I was able to keep track of what was happening when I went into another room.

Some hours later, it appeared Pattie had exhausted herself and was making smaller sounds, while she rested, or so I thought. In retrospect, perhaps she had fallen asleep in the manner the oncologist had predicted, drifting away into loss of consciousness. I don't know.

But believing she was resting, I left the room and, overwhelmingly exhausted from the stress and constant caring, lay down to rest for a brief while. When I returned only a few hours later, the house was quiet. My Pattie was gone. Vital organs deprived of oxygen, I have learned, can result in death in four to five minutes, a type of anoxia.

I cannot describe the sorrow and regret I feel that she didn't pass in my arms as a final goodbye. Never late for an appointment, never one to break a promise, she had departed without waiting for me. Suddenly the days and years that had been filled with the sounds of each other were replaced by an interminable silence.

It was past midnight, sometime in the early hours of August 3, 2013, eleven days before Pattie's sixty-fourth birthday. It was like her to slip away in an unobtrusive manner to avoid upsetting me. I sat without crying on the edge of the bed with her in shock and glumly somber. The weeping would come later, a remaining lifetime of uncountable tears, sorrow, and mourning.

At one point early on, Pattie had fiercely told me, "I don't want to die." Not knowing how to respond, I had nodded agreement to her determination. Her desperate pronouncement permanently buried into my mind. Now I regret that I had not grabbed her and held fast to her, comforting her at that moment. Through all the prolonged suffering and medical treatments, she had fought and willed herself to live, behaved stoically, and tried not to burden others with her condition. Then like that, she was gone. With her departure, a large part of me died, too.

I lovingly folded her arms across her chest and closed her eyes. She did not respond. Already, it was not Pattie. She would have laughed or smiled, or made some amusing remark. Instead her body lay there unmoving as I touched her skin for the last time. No longer of this world, she was already somewhere else. Strangely, though, I felt her presence all around me.

I removed the rings she had treasured and worn always. They did not come off easily in any sense. For years, those rings had tightly symbolized our love for one another—the Montana sapphire ring I had given her the first year we had met and her beautiful custom-made wedding ring. They represented our passionate commitment to each other. We had meant all we had vowed that long ago autumn day in the Tetons on top of Signal Mountain, including "until death would do us part." The full meaning of that vow weighed heavily now. Tight-lipped, another arose in me in its place: *death would never do us part.*

Pattie to her everlasting credit had put up an uncommon resistance. But no matter how long she had fought and endured, the end had come too soon and too sudden. My stubborn inability to relinquish her would become a complicating factor in my bereavement.

I was one of the "walking wounded," the seriously emotionally injured, who, having been left behind, struggled to carry on. Ghastly haunting images of those last days, last hours, and final minutes with Pattie play and replay through my mind, over and over again—a nightmare stuck on repeat. Friends have told me I am symptomatic of post-traumatic stress disorder. I ask myself the question we all seek to know: "Where do those we love go when they die?

The Bereaved's Lament

Where did she go, this love of mine?
I saw and felt her body rigid and cold,
her warmth and smile were gone.
Finality echoed like a thunderclap gavel rap
when I closed her eyes and folded her arms.
I removed her rings, she did not resist,
nor show emotion, fear or pain.
She is gone, somewhere departed,
I am left alone in mournful sorrow.
My affection still burns strong, I yearn for her;
if I follow the pull of those feelings, will I find her?
Does a reunion wait for us behind death's door?
Will we be reunited in another time and place—
walk hand-in-hand throughout eternity,
along the River of Heaven's celestial shores?
Where did she go, this love of mine?
—The Author

CHAPTER 33

A SLUMBERING GIANT AWAKENS

Some of you say, "Joy is greater than sorrow," and others say, "Nay, sorrow is the greater." But I say unto you, they are inseparable. Together they come, and when one sits alone with you at your board, remember that the other is asleep upon your bed."
—Kahlil Gibran, *The Prophet*

As *The Prophet* foretold, sorrow arose from a long dormancy and replaced joy, who alone had sat with Pattie and me all of our years together. The more joy had thrived and grown, so had sorrow, hidden and out of sight, grown, too. Until, when awakened, sorrow appeared as a formidable giant.

The greater the love and joy that had been, the larger the grief and sorrow that inseparably follows . . . opposing opposites, darkness followed the light. One person was gone, but to me, the whole world appeared abruptly empty. As writer Douglas H. Gresham noted, "All human relationships end in pain." While I must agree with Gresham, I would add that some relationships end more painfully than others. I confess that I was ignorant of the full wraithlike power that grief can achieve. Gathering like a black storm cloud, it built upon itself, growing layer upon weighty layer

Our culture does not treat bereavement as an illness, but both Freud and British psychoanalyst Melanie Klein regarded it as a pathological condition. According to psychiatrist and writer Dr. David Peretz, pathological derangement in the grieving bereaved correlates to the extent he or she depended on the deceased for "pleasure, support, or esteem." Yes, but what successful marriage or relationship doesn't seek, encourage, reward, and depend on those things? As close as Pattie and I were, we epitomized Peretz's criteria. Pattie and I always happily designed and endeavored to receive "pleasure, support and esteem" from one another.

I wish no one the task of composing an obituary, the final and fitting words for a loved one. How can one meaningfully describe with words alone a person's life, and a relationship ripped from one's heart? For Pattie, the person I loved most in life, it was penned in tears. It was the third obituary I had written in the course of my life. I had composed obituaries for my father and mother, and now Pattie.

Published in its entirety, Pattie's half a news page tribute appeared in the Jackson Hole and Teton Valley newspapers. I selected a photograph for the obituary that showed Pattie emerging from a two-person tent into the mountain morning holding Benji when he was still a puppy. Her signature shock of long curly hair catches the eye. Recounting an excerpt from her obituary still triggers an overwhelming upwelling of sorrow and grief-filled feelings:

> Longtime Alta resident, Pattie B. Layser, 63, died Saturday from breast cancer . . . possessed with a strong spirit and will to live, she succumbed only after a long and courageous struggle . . . Pattie was a kind, loving and gracious person, who had a beautiful bright smile and infectious laughter. With polite humility she rarely spoke of her many accomplishments. She had a great love and sensitivity for people, beauty, aesthetics, and nature. She was very much loved. Her loss leaves an emptiness that will forever be mourned.

Dazed and preoccupied, more than a little crazed, I personified the vulnerability of the deeply bereaved. Not only mentally distraught,

I was unbalanced physically, too. At a friend's house, where I went to make copies of the obituary three days after Pattie's passing, I missed the stairs and accidently stepped off into space at the top of their foyer.

In an instant, all my years of experience hiking, skiing, and climbing in challenging mountain terrain without injury were negated by a single misstep. I landed on the edge of a bottom flagstone step with my leg pinned under me. The ligaments attaching my quadriceps muscles were torn completely from their moorings above and around the knee. Writhing on the floor in agony, I was unable to bend or move my leg. It was excruciatingly painful.

Major ski towns host a battalion of orthopedic surgeons who are assured a continuous flow of business from outdoor recreation activity mishaps. Loaded into a vehicle, I asked to be taken directly to the local hospital. A surgeon there had developed a reputation for successfully fastening the unfortunate back together.

My injury required prompt attention for the ligaments to be effectively reattached. But the surgery was scheduled for several days later? When I questioned the delay, I was informed that the doctor had a golf tournament he was planning to attend first.

Crippled and despondent, I lay on the couch at home. Helpless, I had to hire a day-care nurse to assist me. Strangely, there was no boundary between where the physical pain ended and my emotional pain began; the two indistinguishably merged and became one. I did not know it then, but emotional pain and physical pain are processed in the same part of the brain. The brain does not recognize them differently.

My son drove up from Utah to help me get to surgery and take me home afterward. While I was sitting dazed in the hospital lobby in a wheelchair waiting after the operation, I could overhear the nurses whispering about my need to be treated with antidepressants. To the disbelief of the nurses, I refused. Through my miasma of physical and mental torment, I was briefed on the proper use of crutches before being sent home.

Once home, I returned to the familiar couch. My son left for Utah and the daycare nurse took charge. She was competent and did a good job, considering my wounds involved a great deal more than just the surgery. A physical therapist made daily trips to the house. PT, as it was benignly labeled, was an acronym for "physical torture." A complication had also been diagnosed—a blood clot. The orthopedic surgeon predicted it would require six months for my leg's full recovery.

Surreally, I was confined to the same bed where only days before Pattie had lain, and where she had died. Lying there was a dreamlike immersion into a world of pain and overpowering emotions: an ethereal presence of Pattie, the bottomless sadness of our last hours together, the intense emotional pain, all overlain with a substantial patina of insistently throbbing physical hurt.

Author Diane Ackerman penned, "Wailing out loud and silently clawing at the world and at one's self, the abandoned lover mourns." In my anguish, my soul scratching and clawing like a caged wild animal, I called Pattie's name out loud. When Pattie was still with us, I used to play a game with Benji. "Find Pattie," I would say. And he would look for her, and go to her. Now, hearing Pattie's name he looked at me inquiringly, then began searching through the house, running from room to room searching for her. It was heartrending. He missed Pattie, too.

Kind friends continued to come by to drop off food offerings and break up the monotony, for which I was humbly grateful. My life became one of reporting for physical therapy and a resigned confinement to the house, couch, and bed. The last days of summer passed, a change of seasons that for me would forever after be marked by melancholy. Eventually I learned to scoot up the stairs backwards like a crab to access my desktop computer and the upstairs bathroom shower. It never occurred to me to use Pattie's laptop in her office in the downstairs bedroom. It had been her computer and space.

In a fog-like state, I occupied myself with preparing a eulogy and planning her memorial service. Part of it would consist of a

PowerPoint presentation of projected images of her from birth to her passing, accompanied by the softly playing gospel hymn, "Amazing Grace." Among the photos I chose were images of her standing among wildflowers in alpine meadows with the cathedral-like spires of the Tetons rising behind her—places she had loved.

I spent days occupied in sorting through the voluminous library of photographs we had accumulated over the years, reliving and saying a sad farewell to the many moments they represented and brought to mind. Amazed by the number of photographs I found stashed here and there in closets and in drawers, I wondered where they and all the memories they represented would end up after I was gone.

Oddly, with the emotional wounds still fresh and gaping raw, I was able to withstand sorting through the photographs. Now, I think viewing those images would be overpowering and impossibly difficult for me. Sensitive wounds would be reopened, and congealed misery would flow forth instead of blood. Floodgates barricading off places too painful to bear would be opened, drowning me in cascades of anguish. It would summon grief's most haunting demons: so painful are they that I have learned to fear and dread invoking them.

Pattie had told me she wanted our ashes mixed, and Benji's included too, and then spread across the Tetons. I was to keep hers until we could all be reunited by the mixing. At an attempt for levity, I said, "It'll be awfully cold up there on the Tetons." She looked downtrodden. I quickly added, "How about on Signal Mountain?" She had smiled. I hope that someday two wild flowers, and a bud for Benji, too, will spring from our combined fertile dust on the mountain summit where we were married.

I had to delay the date for the memorial service until I would at least be reasonably able to hobble around on crutches. Although I know she had foreseen her own end, Pattie never specified her wishes for a memorial service, aside from offhand remarks made at various times. Maybe she did not want to cause me concern; more likely, it was too difficult for her to talk directly to me about it. But her casual way of making her final requests known was effective.

Pattie liked Vanessa William's rendition of "The Colors of the Wind" and played the song frequently in our Alta home. At some point, she mentioned out loud to no one in particular, except that I was nearby, "You could have them play that song at my memorial service." At my mother's service, Pattie had offhandedly remarked that the hymn "My Father's World" would be one to play at her service, too.

One of Pattie's friends had earlier died of pancreatic cancer. Pattie spent time with the person in the last weeks and days. The friend was a strong personality. I believe Pattie was identifying with her own situation, maybe seeking to learn what to expect and seeing how that woman conducted herself. A memorial service was held for the friend at Riverview Lodge, a large newly constructed log building overlooking Teton Valley and panoramically viewing the Teton Range. At the service, Pattie had spoken as if to herself again, but loud enough for me to hear: "You can hold my memorial service here, too."

The Riverview Lodge was one of the first places I inquired at for the services. But because of the large floor-to-ceiling windows, it could not be darkened to project images. I began looking into the alternative of somehow having her ceremony inside Grand Teton National Park, like when we were married. It was a place I knew she would have approved.

I inquired at The Murie Center, a nonprofit conservation organization and facility located inside the park at Moose, Wyoming. Pattie had spent some time there interviewing, writing about, and getting to know the original owner, Mardy Murie. The possibility of conducting the service in the auditorium of the park's Craig Thomas Discovery Center came up—a beautiful venue. It was a long shot, but through the helpful assistance of The Murie Center's director, the National Park Service agreed to it.

They all knew Pattie through her love of the park and her published writings. It would be honoring a dear friend of the park. The entire back of the auditorium was framed in glass, which provided a magnificent view of Teton Mountains. I was delighted. Pattie would have been thrilled to be memorialized in that setting.

In Jackson, we knew a young, gregarious, six-foot-four Baptist minister, who sang Southern gospel music, the kind of gospel hymns Pattie had grown up with in Memphis. We had attended his Sunday services a few times, and Pattie had remarked that she liked him. He likewise remembered Pattie and agreed to conduct the service. Pattie's women friends stepped up and kindly volunteered to help with the arrangements and refreshments for a reception at the park's facility afterward.

After the initial shock of Pattie's passing, sorrow continued to build on itself and to gain emotional impetus. I became progressively more grief-stricken, I could not even bear to say Pattie's name aloud. My grieving continued to grow into a raging mournful torment.

My ambulatory ability was still curtailed by my injury, requiring concentrated effort with crutches. But the memorial service, scheduled for the first week in October, gave me comfort. It was nicely planned and arranged within an exceptionally spectacular venue. The Teton mountain summits, forming the backdrop and viewable from inside the auditorium, were dusted with snow and the lower-slope aspen trees radiant with autumn colors. It was reminiscent of the scene when Pattie and I were married on Signal Mountain.

Then the plans and the location were blindsided. On October 1, only days before the planned memorial, the U.S. Government entered into a "shutdown." Republican Congressmen blocked enactment of appropriation legislation for FY 2014, a deadlock brought about by House conservatives known as the Tea-Party. All nonessential federal government facilities and their personnel were required to cease operating.

What the point was for the Republicans' asinine political grandstanding and disruption to the federal government's conduct of business has been forgotten, but the negative consequences to the personal lives of real people still festers in the minds of many.

Grand Teton National Park and the Craig Thomas Discovery Center were closed to the public. A barrier was erected on the access road at Moose. I postponed the date for the memorial services, hoping the situation in Washington would resolve. It did not. When it might be settled had become unknowable. The grandstanding Tea Party and House conservatives stubbornly dug in their heels. The nonsensical stranglehold on the operation of the park, and other federal facilities and services, as well as on people's lives and livelihoods would continue past mid-month, until October 17. Rather than cancel the service, I was forced to change its location, moving it to the pastor's large, modern Baptist Church on Kelly Street in Jackson. I'm certain Pattie would have understood and approved.

Attended by a large number of friends and family, the service stood out as exceptional and lovely. Shelly and Kelly had volunteered to play in the large foyer as people were gathering. A violinist, pianist and vocalist performed solos and accompanied one another. There were few dry eyes present.

> Like the autumn wind calling home the valley's golden
> aspen leaves, the Lord called Pattie to her heavenly home.
> Her spirit will forever reside among the mountain peaks
> she loved, along the trails she hiked, amid the glory of
> the mountain meadow's wildflowers, and in the sparkle of
> crystalline powder snow. Taken home in the Tetons,
> the place she so dearly loved, she herself has become a part
> of the valley's legends and timeless grandeur . . . for whence
> things have their origin, there they must also return . . .
> The dust returns to the Earth as it was, and the spirit returns
> to God who gave it (Ecclesiastes 12:7).

CHAPTER 34

PATTIE SPEAKS FROM BEYOND THE DARKNESS

Do not stand at my grave and weep.
I am not there. I do not sleep.
I am a thousand winds that blow.
I am the diamond glints on snow.
I am the sunlight on ripened grain.
I am the gentle autumn rain.
I am the swift uplifting rush
of quiet birds in circled flight.
I am the soft stars that shine at night.
Do not stand at my grave and cry.
I am not there, I did not die.
—Mary Elizabeth Frye

William Penn is attributed to having made a similar observation: "They that love beyond the world cannot be separated by it. Death cannot kill what never dies."

As I was leaving the church after the memorial and reception, I noticed a large envelope left lying on a foyer table. It was addressed to me. I opened it, discovering letters and an essay Pattie had written to a friend of hers in Bozeman years before. It was dated from shortly after we had married. The essay was entitled: "An Unlikely Tale of Triumph." I had not seen it before. The hair on the back of my neck prickled. It turned out, Pattie had written about an awareness of her mortal transience years earlier. Her prophetic insights seemed as if she were speaking to me from the other side.

> Fortunately, I was critically ill as a young adult. Because of this, I have been "old" for quite a long while. And, because of this, I will never really "be old."

> I was spared the seeming invincibility of health-filled youth; I bypassed the innocent arrogance, the unintentional superiority, of a calendar assumed full of tomorrows.

> The crisis point of that illness was my initiation into the experience of being alive. I have had 8,200 incredible days since that point [when this was written].

> I vaulted over life's clichés. Eavesdropping on many coffee klatches of aged adults, it is common to hear phrases such as "If I had known then, what I know now," or "You learn too little, too late." Behind the poignant laughter at their common humanity, there are often heart-rending regrets around the table . . . angers too long embraced; missed opportunities; family estrangements left unmended; choices denied; family and personal pleasures, too long delayed.

> Clichés only have a life as common sayings because of the Truths that they popularize. Life is backwards.

> It takes some time to rack up quality life experiences. Maturity and wisdom sometimes enter as health and energy are seen vanishing beyond the back gate.

> I was one of the lucky ones. Clichés were plucked before they could ripen. My life was jump started at age twenty-five. From that day forward, it has been easy to tell family and friends, "I love you." The important happens today;

and pleasures are not on hold for "The Golden Years and Retirement." Patience and tolerance replace youthful sarcasm and exasperations. My new sensitivity overrides the protection of my self-image, extending to consideration of others, our world and our environment. Laughter bubbles up quickly.

On a daily basis, rather than a cumulative one, I have lived a lifetime in the twenty-years since. That is not to say that I always remember the lessons of that day, for I am gloriously human. But often I have been patted on the back for a sense of humor or for unexpectedly opening a window on the collective wisdom of the ages. Being wonderfully human, it is nice to smile modestly and accept the accolades. But I deserve none of the credit.

Let me share how these homegrown wisdoms were harvested. Carried from the hospital after six weeks, I continued my long, slow schooling at home. The day arrived when I felt ready to make my first trip to the small, neighborhood grocery. The noise and motion of daily life seemed riotous. It was fear-filled and overwhelming. But all that was positive was accentuated also. Colors were brighter; smells sharper, sounds more acute, feelings heightened. I reveled in the sensory implosions.

On the coattails of these phenomena, I was ready to discover Nature . . . and Nature heals. She grants a new perspective; she reminds us we have choices.

I was a bookworm and art lover. My experience of the outdoors was largely vicarious; the enjoyment of beautiful landscape paintings. So I started slowly and simply. I stepped outdoors.

Assailed by flower scents and birds' songs, I was teased along by sun on my back and the wind on my face. I started walking. Determined to walk beyond the easy tasks that were now so challenging, I discovered the pleasure of physical exertion; the unexpected perks of stretching the boundaries of my comfort zone. It was good. It was exciting to push myself ever further. Pushing my physical limits often reordered the concerns of my mind and quieted unfounded worries. And I was only scratching the surface.

Years later, I met and married an outdoorsman. Suddenly I was seeing backcountry summer over the tip of a fly rod; ushering in winter, tentatively tracking his skis. I was alpine hiking, seeing a lot of country from my bike, and canoeing far backwater stretches. It was sharing those experiences that opened my eyes to the quiet and benevolent lessons of nature.

But it was my past that made me receptive. I had sipped the intoxication of physical exertion. I knew the headiness of growing strength. I had flirted with the stimulation of considered risk-taking. Illness and accidents seemed more foreboding and offered less hope of control than approaching a mountain well-equipped, and mentally and physically prepared!

And, by this route, I encountered indelible memories. I have taken luxury vacations. The memories of four-star meals or of dioramas of the area have long since faded. But I can see and hear, and I can smell and taste, trips when I camped or climbed, or somehow interacted with my new [outdoor] setting. I may have been mildly uncomfortable, but ... oh, I was alive! And, I have only to close my eyes to recapture the wonder. How fortunate that I was given permission early on to free my soul from old routines and habits and fears.

For me, sickness restored the imagination and curiosity that is often the privileged province of the young. Imagination shelves boredom, while curiosity unwraps energy.

What a leg up I received! I received intellectual strength and stamina—necessities for learning just as surely as is mental acuity. And as long as I nurture the stamina of my restored inquisitiveness, I will learn; I will grow; I will be young.

At times, residual effects from my ruptured and clipped aneurysm prevail. There are days when I feel old. But this invariably passes, and an incredible euphoria follows. Whatever the weather, the days are bright with optimism. They feel sun-warmed and filled with hope. My earlier sense of urgency about discovering life's meaning has mellowed into a determination to make each day meaningful.

It need not be sickness that triggers a deeper appreciation of life, but often, it seems, the turning point arrives "crisis-wrapped." The package looks decidedly undesirable, but please know that it houses divinely wonderful compensations.

There is an insidious leisure to "drifting." This is the dubious luxury of the young. Any philosophical notion of "a well-spent life seems antiquated, stodgy; and histrionic, if not ludicrous.

But there is no overtone of heavy seriousness to my life. Indeed, there is a seriousness about having fun and learning new things. There is a serious pursuit of days balanced with work that engenders pride, and time spent with people and activities that I enjoy. This is joie de vivre.

There is no need to turn your back on being young. Enjoy carefree days of transient pleasures. Enjoy and learn from seemingly inconsequential pleasures.

I would seek only to heighten transient pleasures to the level of lifetime's treasures. I would give you the intense pleasures of awareness and appreciation.

Some of us receive a glimpse of age's insight early in life. It is the most valuable gift that we have to give. For some of us, it is our legacy.

CHAPTER 35

CRAZY-MAKING COMPLICATED GRIEF

Perhaps tragedies are only tragedies in the presence of love, which confers meaning to loss. Grief is not felt in the absence of love.
—Elizabeth Alexander, *The Light of the World*

Profound grief is when one's soul bleeds. Trauma to one's soul lingers. A person's entire neurological system becomes inflamed and festers. It hurts incredibly and all over, but at no one place. Like love, there is no way to describe it but through metaphor. As author C. S. Lewis put it: "One engine is now gone, where there were two engines, and somehow one must chug along until the journey ends."

Like love, everyone experiences grief differently; and like love, it takes up residence in similar neurons of the brain. When I have tried to tell people about my grief, they respond with: "Pattie would not want you to feel that way." But it is not so simple. The grief one feels for the loss of a beloved spouse can be among the most difficult and traumatic of life's experiences.

It is and has been horrendously emotionally painful, measureless pain and tension. Yes, they are right: Pattie was too kind and loving to want to cause any hurt to anyone, especially me. Regardless, I am grievously wounded, engulfed in a state of pathos; living on the abyss's edge, feeling like I am on the brink of dying myself.

By any measure, my bereavement is wickedly complicated. It

manifests, in part, in the form of a devilish double bind, an emotionally distressing dilemma with conflicting messages. In this disagreeable state of mental turmoil, one message results in a failed response to the other; I am automatically wrong regardless of my response. I am unable to confront the inherent dilemma, and therefore can neither resolve, nor opt out of the situation. It could only all be resolved if only somehow magically Pattie were to return.

No, Pattie would never want me to feel sad, immobilized, numb, ill, distressed, depressed, yearning, mournful, suicidal, empty and alone. On the other hand, it would be like betrayal, disloyalty, dishonoring our love and closeness, and disavowing to the meaning of all we shared not to feel this intense crazy-making grief and despair. One might turn it around, too, and say, it is Pattie's love, our love, that I feel; the pain is the counterpoint of great love.

I never fully anticipated the psychosomatic, neurological, and heartrending misery triggered by the death of my beloved Pattie, nor the subsequent interminable mourning. I find many are uncomfortable with the subject (and my grief) and turn away in the face of such sorrow and suffering. Given a choice, many chose to avoid it. C. S. Lewis made a similar observation, describing himself as "an embarrassment to everyone he met."

A few years ago, I knew or understood little about complicated grief and the misery of bereavement and mourning. Oh, certainly, yes, I had had other serious encounters with grief—divorce, relationships dissolving, children leaving home, parents, relatives, and friends deceasing, and pets dying. And I had lived for a long time with the constant and mounting grief associated with Pattie's progressive illness and my own brush with death through cancer. But I had never felt bereavement's deepest sting.

Not all people experience deep or complicated grief. Confounding grief and grieving, everyone's experience, intensity, and understanding of it will differ from everyone else's; although, in our humanity, we will all share a certain commonality in how the potentially devastating emotional effects manifest and impact us.

It is not something new to humanity. Ovid said, "Welcome the pain for you will learn from it." There are no doubt those who over the course of a lifetime escape or experience such hurt only minimally. Some of those people might be characterized by an inability to deeply invest emotionally in relationships. Minimally invested in love and emotionally detached, they do not grieve as deeply. Others may call upon religious beliefs to help cope with grief and grieving.

The only time I ever saw my father weep was when his father died. At the time, it surprised me. Men from his generation rarely cried, at least publically. When I sat with my oldest son in the airport on my way to arrange my mother's funeral services, he curiously showed no sentiment whatsoever. Likewise, he expressed little outward emotion when his mother died. For some, non-commitment and non-involvement can be a means to control or avoid potential emotional pain. While I cannot speak for others' experiences with grief, I can only say that mine for Pattie has been devastating—the deepest of all despondencies.

CHAPTER 36

TORMENTS OF THE DARKNESS

If the light was bright and heavenly, the comparative darkness that can follow affords a type of unrelenting perdition. It is up to each of us to decide the limits of our own torment.
—The Author

What I have chronicled here are my feelings at the time of this writing regarding running away and beginning anew, the urge to join the loved one, and the hauntings engendered by memories and personal possessions of the deceased. They deeply involve matters of the heart, but are not necessarily static. With passage of time, one's state of mind can change. Emotions and their intensity can transform, increase, or moderate throughout the course of one's life journey. One might even clutch desperately onto the very things that cause pain, fearfully agonizing that any lessening of grief is but a result of dimming memory.

Finding one's way in a wilderness landscape is relatively easy compared to navigating the mindscape of the brain. The former is fixed terrain with recognizable landmarks, maps and compass bearings to follow; the latter, an uncharted emotional wilderness—a whirling vortex, kaleidoscopic, unfamiliar and changing, unpredictable, chaotically spiraling out of one's control at times. The former is a physical journey and dependent on one's sensory ability; the latter is spiritual, perhaps even mystical.

Fleeing the Pain

I identify with a journal entry Theodore Roosevelt made in 1878, describing his first meeting with his future wife, Alice: "As long as I live, I shall never forget how sweetly she looked, and how prettily she greeted me." The statement echoes my feelings when I first met Pattie in Bozeman.

In 1884, Alice, Roosevelt's beloved young wife, died suddenly without warning. Sensitive people from all walks of life are not spared grief's despondency. Roosevelt scrawled a single sentence in his diary: "The light has gone out of my life." A friend observed: "Theodore is in a dazed, stunned state. He does not know what he says or does."

Roosevelt undertook draconian measures to dislodge Alice from his soul. He forbade anyone to speak her name out loud in his presence. He packed up, abandoned his promising political career, and moved to the far-flung Dakota Territories for four years, seeking solace, erasing pain-filled memories, and beginning a new life far removed.

Faced with similar bereavement, the Apache Indian is said to have responded by burning the deceased's house and possessions; after which, they also moved on to a new place to escape the dead family member's ghost.

I understand it. I think about running away, too. Escape the haunting by fleeing to someplace unfamiliar—maybe somewhere languorously tropical like the Caribbean, Baja Mexico, or Costa Rica. But, rationally, I am anchored by real property, our personal possessions, and, particularly, my age. Lame excuses, I suppose. But if I were younger, yes, moving somewhere new might be advisable. Move and begin anew.

Last holiday season, I fled to the semi-deserted beaches of the National Seashore near the southern tip of Coastal Texas for a few months, the seasonal habitat of a small population of northern snowbirds. Like a lonely island bound castaway, I experienced little social contact there. The setting provoked fewer reminders. Empty beaches and the eternal ebb and flow of surf and tides provided some solace. Maybe it was a return to when, as a child, I spent time with my parents on the beaches at Wildwood, New Jersey—sand, water, eternally restless waves, shorebirds, and a pain-free innocence.

From the National Seashore, I drifted south paralleling the Laguna Madre to Port Mansfield, the Texas Tropics. A different local culture, the primary language in the Rio Grande Valley is not English. But even there reminders waited. In Port Mansfield, I found myself walking along a street named Bell, a Bell Street. As I mentioned earlier, Pattie's family name was Bell.

My aimless and mindless wanderings reminded me of the lyrics from the song, *They Call the Wind Maria*: "I had a gal. She had me and the sun was always shinin' . . . now I'm lost, so gol' darn lost not even God can find me."

While there were fewer mental triggers in Coastal Texas, the different setting did not afford total escape from feelings of loneliness and depression. Muted perhaps, my grief merely manifested in a different setting, though I did not sink to the condition C. S. Lewis describes as "untidy, dirty and disgusting." I could not differentiate between feelings of homesickness or missing Pattie. My mourning remained a soggy weighted shroud that depressingly enwrapped me wherever I went. It colored everything. Frequent overcast and rainy days did not help my melancholy.

Early one morning, I imaged that a lone woman walking toward me in the distance on the beach was Pattie. From a distance, a look alike, she moved like Pattie. I knew it could not be her, but I allowed my mind the deception for as long as possible. And for a brief while, it sweetly felt like I was meeting up with her on the beach after our having been separated for a time.

When I was leaving Texas to return to Wyoming, I turned the local radio station on in my vehicle. Hauntingly, our song, "Could I Have this Dance for the Rest of My Life," began playing. An uncanny coincidence, I suppose?

Fleeing and beginning anew may be a workable solution for some, perhaps. For me, at this time in life, at my age, it does not appear that escaping to the equivalent of the Dakota Territories and a totally new life is a realistic or reasonable course of action. I confess, though, I totally understand the appeal.

The Urge to Join Her

No human culture is without suicide. Unwillingness to be separated from a loved one because of death ranks high among the causes. When joy has been replaced by hopelessness, trying to find peace and end the pain can be a reason. One might adopt Ernest Hemmingway's nihilistic philosophy on life and determinedly seek to control one's own destiny.

In Greek mythology, Orpheus attempts to join, Eurydice, his bride, in death. He travels into the darkest depths of hell and back again in search for her. For three years he wanders alone, trying to erase his thoughts of her. The intense feelings generated from the loss of a beloved spouse and a fixation on reuniting with them has been a recognized theme since ancient times.

In some highly social cultures, if a person goes off and lives alone, it is thought he or she is preparing for suicide. In our society, widowers, particularly, frequently and unintentionally, find themselves in that situation, living very much alone; just as I now find myself, alone. And, in a type of liminality, the survivors find themselves fitting neither into the world of single nor married people.

Reckless thoughts? High suicidal risk? Those are simplistic phrases for the dark path my circumstances have led me to contemplate. Since Pattie's passing, my thoughts have sometimes led me down that shadowy and foreboding passageway to stand before death's doorway; there I have paused. I have not taken the final step to pass through to the other side. But I have become familiar with the emotional path leading there. It is a way that beckons to the most grievously tortured souls. As the Hindus describe, it represents a desperate attempt to "escape divine will" or to control fate.

A taboo topic in our culture, mention any of it to most practicing psychologists and you will be diagnosed as suffering clinical depression and as mentally ill—pathological bereavement. The big, one size fits all "D" is stamped onto one's forehead. It could stand for "the damned" instead of "depressed." Typically, one will be prescribed with the standard treatment regime of anti-depressants, sedatives, and vitamins D and B12. The Merck Manual lists pages of potential drugs for the treatment, as if a pharmacological cure exists for a broken heart or a pill and vitamins will truly alleviate the pain of long and sorrowful bereavement.

Conversely, in *Care of the Soul*, psychotherapist Thomas Moore presents another side: "Melancholy gives the soul an opportunity to express a side of its nature that is as valid as any other, but is hidden out of our distaste for its darkness and bitterness." I find the hiding aspect applies in our society. I was advised by some reviewers to limit this story to the lightness and extraordinary love Pattie and I shared, and to dispense with the part chronicling the darkness that followed, or else make it into two separate stories. But grief became as much a part of our love story as the joy. To exclude the darkness and bitterness would be to try to deny a tragic inevitability of our humanity.

It is not uncommon to learn of a surviving spouse deceasing not long after the other has passed—days, months, or perhaps a few years later. This is not coincidence. I have come to appreciate the phenomenon. Teetering at the abyss's brink at times, I recognize the pull to join a loved one can be a very real and compelling force. Emily Dickinson captured the essence of such a breakdown:

And then a Plank in Reason, broke,
And I dropped down and down—
And hit a world, at every plunge,
And Finished knowing—then—

In recent years, researchers have statistically determined that bereaved spouses have a 66-percent greater chance of dying within three months after their partner dies. It applies to all ages. The incidence is variously termed the "widowhood effect," the "anniversary effect," or more simply, that the bereaved "died from a broken heart." Widowed men have the highest suicide rate of all.

Scholars have attributed causation for the widowhood effect to various reasons: depression, a way to relieve the emotional pain, isolation, loneliness, stress of grief, to avoid the dramatic changes in life type, and a result of lack of family support. It's a long unparallel list of possible reasons. And, yes, for me, I can check all of them off. In my opinion, the effect does not result from any one factor alone. It is driven by an overwhelming simultaneous multiplicity of factors—a gathering of despair to the point of death.

The type of suicide I am writing about is *not* an impulsive act; it is calculated. It is based on the assumption that the hurt and sorrow will exceed any remaining joy in life. Some simply and rationally do not wish to continue to experience the continuing painfulness of life. The common counter argument appears to be that things might change for the better if you stick around.

Where a deep relationship existed, where two people had become one, where they had become agreeably dependent upon one another for "pleasure, support, and esteem," as Pattie and I had, there can be an all-consuming urge for the survivor to join one's life companion, wherever that may lead. Death does not erase the bonds shared in life. It only physically and tortuously separates two people, who in life were inseparable. The dead cannot return; choices remain only for the living.

While I search for words to explain, perhaps only those who have experienced the descent into the darkest passageways of sorrow—Orpheus's hell—can understand. In life, Pattie and I knew the joys of an exceptionally strong bond. We worked at making it that way; others professed to envy our relationship. For more than twenty-two years we slept closely next to each other, and happily spent all our waking hours together. We were passionately in love, and were each other's muse and partner in all things. No cranny of the mind, heart or body remained apart and unsatisfied. Suddenly, all that intimacy has been stripped away; tragically gone, vanished; and I am left alone. It defines all that the concept of loneliness encompasses.

My whole being cries out in yearning for her. It is a wailing lament. With her departure, a large part of me is gone, too. Logically, why shouldn't I ask: If I can no longer physically be with her in this life, could I possibly be with her in spirit? At times, I feel disloyal, guilty, and lacking in courage for not joining her, for having let her proceed on life's most mysterious journey alone and by herself. We walked inseparably hand-in-hand in life through all kinds of places and situations, so it is not unreasonable to ask: Why not also in death?

Earth hurtles along through boundless space; time rushes on, unstoppable. My life and time with Pattie is inexorably being left behind, becoming history, and fading away. I can feel it happening. It generates remorse, conflict, and anxiety. A fading memory generates huge fear. On one hand, I clutch and grab desperately for every memory; on the other hand, each memory stabs sorely back at me. Stop the world; I want to get off of it. I find myself engaging in writer Joan Didion's "magical thinking," as if somehow Pattie's passing might be reversible. I want to travel back in time to where Pattie and I lived and loved and to find each other again.

When I have tried to discuss these complicated feelings with people, they are, of course, uncomfortable or appear alarmed. Some have been quick, again, to recommend psychiatric counseling and anti-depressants or sedatives. Some further raise an eyebrow, they are thinking: "He really is mentally unbalanced." Yes, of course, I am, but as painfully difficult as it may be, I do not believe these feelings are unnatural, nor are they necessarily depression driven. A worried relative counseled, "You will have eternity to join her, there is no rush."

Recently, I met a grief-stricken young woman who had been widowed for two years. The subject of suicide came up. When I said,

"It would take courage," she responded, "Thank you." She obviously had been down Orpheus's path to that mysterious doorway, too.

The young widow lived alone in a rural area in snow country. After her husband died, she had spread his ashes on top of the snow around the house. As the snow receded, all spring long, the ashes would rise to the surface, a recurrent reminder visible outside her windows. Imagine the emotional pain and mourning each resurfacing reawakened.

I have been asked by several: "What is it that stops you from acting on the urge?" I am not sure. I have a number of pathetic reasons, I suppose: The courage required? A sense of social responsibility? A societal stigma, maybe? Perhaps I still have something yet to accomplish in life—this book? Perhaps as the Hindus' believe, my misery is somehow part of a divine plan. Maybe it is because, as some have told me, "Pattie would not approve of it." And I feel a responsibility for Benji, Pattie and I both loved him. He mirrors the joy and loyalty that existed in Pattie's and my relationship. He is a wonderfully happy companion and a living connection to Pattie.

For better or worse, things can change. The pull to join her varies at times. But the thought still arises, and the urge is incredibly strong, almost physically palpable at times. Shutting my eyes, I see her smiling, her image beckons. It would be an elected choice; the most basic of freedoms; a peaceful, loving reunion, and an escape from the continuing dreadful emotional pain of my bereavement.

We vowed "for as long as we both shall live." It was never work or difficult; rather, it was pleasure, to keep that promise while we lived. Even with both of us ill, what one of us would do after the other was gone was not something we gave much energy or thought, or dared to verbalize. We were too busy living. Our wedding vows should have been more accurately stated not as "until death do us part," but rather *for all eternity*.

Now, there is a dirge engulfing loneliness and sadness to endure. Amid it all, I can still visualize her beautiful countenance, feel her eternal love. I gropingly wonder what is really "on the other side?"

Where has she gone? I do not know; no one knows. The other side may simply hold eternal darkness, an escape from the numbing grief and pain; or, at the wishful best, comfort at being reunited with her again, in some way.

To endure, to continue to go on, implies one can visualize a future. Simple as it might sound, I believe one should have a plan or a purpose in life. But the older a person is when their loved one is lost, the more difficult envisioning any future prospects or life's promises becomes. It is another cruel catch-22.

Only the living are faced with choices. Time may erase or lessen the stigma of a self-chosen departure. The possibility of losing the capacity to act is very frightening to me. Like Hemmingway, at some level we all seek to control our own fate. And those that recognize the amount of suffering that terminal illness can engender might understand and forgive. The act of joining the deceased is a way to escape the suffering, tortuous heartache, and the disparate and conflicting feelings that can stab at a person for the remainder of their life. The sorrow engendered by just one person remaining can be harder to bear than if both were gone.

True love trumps all. It does not die when the other person is gone. Finding ways to continue to honor the beautiful bonding we shared in life is essential for my wellbeing and my very existence. For anyone's existence, for that matter, who unfortunately finds themselves in my situation.

A Riderless Horse Elegy

Everywhere I go, everything I do, inescapably summons memories, flashbacks, replays. Through those memories, Pattie is still with me, but it is all in the past. Nowhere can I realistically envision her physically on this Earth with me, now or in the future. Coming up against that hard finality is achingly difficult.

By any standard, we enjoyed a great marriage and enviable life.

Pattie and I did everything together: we shared our thoughts and dreams, experienced adventures of a lifetime together, played and made beautiful love together, served as each other's muse, and looked out for each other. We were elated by the intimacy and each other's company and friendship. For some less compatible couples, it might have been too much intimacy and not enough space. But it delighted us. Hand-in-hand, we happily skipped down life's road together, living our lives as one. It was a romantic dance in the moonlight under the stars; a walk in warm sunshine after a spring shower. "Every pot has its lid," and we were among the fortunate who had found theirs.

Neither of us knowingly tried to control or manipulate the other. We were open and honest and took pleasure in pleasing and supporting one another. There was little negativity. Perhaps we were both a bit codependent, or maybe we had been love-starved as children. That was okay; it totally worked for us. "Grow old with me, the best was yet to be," we both happily exclaimed. Few would ever dwell on the unexpected or worse case when life is at its best.

Now, with Pattie gone, metaphorically, I lead a horse with an empty saddle. I go to the same places, try doing similar activities, visit with the same friends; yet it all seems hollow and empty. There is no joy. I am simply going through the motions. I dearly miss the person who had so closely, lovingly, and cheerfully ridden side by side with me in life. Now instead I lead a riderless horse. The apparition follows me everywhere, accompanying me in everything I try to do.

The empty saddle—or similarly her empty dinner table chair, car seat, and ski lift seat beside me, too— symbolizes my missing life companion, the person who for years so capably and willingly cantered side-by-side through life with me. Gone now, she nevertheless continues to accompany me everywhere in my thoughts. But symbolically her empty boots are reversed in the saddle's stirrups.

I am endlessly and inescapably reminded of the life we once shared as I lead this phantom into eternity. The apparition only allows me to look back. I am compelled only to recall what had been; only remember the past and immense joy and love we once shared. The promises the future formerly held and all our attendant plans are vanished, gone. Looking ahead there is nothing but dark emptiness, a future for us no longer exists. My sense of the world and my life's geography have vanished, shattered. It is more than just loss of direction, too. If there is a discernible direction or future for me, without Pattie it appears paltry and empty in comparison to that of the past.

Memories, Personal Possessions, and Places

Persons, places, and things are the nouns and subjects comprising people's life's stories. Disposing of those things or separating from them presents a dilemma. It results in removing the reminders of loving and having been loved; it purges the stuff that represented or symbolized our lives and who we were; it renders our life stories incomplete and into tatters.

Tao Te Ching said, "He who is attached to things will suffer much." How true, but we never intended to live our lives as Buddhist monks.

Our personal possessions have taken on lives and meanings of their own. More than just things, it is the stuff of memories. Memories are invoked by and attached to nearly every item. It includes everything from our house itself, the automobile we last bought for her, furnishings, the art pieces on the wall, mementoes from our travels, photographs, journals, her sports equipment, my sports equipment (gifts), Christmas decorations, articles of clothing, jewelry pieces that were gifts and worn on special occasions, our published writings . . . on and on, all the stuff of our once active life together, it represented our identity.

It all triggers memory flashbacks and is emotionally charged. Pick up one thing and it is attached in complex ways to others. Not just her things; in many cases, the stuff represents what were our things. In some cases, it invokes poignant memories of loving and being loved. Emotionally entrapped, I am prevented from acting and disposing of our or her things. It would be like discarding parts of us, and with it, all the associated memories. The web we wove, and its association with things, it seems, is extremely complex and emotionally charged. I cannot disentangle myself from it. For me, it is not just material stuff.

When we married and combined furniture, decorations, kitchen items, and more, from two homes into one–it all became ours. And our lives likewise became one. Mentally, it is impossible for me to untangle it all. Monetary value of the items has little or nothing to do with it. It is the extent and manner to which feelings, memories, and our lives are connected with those possessions that determines the degree of anguish or attachment they can elicit. Our stuff and my memories appear inseparable.

People tell me, "You'll do it when you are ready." But getting rid of her things, our things, is like giving away parts and pieces of our lives, parts and pieces of who we were, and who I am.

I have agonized over what to do with Pattie's emotionally charged and precious wedding and Montana sapphire rings. But Pattie had slender fingers, and the rings would never fit anyone in our families. The thought of them being disposed of as objects in an estate sale, and passed around to no one in particular or melted down, their provenance lost forever, is dishonoring and deeply disturbing. I have decided to bury them on the mountain summit in the Tetons where we were married, and where our ashes are to be spread.

For people like Pattie and me who were sentimental and nostalgically inclined to hang onto stuff, and who practiced "making memories," the feelings attached to personal items can be greatly intensified. Intimacy deepens memories and strengthens the associated feelings. Some people are not sentimental and others avoid intimacy or involvement. Those people are less likely to be bedeviled by memories. They are able or apt to put any such feelings aside or out of their minds, if any such sentiment arises for them at all.

It may be difficult to understand, but for me, simply opening a closet and seeing things that Pattie enjoyed summons an overwhelming onslaught of memories. A rush of ghosts hauntingly spring from opened closets. Seeing the gifts I gave her—a coat she had proudly worn on special occasions and looked gorgeous wearing, or dress boots that she prized—sends incredible pain-filled emotions deep into my very being. So incredibly hurtful are those feelings, the triggering of those neurons, that I have become apprehensive and fearful of them. For now, I have learned to try to avoid or minimize doing what I know will summon those awful hauntings.

It is not easy. I am everywhere surrounded with the artifacts of our life and love, constant reminders—places we frequented, photographs, the clothing and jewelry she wore, the words of love and promises written in cards and letters, the gifts we gave each other, furnishings and home decorations, Pattie's breakfast coffee cup inscribed with the words "True Love." The list goes on and on. All of it generates flashbacks, reawakens images and memories, and invokes feelings that torture my soul and constrain my very existence. Those thoughts pummel my soul into what feels like a gaping and oozing hematoma.

In the materials for Pattie's memorial service, I included a naïvely wishful declaration: "May passage of time diminish our grief and sadness, so that the memories of her instead bring only joy." Maybe it will happen someday, but I now realize that wish can have conflicting elements. For me, memories of the deceased at this point do not necessarily bring joy; they also can hurt. Given time, a poignant sweet sadness may linger, perhaps, but never joy or pleasure. While time may diminish sorrow's intensity, what were once joyful and better times are now overridden and trumped by sadness. For me, sorrow has truly replaced what was once joy.

At one point, I confided to a person I had known since childhood that I was unable to open the closets where Pattie's clothing and things hung. Acting annoyed, he replied, "Oh hell, tell her sisters to get up there and clean that stuff out." Revolted by his crude insensitivity, I said nothing.

However, I knew he had lost a teenage son in a horrific hunting accident many years ago. The boy died in his arms while he was carrying him out of the woods. If you go into this person's home, there are no photographs, mementoes, or any visible reminders of the son setting out. All such reminders of the child were expunged. Years ago it was one method recommended for coping with and surviving profound grief. It was similar in a way to Theodore Roosevelt's leaving everything behind and moving to the Dakota Territories to begin anew.

Shortly after Pattie died, a friend volunteered to take a box of Pattie's shoes from the closet to Goodwill to make space in a closet next to the front door. I agreed. Ever since then I have been stricken with remorse. Among the shoes were Pattie's hiking boots. Whenever I think about that box of shoes, I visualize her sitting on the bottom stair steps tying them before a hike. Utterly sad and irrational, I nevertheless wonder now how she will ever go hiking with me again since I gave her boots away. I suppose a psychologist might identify this to mean that I have not accepted her death and I am still expecting her to return.

Clearing out all Pattie's personal belongings is simply not workable for me—at least not at this time. Where someone may have had only a single closet of clothing and a few personal items, it is more reasonable and doable. I know because we were able to do it for most of my mother's and father's personal belongings.

But where two people combined, contributed, gifted, and comingled their things until it all became theirs, and there is an entire household full of things representing our prime of life, it is a difficult quandary and not so simple. There are associated layers built upon layers cemented together by soul memories. I know rationally it is not the memories themselves that are being given away, just the physical reminders. Still how can one bring oneself to give away the stuff of life's precious memories?

If I were to try to remove or dispose of all Pattie's personal property or objects that invoke memories of her, I would have to literally empty out our home and start over. But then, too, even the house itself represents memories; we built parts of it together. Bottom line: I would need to sell our home, too, and move somewhere else, and literally start over. And just what would or should I set up in its place? Besides, when I indulge my pathological yearning—"magical thinking"—it occurs to me, our home in Alta would be the place where Pattie would return to if she were to somehow come back.

For now, I am resigned. It will all always be our home, our things, our memories; it all represents our life together; how we loved and lived together as one. Our house is a museum, my heart a living museum. I find I am incapable of undoing it all and beginning anew. Maybe someday I will, but at my age, it is unlikely, perhaps impossible. Time will tell.

Favorite places and our related activities at those spots generate memories not unlike those linked to personal possessions and mementoes. I find visiting those once familiar places, which have strong emotional associations attached to them, is like opening closet doors and can be just as frightfully haunting and painful. They are places of the heart that I can no longer return to, but that will always haunt me.

We had long-time friends in Bozeman, but I have simply been unable to return there. The strong memories of Pattie and me in our early years together, which are connected with Bozeman, would be so horrendously excruciating that I am frightened by the thought of them. Seeing Pattie's house or going down Main Street would result in a flood of images from those earliest years together. When Pattie and I used to return to Bozeman, we reveled in those reminiscences. Now I am terrified of invoking those memories. I'm afraid it would lead to an overwhelming storm surge of grief.

Likewise, there are natural features and places in the mountains that we fondly frequented that I am apprehensive about visiting. Pattie's absence at those places is now as profound as her presence had been. Hauntings at those spots are analogous to my opening of Pattie's closets where her favorite personal possessions reside. A rush of over powering memories and images await me behind those doors and at those places and would leap out to haunt me if I dare to go there.

In my anguish, I dreamed the Devil offered me a deal, a way out. The Devil proposed to rid me of all my pain and heartache, if I would agree to let him erase the memories I find painful. I recoiled, repulsed by the idea. It put my misery and hurt in perspective. I would never deny or betray all that Pattie and I had cherished and the love we had known to escape from my personal misery. Turn it around, and underneath it all, I realize the depth of my despair is a reflection of the deep and profound love we shared.

CHAPTER 37

THE WINTER OF MY LIFE

Perhaps you have noticed that some people die a long time before they stop breathing. They have no more promises to keep, no more people to love, no more places to go. It is as if the souls of these people have already died.

— Alan Wolfelt, *Understanding Your Grief: Ten Essential Touchstones for Finding Hope and Healing Your Heart*

I have not yet sought professional psychiatric help. My only approach to reconciling my loss has been to try to gain some partial understanding of it all through a kind of bibliotherapy. As if by knowing more about my malaise, I might come to terms with it.

It is a devious malady, comprised of continually changing emotions and feelings—up and down, back and forth, unstable and indefinable except for the unrelenting sorrow and painfulness of it all. And I am still unable to control my frequent upwelling of tears. But regardless of how much I agonize, I cannot call back what has been lost. I am unable to bring Pattie back. And that is the root of it. You do not get over it. As acclaimed poet Edward Hirsch identified in his elegy, *Gabriel: A Poem*, "the work of grieving never ends."

In the seemingly short time since Pattie's passing, I feel like I have grown to be an old man and very much alone. One morning when I awoke my hair had suddenly become silvery grey overnight, whitened like a frosty winter morning. I am reminded of the solitary old bull elk one occasionally sees in the mountains. Turned nearly white with age, they leave the herd to live out their remaining time by themselves, alone.

Aloneness does not necessarily mean loneliness, but in my case how could it not? Yes, I say hello to people I know, and do occasional activities with friends. They come and go, we laugh and talk; they tell me I look well. I appreciate their kindness. But my life without Pattie is dismally empty. I grieve for her and our lifestyle. I am deeply disturbed and haunted by the loss of her and sorely miss the beautiful relationship, companionship, and joyfulness we had shared.

It was unjust and tragic that Pattie should have suffered and died so young. She was such a beautiful, kind, and happy person. I have never known a person who appreciated life more. She has been gone for some time now, but a part of me crazily still waits for her to walk back through the door again, as though she had merely been off visiting somewhere without me. I am certain Benji is expecting her at any time, too. And there is still a powerful urge tugging at me to join her.

In *Shadows on the Grass*, author Isak Dinesen wrote about the death of her beloved servant, Farah: "Then I recognized ... [he had gone] ahead to some unknown place, to pitch camp and wait for me there." I like to think of Pattie that way, she has gotten ahead of me on the trail and now is waiting for me up ahead somewhere.

Odd how the mind works, Pattie resides in my thoughts not as somebody who had been sick or who has died, but rather as the gorgeous person I knew and loved, who was vibrantly full of life and happiness. I guess it is true, a part of me has not accepted her death. There is hardly a waking moment that I do not think of her. I am awash in memories that we purposefully designed and built; reminisces and images that invoke powerful feelings. And, while it may seem silly to some, those feelings dominate my thoughts and channel my remaining life.

I find that everywhere, I am now being confronted with the passage of time. But our home in Wyoming remains the same as it was when we were both still happily living as one. Pattie's spirit remains a powerful presence there. So far I have been unable or unwilling to change much; likewise our Pine Creek home. It is easier emotionally to simply leave everything as it was—frozen at a point in time—

rather than attempt to change or decide what to do with things. That can change, too, but for now that is the way it is. In a large way, our possessions and things, along with the associated memories and stories, communicate who and what we were, and who I still am.

Pattie's large office space and our downstairs bedroom look just as they did when she departed. Her purse with her car keys, credit cards, and personal items still hangs on the chair were she customarily left it. The book that I read from to her still lays open on the bed. Like some macabre scene with an accumulation of cobwebs, it will soon all require dusting; no doubt it already needs it.

Not intentionally, but inadvertently I suppose I have created a shrine. Some might worry whether or not it is healthy for me. I have not purposely made an effort to keep everything that way. Rather, my inattention is the course of least resistance.

Because of my inability to proactively deal with these things at this stage, to get on with life and reorganize what was our home, it seems by default to have emerged as something like a memorial. I know most psychiatrists analyzing my behaviors, following professional protocols and criteria, would determine me to be mentally unbalanced. Among society's functioning members, I am the walking wounded; with my neurotransmitters allowed to run wild, I represent a bleeding and afflicted psyche.

Over the past several years, when Pattie and I were both sick, I put off much of the maintenance work that needed to be done around the house and yard. I am reminded the weathered redwood deck sorely needs staining every time I go outside the backdoor. The flowers in our gardens were unusually beautiful this year, sort of a last hooray. Weeds have recognized a potential opportunity and now are invading in force. In my mind, I see Pattie sitting alongside the flowerbeds, exuding her happy persona, wearing her signature broad-brimmed hat and gardening gloves, patiently pulling the weeds, contentedly making little piles of the unwanted intruders.

My pride in having everything looking reasonably at its best, something Pattie and I endeavored together without interfering with other activities and priorities, has waned; at least for now. Maybe this coming spring or whenever, I will feel more like doing what may be needed. Some might be inclined to attribute my lack of motivation to depression disorder which seems to be all-encompassing in the minds of many. But some chores, when I try to look ahead, seem pointless anymore. My vision for life has been turned upside down.

I try to continue going through the motions of day to day living, numbly engaging in some of what were our traditional seasonal activities. Last year I picked raspberries and huckleberries and froze them, grew a garden, hunted and killed an elk for the freezer, caught a few trout at places where we used to fish, and occasionally went to the fitness center. For those observing me, it no doubt appears I have returned to going about my normal life. But my concentration is weakened; it is a detached and half-hearted existence, without enthusiasm or excitement. Without Pattie, the joy of living is gone.

People ask me, "How are you doing?" Although I have been asked that question hundreds of times, I invariably grope for a reply, finding it difficult to answer. At one time it was not. I know all they want is a smile and a simple upbeat word or two of pleasantry. They do not really want to hear how I feel, how I am doing: miserable, dismal, sad, lonely, and not very well. "How am I doing?" Relative to what?

My response to the other frequent question, "What have you been doing?" is generally to mumble about some activity—writing, cycling, skiing, hiking or visiting somewhere. That often elicits surprise. "Good," they respond smiling, "I am glad you're not just sitting." I don't know what they expected me to say. I have never "just sat" anytime in my life, but I smile back and nod. However, it would seem I have been written off as unlikely ever to accomplish anything significant again. It is as if they are confirming my life is over.

I go cross-country skiing on the fastidiously groomed track in Teton Canyon—in our early years in the valley the canyon's unbroken snow attracted few skiers, we had it all to ourselves—nowadays, it is promoted as "one of the most picturesque courses in the world." It is not so picturesque now that the canyon's track is overrun with dogs and people. Some individuals have three or four dogs running out of control in every direction. We used to spot deer on the hillsides and moose along the bottom, cougar tracks at times, even a cougar-killed yearling moose once, and always pine martin and ermine, and sometimes even great gray owls. It was quiet and peaceful back then—solitudinous. Now there is none of that, the animals have been displaced by the commotion of people and dogs. The State Game and Fish Department notes the moose population has declined, they suggest it is due to predation. Any cougars in the canyon have already been removed, so the scapegoats are wolves, again.

I am reminded, after all, that we have entered *The Human Age* and, as Diane Ackerman eloquently points out in her new world paradigm, what constitutes nature is no longer natural. I find myself to be an anachronistic Luddite, rooted in old-fashioned nineteenth and twentieth century precepts and attitudes towards Nature, and relationships, too, and reluctant to capitulate.

Prepping my skis with green kick-wax, I do classic diagonal-stride for five or six miles in the canyon at a dogged pace, my knees protesting. Where I once knew the few people I might encounter, if any, now I rarely recognize anyone. There is a whole new generation—another sign of the passage of time.

Although he still greets me playfully every morning, Benji no longer runs "joy circles." But he is my constant companion. I worry about him. He sleeps a lot. In dog years, he is very old. We are both old dogs.

While my mountain trail running is over, in late summer, Benji and I set out together on a challenging day hike to the 11,000-foot elevation Hurricane Pass in the Teton Mountains not far from our home. We went by way of a little-known route, up the Roaring Fork. I wanted to return to the high elevations in the Tetons and walk among the peak's grandeur and the profusion of wildflowers one more time; perhaps, one never knows, it might be my last time.

I went alone with Benji, because if I became unable to complete the hike, I did not want to spoil someone else's outing, too. It was a calm late summer day, and we saw no one else the entire time. A favorite alpine wildflower, old-man-of-the-mountain, firmly rooted in limestone crevices, probably since before I was born, was in blossom.

At Hurricane Pass, sitting behind a boulder for a windbreak, Benji and I had some lunch. Viewing the awesome panorama of the Three Peaks rising directly before us across the abyss of Cascade Canyon, I could see and trace the climbing route Pattie and I had taken from the Lower Saddle to the top of the 13,776-foot Grand, fifteen years earlier. In my mind, we were on the mountain again en route to the summit, the mica in the gneiss and schist rock glittering all around us in our full moon and headlamp-lighted predawn ascent. It was another inescapable memory flashback—vivid, detailed, and palpable. We were both the picture of health and strength back then.

Curmudgeon-like, I mull over how much the world has changed in the short time since. Today, without any mountaineering skills, breaking a sweat, or being exposed to icy couloirs, people can electronically summit the Grand in the park's visitor center by virtual reality. Likewise for other hikes in the park, too—a sedentary electronic reality in place of multisensory experiences. What are we humans becoming? It is commentary on the fact our species is separating itself at warp speed from nature and the natural world.

I returned to Pine Creek this past autumn. Alone, with only my thoughts and memories, and Benji sleeping in the seat next to me, except for the roaring background noise of truck traffic, it is a silent, long and lonely drive.

At Pine Creek, when I went to pick a few apples from our favorite tree—a wonderful heritage variety, located at an old abandoned farm site—I jarringly discovered only a broken stump. The gnarly old tree that had stood for over a century was suddenly completely gone. Someone had even removed the wood and cleaned up the limbs. Just a year ago, it appeared Malthusian, as though it would tenaciously cling to life forever. In my mental state, loss appears to be on an accelerating trajectory, and my reaction to every loss is compounded.

I thought about picking cranberries at the colorful mountaintop bog. It was one of Pattie's favorite spots and things to do in autumn. Wearing knee-high rubber boots, she was reluctant to leave the bog until every last wild cranberry had been hunted down and captured into her bucket. Then I cringed before the onslaught of haunting memories and images. The bog is relegated to another one of those places, where the aurora of her presence is so powerful, I shrink before the images clutching and clawing at my soul. There are beautiful memories residing there, but when awakened they are frighteningly overpowering.

Perhaps I am overly sensitive or lack a necessary emotional toughness. But so far, I cannot bring myself to go into the bog. I have never been there before without Pattie. Like the cotton grass, pitcher plants and sphagnum moss growing there, I would expect her to be there, too. Her absence would be as palpable as her presence.

Similarly, for now, at least, I am unable to visit certain mountain top vistas, mountain meadows, favorite streamside places, and other natural features and places we once happily frequented, places where her spirit is hauntingly and overwhelmingly present. In spite of knowing it would not be what Pattie wanted, I am entrapped and my life controlled by the intensity and intimacy of our past.

Through the window of our Wyoming home, I watch the wreathlike clouds gathering, surrounding the snow-clad summit of The Grand. "Benji, come," I say, and he hops up beside me. Benji and I sit there sharing the moment. We live in the shadow of the mountain. Mortal endings are destiny. Soon only the mountain will remain.

As I view the mountains Pattie loved, I am transported back in time to that snowy April morning in Bozeman long ago. Dreamlike, I follow along the street in the blowing snow to the doorway of Quest Gallery once more. As I enter her gallery, the love story of Earle and Pattie begins replaying once again. In my mind, I hear her happily call out, "Hello Earle," as if she had been patiently waiting for me.

Earle and Pattie—
Remember them …?
They sang and danced,
worked and played,
hoped and prayed,
believed and trusted,
laughed and cried,
loved and romanced,
lived … and died.
Remember them,
Pattie and Earle,
they knew an
uncommon love.

ACKNOWLEDGMENTS

My sincere appreciation for fellow authors, relatives, and friends who stepped up to read my early drafts, either in whole or part, and who provided comments and criticism. Some went the extra mile and generously provided the cover jacket praise, too — Matt Daly, Donna Hulsey, Alexandra Fuller, Kristine Kopperud, Susan Marsh, Michael McCoy, and Todd Wilkinson. Social worker Carol Taylor read portions of the Introduction at a Wyoming conference on bereavement and provided me with the resultant comments.

The positive support and encouragement from these folks allowed me to overcome insecurities about publically sharing the personal and intimate details of my grief and of Pattie's and my life together. The freely given suggestions, comments, and criticisms received were invaluable. I owe all a debt of gratitude.

Melanie Austin of Seattle Editing conducted the preliminary editing of the manuscript. Gaia Layser kindly lent her practiced eye and editorial experience to a final proofing. I realize in spite of all our best efforts, imperfections undoubtedly exist. Those remain the final responsibility of the author.

Miga Rossetti of Rossetti Designs applied her ample skills in designing the cover and in the artful layout and design of the book. Her capable assistance is reflected throughout the book.

My thanks to photographer Katrina Giosher for the use of her image in the design of the dedication page and Yongyut Kumsri for the cover photo. All other images were by the author.

I referred to literature by a number of other authors who also described their emotional experiences with complicated grief and bereavement. We are all indebted to those people for baring their souls. It is not literature one normally seeks out, perhaps, until we find ourselves in unintended similar circumstance, adrift and searching for answers.

Some of the excerpted materials herein were published by Earle and/or Pattie Layser previously in different form and formats in the following newspapers, magazines or anthologies: *Teton Valley Magazine, Teton Home and Living Magazine, The Denver Post, The Jackson Hole News and Guide, Rhodes Magazine, Images West, A Grand Wedding Planner, Teton Valley News, Bugle Magazine, Southwest Art, Persimmon Hill, Wyoming Magazine, Yellowstone-Teton Country, Jackson Hole Magazine, Jackson Hole Wedding Planner, Stories of the Wild Anthology, Spindrift: Stories of Teton Basin Anthology, High Country News, Crone Chronicles, Bozeman Daily Chronicle, The World and I, Pennsylvania Magazine, Pennsylvania Game News, Grit Magazine, Great Falls Tribune, Log and Timber Style Magazine, New Holland News, Paddler Magazine, Mountain Gazette, Montana Magazine, Webb Weekly, Acres Magazine, and South American Explorer.*

ABOUT THE AUTHOR

At this writing the author and Benji still reside at what was his and Pattie's home on the west slope of the Tetons at Alta, Wyoming.

Other Titles by Earle F. Layser

Flora of Pend Oreille County, Washington

Green Fire: Stories from the Wild

Jackson Hole Settlement Chronicles

*I Always Did Like Horses and Women:
Enoch Cal Carrington's Life Story*

*I Always Did Like Horses and Women:
Enoch Cal Carrington's Life Story* (New and Updated Edition)